THE BELGIAN B]
by
Richard F.A. Whi†

Dedicated to the memory of my dear parents and grandparents. It is also a tribute to the unsung heroes and heroines depicted throughout the book.

Every effort has been made to trace the copyright holders of material quoted in this book. If an application is made in writing to the publisher, any omissions will be included in future editions.

ISBN: 9781719915953
Book design including cover by Richard F. A. White.
Typeset in 11/16 point Adobe Palatino.

Prologue

Alan Granville White was born in Nuneaton, Warwickshire on September 20th 1921. Five months after Britain declared war on Germany in 1939 and like so many of his friends, he volunteered to join the Royal Air Force out of a deep sense of duty when bombs started to fall on Britain's cities. The following story reminds us of those dark days of conflict and the urgent demands made upon the young men of the RAF who gave their all to counter Adolf Hitler's plans. Propelled into a dreadful conflict and facing an uncertain future, we are able to catch a mere glimpse of what was expected by a nineteen year old trainee radio operator and his aircrew friends during the early stages of the war. Later, after being grounded due to health issues at high altitude and now promoted to Flight Sergeant, Alan cast aside his disappointment and became one of the few pioneers operating recently developed early warning detection systems at the 'Chain Home' stations. Although in its infancy this new science eventually became better known as RADAR.

The story also throws light on the bravery of a Belgian girl from Mons. Odette Fernande Moreau along with her family and friends, tried to avoid occupation by joining a column of refugees heading towards the French coast before being turned back. They walked a total distance of well over 300kms carrying their few precious belongings. On the march, they witnessed numerous horrors at the hands of the Germans and once back in Mons, survived four more years of oppressive rule until liberated in September 1944. A head strong but intelligent girl, Odette nevertheless ignored her parents' and friends' advice to avoid members of occupying or liberating forces. After four years of brutal German occupation and only eighteen, she was looking forward to some fun and happier times.

Alan was posted to Mons in the autumn of 1944, four months after the D-Day landings. The town had already been liberated by the US Army but it was still a dangerous place to be out and about in. Occupying forces had retreated in the face of allied advances, but there remained well-hidden pockets of German snipers, as well as Belgian Rexists, regarded as traitors on account of their loyalty to the Führer. They were there to hamper liberating forces, slow progress and cause maximum inconvenience where possible.

RAF flying and non-flying personnel, particularly radio, wireless and radar operators, along with a small number of USAAF personnel, and US 1st Armoured Division troops had taken up residence close to the town centre. The RAF boys made up from 109 Squadron and 72 (signals), had been flown in to Chièvres air base by Dakota C47s in late 1944. Their destination and home for just over a year would be the *Ecole Normale* in Mons, an imposing large red brick school building built in the 1880s, just off the Boulevard Dolez. Although not involved in combat, they were part of 'Operation Oboe', the code name for a special detection and surveillance task. Their job was to prepare for any further action in the Southern Ardennes where the German 6th Panzer division eventually attempted an audacious counter attack during the worst winter on record. Late one evening, amidst the chaos and joy that often accompanies liberating forces, Flight Sergeant A. G. White, ignored advice and official warnings not to fraternise with the town's people.

Along with a few RAF friends, heavily wrapped up against the chilly autumn winds, they ventured out to a dance party jointly organised by the RAF and the USAAF. Amongst the people attending, were a few Belgians who had eagerly offered to help out. They were hardly to blame. After four years of occupation, this was a rare opportunity to laugh the night away and let their hair down. Beyond the heaving dance floor and the loud but unmistakable tones of Glenn Miller on some well-used 78s, Alan met Odette, but only because the music came to an abrupt stop. With an attractive French accent, speaking in schoolgirl English, she asked for a volunteer to mend a petulant and annoying gramophone.

Chapter 1: Escape from Mons

"Laure! I've managed to find a cart that once belonged to Marcel Bouvier, the old farmer. It's a little heavy and rough but I'll be able to manage it without a horse."

Fernand paused, shifted uncomfortably and breathed in deeply before continuing. He looked pale, tired and anxious.

"Bouvier has not been seen since his farm was ransacked last month. The place is in a dreadful state. It's a terrible sadness, but we must now gather together our most precious personal possessions and essentials and load them into the cart before the Germans arrive in the next few days. Tomorrow, our relatives and friends will join us since we have no choice but to walk to the French coast. We'll head towards Calais or Ostend, where it will be possible to find a boat that will take us to England and safety."

There was a long silence before Laure, with tears in her eyes and outstretched pleading hands, trembled in her response.

"Fernand, please, don't let us do this; it's such a long way and too dangerous. Odette is much too young and besides, I can't bear to leave our beautiful home to the Boche. They'll destroy everything. Maybe we can stay and plead with them."

Fernand reflected and took both her hands. With tears in his eyes, he spoke softly but firmly.

"The Germans are closing in on Charleroi and heading this way. Tomorrow, they may be in Binche, who knows what they'll do with us? I've heard they put poison in chocolate bars and smile when handing them to children! We cannot linger. These Germans are not to be trusted and in any case we all know what they are capable of after the last war. Please understand, I don't like this any more than you do, but we must make haste."

At that moment, Odette skipped in smiling but seeing the anxious sorrowful looks on her parents' faces, quickly realised something was very wrong. Born in 1926 and an only child, she had grown into a mature, pretty girl. With her big dark hazel eyes, impeccable complexion, shock of mid-brown wavy hair and gregarious nature, she was already attracting the attention of several older boys at school, much to her father's chagrin.

Odette was clever, confident, amusing and full of ambition to succeed. Her main regret and a great sadness for her and her parents, was the brother who had unexpectedly died in 1932, just a few days after his birth. She looked at her parents with fear in her eyes and blurted out with trembling lips, "What's happening?" although she was bright enough to realise it probably had something to do with the approaching Germans. Forecasts had been coming through for several days in May 1940 about the imminent collapse of Belgium, following the Wehrmacht's rapid progress from the East.

Her father kindly asked her to go and start packing essential items for the journey but mainly clothing for the long walk to safety. At least, close family members and some good friends would all be together for the extraordinary journey. Before climbing the stairs, she paused, hugged her mother tightly and both burst into tears. She looked around and in a moment took in all the familiar items that made this her home; the wall pictures, the bronze figurines, the dark oak furniture, the ornate mirrors, the black and white marble floor, the coat stand in the hallway and, above all, the distinctive clean smell of the house after being scrubbed with 'Savon Noir' by her ultra tidy and house-proud mother. At the same time she reflected why it had been necessary to clean the house ready for potential new unwanted residents. It also dawned on her that she might never see her home again.

During the night and taking over three hours with pick and shovel, Fernand Moreau had managed to bury his entire collection of St Emilion Grand Cru wine in a deep hole he'd dug in a secluded part of the garden before covering it all with a tarpaulin, soil and a huge pile of smelly horse manure and rotting compost.

In World War One, after internment in a prison camp as a 17

year old and suffering badly at the hands of the Germans, Fernand was determined to avoid the 'Boche' any way he could. His impression of Germans had been forged after 2 years of beatings, forced labour and digging up beet from frozen ground just to survive. It pained him to leave behind the home he and Laure had worked hard to provide for them as a family. He and Laure carefully chose the essential items they would need for the road ahead; shoes, clothing, an assortment of small tools, a couple of spades, cushions, towels, water carriers, eiderdowns, photographs, jewellery, birth certificates, identity cards and a few loaves of bread, fruit, pots and pans, cups, plates and cutlery.

Right now however, apart from hiding a few precious items and sentimental possessions, the only job remaining before they took their leave was to make sure the family's beloved horse 'Hercule' was released in the woodland and fields at the rear the house called Mont Panizel. Odette was devastated to say goodbye to her gentle friend and broke into sobs as her father led him away.

"Filthy Germans," she muttered, "I hope you are all punished by God and rot in hell!" before she quickly made a sign of the cross. She then fretted that God may not be too pleased with her and take an exception to her choice of words.

The next morning, after a very restless anxious night, there was a knock on the door just as the old Westminster clock chimed ten o'clock. It was cousin Jean-Baptiste Clarifié. Fernand, tying back the last of his grape vines in the veranda, shouted to his wife and daughter, "Everyone is waiting outside, it's time to leave." They could hear distant rumblings in the direction of La Louvière.

The three of them stood outside for a few minutes, looking pale faced at what had been their home for 16 years. It was May 2nd 1940 and might be the last time they would ever see 10 Chaussée de Beaumont again. Tears and sobs were understandable even when Aunt Hélène consoled them with her fresh warm soupe aux légumes which she'd prepared in a large brown tureen and hidden under coats and blankets in a ramshackle cart pulled by a black shire horse.

Fernand, a strong tall 43 year old, used to farm work, was able to harness his old wooden farm cart with thick leather straps secured around his chest, shoulders and waist. Most of the other families carried items in old prams, improvised wagons, hammocks slung between poles, converted cycles, various wheeled contraptions, suitcases and even children's trolleys. There was also a rare Renault Monaquatre open top tourer owned by the family Léonard on the Chaussée de Binche. Apart from Haute Couture clothing from the best fashion shops in Bruxelles, the car was filled with oddities including an odd shaped wooden carving of a monkey, an art deco pewter lamp, a bronze statuette of King Leopold and a collection of parasols. Most of the families and friends, including three of Odette's school friends, had only packed basic clothing and a few personal belongings. Most had listened to advice not to take anything that would attract the attention of German soldiers should they be stopped at any point. Sadly, some, at a later stage on the march, would ignore this advice with devastating consequences.

"Bonjour! Hello Monsieur Delage," shouted Fernand. "Laure, Odette, look! It's Monsieur le Curé from Jemappes."

The old priest, a good family friend heard him and smiled. He waved and hurriedly ran towards them but his black cassock got in the way and he stumbled across cobbles and tramlines at a place called 'La Bascule'. This was a well-known memorial, dedicated to the British soldiers of the Middlesex Regiment, the Royal Irish and the Scots Guards who had died during the defence of Mons in 1914. He joined and stayed with the Moreaus as they walked amongst the growing procession heading west towards Beloeil some 16 kilometres away and where they would try and find shelter for their first overnight stop. Father Delage was a genial man and very well read. Odette discovered he'd brought along a few of his favourite books including a well-thumbed copy of Baudelaire's 'Les Fleurs du Mal'. There were others by Flaubert and Victor Hugo all of which kept her occupied, often sitting on one of the horse drawn carts belonging to friends. Odette'sparents were more inclined to chatter with fellow travellers but it was the well-meaning Curé with his fixed broad smile that kept them from the sadness and anxieties that came with a realisation they were homeless refugees. He was also wise in most things and somehow managed to glean news and information about German activity. As they approached Beloeil, Father Delage came across a few of his fellow clerics hurrying towards the column.

"Father, Father!" one of them cried, "There are German troops near Tournai. Please caution your friends to be very careful. Hopefully they are not interested in civilians and seem to be looking for any signs of the French and English armies who were last seen retreating beyond the town, heading towards the ports."

"God go with you Father," answered one of the young pastors.

Most of the travellers were feeling weary and in need of sleep by the time they arrived in Beloeil. Deep lines of worry and tiredness were etched in a few gaunt faces. Somewhere, someone played an accordion and a few people joined in with well-known popular songs, which lifted spirits considerably. Laure quickly discovered a hotel and restaurant, after going on a short walk looking for a lavatory. She summoned Fernand and Odette to join her at the head of a small queue. They were fortunate as they managed to persuade the owner, Louis Delvaux, to let them have a large bedroom at a reasonable charge. Despite the room looking like it had not been touched for 20 years or more, they were delighted to find an oversize double bed and what can only be described as a small child's bed, which Odette could only just fit into. Looking out of the dusty slats and tall grimy windows, avoiding cobwebs, they could see the crowds milling around in the town square. The majority were desperately looking for somewhere to stay for the night but the unfortunate ones would have to sleep rough.

Jean-Baptiste, his wife Julia and their five year old daughter, Jacqueline, ignored those who were doing little but complain and, along with Aunt Hélène and Father Delage, they found an old farmhouse two kilometres from the edge of town. They decided this was better than risking the outdoors and took advantage of an upper hayloft. They were later joined by a young woman, called Veronique,

8

who was three months pregnant. She had travelled with friends from Mauberge just across the border in France. The ground floor was filthy, occupied by two pigs, a few hens and a cow suffering with chronic flatulence and other bowel problems.

Others were not so lucky since the nights could still be quite cold in May 1940. A few of the younger men had found a café just off the Grand Place, whose owner was more than happy to keep the place open all night and allow his countrymen to consume as much as they could and have some fun before the Germans arrived. Needless to say, there would be some very sore heads by the time dawn arrived. Anyone assessing the gathering storm on the horizon would have been surprised by a general lack of anxiety in the majority gathered there. It was a misplaced belief that it was a big adventure and that if they did not go looking for trouble, they would reach the coast and find a boat without too many problems. Some were even predicting they'd all be allowed to return to Mons within a few weeks.

That night, they ate well. The restaurant's young Chef, Henri, had created one of his specials. He'd already taken a shine to Odette and decided this was his way of advancing his ardour with a twinkle in his eye. Unfortunately, any 'ardour' was short lived after her father bristled and gave him a piece of his mind, but not before they'd wiped their plates clean with some wonderful rustic bread. They'd dined well on ratatouille and bacon washed down by a crafty bottle of red Bordeaux that Odette's father had managed to hide in the handcart, now out of sight and chained down in the dark recesses of the rear courtyard.

Odette and her parents settled down for the night. She lay back in her tiny child size bed and thought of home and then school at the *Ecole Normale* in Mons. She thought of Hercule and wondered if he'd be happy living free in the woodland near home. Luckily, she would never know that Hercule would become Sauerbraten, gracing the dinner plates of senior German officers. Above her, on the ceiling, a very old chandelier rustled and shimmered in the evening breeze, but her eyes glazed over and she fell into a deep sleep despite the heavy snoring already coming from her parents. Sharing a room was not something any of them were used to or wanted to endure for longer than necessary. Privacy was already becoming more and more compromised. Ablutions consisted of one basin with its single cold-water tap. Toilet visits, either using an under bed Jerry, or taking a long walk to the hotel toilet, often resulted in hysterics or sheer embarrassment. Fernand had already lit a few damp sticks and some coal in the fireplace but the chimney was either blocked with a bird's nest or full of soot causing smoke to drift out into the room. This meant keeping the windows open, although it had been possible after some persuasion, to shut the tall pale green outer shutters still showing damage sustained in the 1914-18 war. They slept with their coats on, wrapped up in layers of blankets. Even with the windows open, the sounds of music and singing coming from the Café Les Mousquetaires failed to disturb them. It had been a tiring day but this might be the last time they would manage to have a good night's sleep for some time to come.

At 07:00 hours, they were suddenly woken by what seemed like thunder somewhere in the distance. Loud noises from downstairs jolted them out of any sleepiness and brought on anxious frowns as they heard Louis Delvaux shout from the front doorway, "Quickly everyone, the Boche are coming!" Odette and her parents dressed in double-quick time. Laure, ignoring her husband's distasteful glance, insisted on wearing a wide-brimmed beige hat and a fox fur stole.

"So, you've dressed up for the Germans, eh?" said Fernand. Laure shrugged and gave an agitated flick of her head, causing the fur stole with its grisly glass eyes to whip around her neck and clatter against a half-open wardrobe door.

"Of course not! I want them to see that a lady from Mons is not scared or cowed by the Boche."

Odette chuckled. She admired her mother's defiance but like her father, had doubts that any German troops would notice. She suspected it was more to do with her mother's flamboyance. People, had now congregated outside in silence and were lining the streets

10

waiting for the Germans to arrive.

"Stay close together," said Odette's father, "and do not wave." Father Delage and the other family members now joined them. They had endured a frightful night of animal noises and odours in the barn and were looking quite ill. In the distance, the town's gathering could hear the sounds of motorised armoured vehicles and the steady thump of boots on the road. Odette looked up, letting her thoughts meander as she watched doves flitting about on the opposite roof tops. The sun was casting a warm glow and beaming through fast moving cumulous clouds as the head of the German column arrived, preceded by a staff car, four armed personnel carriers and motorcycle outriders.

Chapter 2: Drawn into Conflict

At the outbreak of war, back home in Nuneaton, Alan's two older brothers, Graham and Gordon had also volunteered to join the army for King and country. They would eventually, through strange twists of fate, see action against the Italian 10th Army in Libya and later Rommel's Afrika Korps. Prior to 1939 the older boys had devoted little time to their young brother's interests other than enlisting his support for the occasional foray into misdemeanours and risky, death-defying adventures. More often than not, it all ended in cuts and bruises.

On one occasion, a week before Christmas 1937, the two older brothers decided it was time to find a Christmas tree and they knew where to find it, in a forest beyond Higham, a village seven miles away on the border where Leicestershire meets Warwickshire. Much to their chagrin, they had not thought about practicalities such as how to sneak back without being detected or how to transport the tree back home. In addition, they had little idea of how tall the tree should be to fit its eventual destination in the house. The answer was to transport the ten-foot tree strapped to Gordon's bicycle with him sitting astride but mostly inside it, trying desperately to peer through the branches and not fall off. Graham decided it was safer to walk home. It was a long meandering ride back, avoiding other road users and observed by curious residents of Higham Lane. Gordon miraculously made it without falling off although one neighbour was heard to say rather anxiously, "A tree has just cycled past but there's no sign of the rider." When the tree eventually arrived, there was a big discussion about how to fit it into the house. The conclusion was to chop nearly three feet off the top!

Alan secretly wished he could be unhindered by nerves and more like them, even if admiration was sometimes undone by fright. They were a mix of raconteur, adventurer, eccentricity and charm, as well as being the life and soul of the party whenever the family or friends came together. They were also musical, able to play piano even if the style was more in keeping with rowdy pub singsongs. As a consequence, Alan spent much of his boyhood playing third fiddle, often a loner and quite shy. He was also a sickly child, prone to illness with persistent aches and pains, coughs, colds and sinus problems. Fortunately, he had a younger sister, Barbara, whose friends provided a female orientated social life. What made him stand out was his gentle creative spirit. He was a poet, an artist, student violinist and very good at making things. Barbara's friends loved all this and so he found it easier being in their presence than with the lads. It was rumoured that when sixteen, Alan fell for the charms of a certain Elsie Hammond, a woman in her late twenties with a rather troubled reputation for liking far too many men!

In 1937, George and Alice White had moved the family from their two up and two down back street terraced home in Bracebridge Street, Nuneaton to a quieter, up market and more desirable three bedroomed semi-detached house at 195 Higham Lane. It was only two miles from the town centre, close enough to good schools and surrounded by fields and friendly neighbours. This was where the Whites found a new lease of life. George had spent time in a local sanatorium recovering from poor health as a result of malaria picked up whilst serving in East Africa during the First World War. He'd taken up his old trade as an electrician but in 1932, he took up a new position as the manager of the Scala Cinema in Queens Road. Here, his work was more in keeping with his fun loving character and George could be seen every day dressed immaculately, if not a little eccentrically, in formal evening attire, welcoming the towns folk as they queued for each show.

He staged many spectacular events, often with elaborate, amusing or bizarre promotions. When the film Zorro starring Tyrone Power was premiered in February 1940, he hired a local Rag and Bone man dressed in a black cape sporting a lethal rapier and sitting astride a huge, agitated, black carthorse. After two hours of restraint amidst well-trodden droppings, the fractious horse decided it was time to go home at a fast gallop, complete with a protesting Zorro still mounted on his back. George's hard work turned the cinema into the place where the miners and factory workers of Nuneaton wanted to be. He established a big reputation as a man of importance and a leading benefactor in the town, providing an invaluable public service.

"Alan, the post has just arrived, can you bring it through? I'm in the kitchen." His mother was ironing and listening to the news on the wireless. "There might be a letter from Graham letting us know if he's coming home on a week's leave."

Alan rapidly scanned through the four letters but there was nothing from his brother.

"Nothing from Gra'," he shouted, "but there's something for me." He could hardly conceal his excitement.

He walked along the hallway, taking in the smell of drying cottons from the kitchen ceiling clothes airer and handed three other letters to his mother, before opening his own.

"It's from the RAF and they want me to go to Coventry next week to attend an interview."

Alice White breathed out deeply and held her face between two hands. They looked at each other and Alan knew exactly what she was thinking. All three sons might well end up out there in some god-forsaken war zone fighting the Germans.

"It's OK Mum, I doubt if they will let me fly planes. It's more likely I'll be joining the ground crew." He was only trying to placate her, as he really did want to fly.

Alice pondered the implications and dabbed the tears running down her cheeks. It was May 12th 1940 and she missed her two sons. To make matters worse there was little news coming through about the campaigns in North Africa, where they were last reported. Alan had felt a need to do his bit by applying to join the RAF along with

14

three of his old school chums, Bill Bennett, who lived across the road, Johnny Westcott from Weddington and Harry Shaw from Attleborough, all districts in the borough of Nuneaton.

The front door opened and slammed as George walked in after another difficult day with staff at the Scala cinema.

"Have you heard the latest?" he said. "Those bloody Germans have marched into neutral Belgium without any warning and the Belgian Government are all at sea. God knows what their King and Queen, as well as their government and forces, are doing about it. Also, our boys are being pushed all the way back to the French coast." His face was red from anger reminding Alice that he had to mind his blood pressure.

"Sit down George, you don't need to get so excited and please stop shouting and watch your language; you know it upsets the neighbours. I'll make a cup of tea."

He turned towards the wireless intending to switch it on just as the grandfather clock in the hall struck 11.00 am. Alan walked in, excitedly glancing at his parents.

"Has Mum told you the news, Dad?"

"What news are we talking about, son?" He looked up from the wireless expecting some other depressing news from the war. "Bloody Germans are bad enough. What's happened now - tell me quickly, I'm tired."

"Next week, I've got a request to drop in at Coventry's Combined Services Recruiting Centre located in the old 'Swift' roller skating rink," said Alan. "They've asked me to attend a day's interview for the RAF Voluntary Reserve."

George's red face deepened in colour as he coughed loudly for several minutes. The signs of his debilitating respiratory malaise, as a consequence of malaria in Africa, was already evident and would eventually bring on pneumonia and death eleven years later. Alice frowned at the bad language but stayed silent. She knew better than to interrupt him but she did click her lips in annoyance

15

"That's what you think. Do you believe that your mother, sister and I want to sit here for the duration of this damned war waiting for a 'Missing in Action' letter? Your brothers are bad enough; it will break your mother's heart! We'll discuss this later."

Alan shut the front door gently, leaving his fuming father ranting on about the war and walked over to the Bennett's house. He knew his father and mother were scared because their three sons would be away facing danger, but hoped that Bill and his parents would show more understanding and sympathy. He saw Barbara with a couple of friends some distance away walking home from school and waved just as Bill opened the door.

"Hey Alan, please come in!"

Somewhere in the background, the strains of Benny Goodman playing the popular 'Don't be that Way' could be heard on a Marconi Radio. Bill's mother, Irene, appeared in a floral pinafore and beamed her usual ear-to-ear big smile. She was a well-meaning large lady with kind eyes and a positive outlook, even if her unimaginative dress sense and heavy local accent was not to everyone's taste.

"Hello Alan, fancy a cuppa'? I'm about to brew up for 'mysen' and Peter. There might be some biscuits too."

"Ok, thanks, but I can't stop long. Dad's not happy at all with me wanting to join the RAF."

"Oh dear, well don't worry, they'll come around to it. You know we had similar concerns and realised that we can't stop you young'uns from helping the war effort, especially as they are dropping bombs on London. If you want, I'll nip over the road and try to console them. Maybe they'll understand."

Alan and Bill sifted through some old comics and photographs lying on the kitchen table, helping themselves to ginger and short cake biscuits on a plate, waiting for Irene to return. Food shortages had not yet fully kicked in. Over large mugs of tea, they chatted about their impending visit to the recruitment office in Coventry.

Peter, Bill's father, fingered his braces, drew heavily on his Woodbine cigarette and scanned pages of the Nuneaton Observer, while the two lads imagined what they would be doing once they were wearing Royal Air Force uniforms.

"I'd love to apply for aircrew in Bomber Command, don't mind what I do so long as they'll have me," said Bill.

He would have never guessed that in less than three months and still only nineteen, he would be flying with 21 squadron as a trainee radio operator in Bristol Blenheims with 139 Squadron based at Horsham St Faiths near Norwich.

Alan thought about it for a few moments. His deep blue eyes flashing wide as he dreamt of flying in anything with wings, "I'd be happy flying a magic carpet," he said grinning.

Peter looked up and with a chuckle said, "Be careful what you wish for. From what I've been told, those new-fangled planes are about as comfortable as a motor car with square wheels!"

The two friends laughed just as Bill's mother opened the back door and walked in. With another of her wide smiles that lifted everyone's spirits, she looked directly at Alan.

"I think you'll find your parents are alright about it. They are bound to be worried but realised that, if you stayed behind, there would be many wondering why you are not helping the war effort and that could be awkward for you and them. Off you go and have a nice chat with them. Try to make them feel more at ease."

Alan thanked her and hurried out the back, helping himself to a couple of ginger nuts on the way.

"That lad has a terrible sweet tooth," said Bill's mother. "It won't do him any good at all. He'll end up with the worms! Never mind, I'm sure his teeth are the last things on his mind right now. Bill, until such a time that you are sent different ways by the RAF, make sure he doesn't get into trouble or come to any harm. He's a good lad and his parents and sister, already concerned about the two eldest boys are fearful about him entering the war."

17

Chapter 3: Approaching Tournai

Odette was beginning to feel the effects of walking. The column had travelled over sixty kilometres in very warm weather. Her feet and legs were aching and swollen despite spending time sitting on a horse- drawn trailer belonging to Monsieur Haché and his family. She and a few others had climbed on board after leaving Beloeil four days before.

Occupied with Baudelaire's 'Les Fleurs du Mal', belonging to Monsieur le Curé Delage, she had nevertheless found time to make friends with Suzanne Decours and Vivienne Van Damme, two girls of the same age from St. Ghislain, west of Mons. Other relatives, including her parents and friends were still pretty much together, trying their hardest to look cheerful and positive, but they too were also beginning to feel the physical demands of the march.

Veronique, the pregnant lady from Mauberge, had also joined Odette and the two girls. Although much older, she possessed a good sense of humour and was much more worldly than the other three. Veronique explained that she'd had a relationship with a married man and carried his child. She also said she'd marry any man within reason who was prepared to care for her and the child.

"I'm not concerned if he's Belgian or some other nationality, BUT certainly not German!" she quickly added. "I'm two months' pregnant and the baby will need a father. I will love the child but I don't think I will have the ability or patience to be a single mother. Every child needs a father figure, that's how it should be."

"What about love?" asked Vivienne van Damme coyly. "Surely if you find a father, you'd have to love each other too?"

"Love is hard to find in war time. So long as he can work hard, keep his family secure and be kind, I'll be happy. If he knows what to do with his you know what, I'll be even happier!" She gestured lewdly towards her lower torso. The three girls giggled loudly but their laughter was brought to a halt by the sounds of approaching aircraft. Jean-Baptiste Clarifié was the first to spot them and with his loud baritone voice, despite traces of panic, shouted so loudly that everyone suddenly forgot their tiredness and ran for cover.

"Everyone scatter! They are German! Take cover or lie low in the ditches." Two Messerschmitt bf 109s flew level and low, so low that Odette could see the pilot in the closest one. The Balkenkreuz black and white cross on the fuselage, the distinctive deafening noise of the Daimler Benz engines and the bright yellow nose seemed to transfix her along with most of the others. The two aircraft disappeared into the distance as quickly as they had arrived.

"All clear!" someone yelled. Fernand and Laure reassured Odette and the girls that the pilots were only observing the column and probably had no intention of causing harm.

"What purpose would it serve for them to attack harmless crowds?" said Curé Delage.

An old man sitting in a squeaky small cart pulled by his grandson replied, "They are German barbarians and they have the upper hand right now. It will pay us to keep in mind the atrocities they committed in the Great War only 22 years ago."

Most people, despite vivid memories of 1914-18, settled down again and resumed their walk. The evening light was rapidly fading as dirty grey rain clouds gathered and the nearest habitation was some way ahead.

Fernand and Laure, along with most of their closest family and friends, decided to bivouac amongst the trees in a forest outside Leuze-en-Hainault, less than 10 kilometres from Tournai and make themselves comfortable. Others carried on for a couple of kilometres but were ultimately forced to do the same. It was just after 21:00 hours and it was raining.

It took nearly an hour before Odette's father and mother had erected something resembling a tarpaulin cover, supported by old tree branches. Inside the makeshift tent, they spread out old blankets and cushions whilst outside, the wind had picked up and the rain became heavier. Jacqueline Clarifié, Odette's young second cousin, had joined the Moreaus for the night, mainly because she had become attached to Odette. The two of them wrapped up in extra blankets and coats before settling down chatting quietly after Fernand had reprimanded them for being noisy. The two girls spoke in whispers and giggled as the sounds of gentle snoring drifted over from the older couple.

"I'm scared," said Jacqueline.

"So am I," replied Odette quickly. "What will we do if the aircraft return? We have nothing with which to defend ourselves."

"I'm sure that a couple of boys in the leading party have a few guns. They might help." Odette shuddered as she repeated what her father had warned them about.

"If we are stopped by the Boche and they discover the guns, we'll be in big trouble."

Both girls pondered this before Jacqueline said nervously, "They must get rid of the guns. I'll talk to my father in the morning."

Rain started to drip from several places in the tarpaulin. Fernand woke up a few hours before dawn while everyone still slept and crawled outside to cover the leaky rubber sheet by lashing down another bigger tarpaulin. He retreated to lie beside Laure even though still quite wet and shivering. The heat from her body enabled him to find some more precious sleep.

Next morning the dark clouds had mostly gone and the sun was breaking through. The sounds of the camp coming to life filled the air. A few enterprising people had formed a raiding party and luckily discovered a couple of deserted farmhouses. The owners had fled, leaving quantities of food, salted bacon, eggs, dry biscuits, cakes, coffee and edible bread. These were eagerly distributed along the column.

Odette and Jacqueline were joined by Suzanne, Vivienne and Veronique. While munching handfuls of dry biscuits, they decided to wander slowly through an adjacent wheat field, chatting incessantly about nature, home, boys and food. Odette held back and took in the surrounding fields. Smoke drifted up from a few fires on the edge of the woodland where the travellers were busy preparing the déjeuner du matin. She watched a couple of rabbits sitting on their haunches, acting as lookouts and reflected on how their simple lives were so unaffected in this awful war. She then watched a nest of ants, disturbed by her footsteps, fascinated by how they were able to just move around so easily without conflict, unlike the human race.

A blue sky and a gentle breeze blowing the rustling wheat seemed unrealistically peaceful, almost musical. Somewhere beyond the horizon, muffled sounds of explosions drifted towards the girls. They decided to hurry back to the column.

"Hurry up!" Laure was standing at the edge of the road beckoning her daughter. She appeared quite agitated and like everyone close by, had also heard the sound of heavy artillery.

"Where have you been? I've just spent the last thirty minutes preparing a good breakfast. Come quickly as we have to start walking again and you have to help."

The other girls ran off to join their groups. Odette quickly wolfed down bacon eggs and fried bread while watching her father pile up their belongings in the cart. The air around them smelled of cooking and damp clothes after the rainy night.

"Some of the men near the front of the column have guns." Jacqueline paused before identifying the culprits as the Delvaux twins, Hector and Pierre. Jean-Baptiste, her father gulped in disbelief and turned to Julia.

"What stupidity is this?" he muttered. "I must talk with them before anyone starts asking awkward questions."

He ran towards the front as the column started to close up. On the way he shouted to Fernand to come with him. The two of them hurried forward just as a parade of motorbikes and armoured vehicles reached them and came to a halt in a cloud of dust.

Jean-Baptiste quickly turned to Fernand, "Leave it. Let's get back to the women and hope that the Germans don't stop and search us." At the head of the German patrol, a major and his driver stopped. Behind them, a number of outriders on motorbikes and two half-track personnel carriers with over two-dozen armed German troops, glared malevolently at the travellers.

"My name is Major Reinhardt Rödl of the Wehrmacht 7th Infantry Division. I have to warn you, it is my intention, following orders from Herr Generalleutnant Eccard Freiherr von Gablenz, to search out and detain anyone connected with resistance against German occupying forces." He spoke with immaculate French using a megaphone so that everyone could hear and understand.

"If anyone knows of such activities or suspects those engaged in sabotage against the Reich, stand forward. You will be treated well and rewarded if you comply. It is my mission to offer the hand of friendship to you all but only if you go about your business without trouble. On the other hand, I will show no mercy if I suspect that one or more of you are troublemakers. We will now search through your belongings and I demand that you stand aside."

The Major motioned to his unit and troops jumped down standing in line. There was much shuffling and whispering, but the entire column of refugees seemed resolved to stay silent. There had been some earlier talk of a few patriots joining resistance groups as soon as an opportunity presented itself but, by and large, the invasion had been so quick following the King's capitulation of Belgium that few had found time to show any reaction. They were more concerned in getting to Calais and knew that beyond Tournai, the British BEF and French Troops were waiting for the German advance towards the coast and Antwerp.

After shouting orders to his troops, Major Rödl stood aside and watched as soldiers randomly began searching possessions. They threw items into road as they climbed all over the various carts, bicycles and packs. The crowd started to grumble as their personal items were searched. Fortunately, a more considerate officer who could not keep his eyes off Odette quickly searched Fernand's cart and found nothing.

Pierre Delvaux, one of the twins who, along with his brother had just turned eighteen, shouted out, "Is this really necessary? Show some respect for our few belongings. We are only travellers trying to find somewhere safe." Several in the group gasped.

Rödl heard the outburst. He stiffened and clenched his fists, demanded the perpetrator show himself. Pierre shuffled forward. The major along with three of his men, strode briskly to where Pierre was standing. A few women nearby started to cry.

"YES! It is necessary!" he shouted, less than a foot from Pierre's face. The German's acrid Bratwurst breath caused Pierre to wrinkle his nose, sneer and turn away. The atmosphere soon became very tense as the German soldiers menacingly raised their guns.

"And where is your family and where are your belongings Monsieur?" demanded the Major, his voice calming down as he detected nervousness in the man standing before him. Pierre pointed to a wagon ten feet away and his family standing alongside.

The Major motioned to his troops. They rough handled the family to one side and immediately emptied their cart throwing everything onto the road and verge. Lying in the bottom was a wooden box in which lay five Belgian bolt-action service rifles and three old Mauser pistols. There was also another box containing ammunition.

"So, you were hoping to walk to safety and yet you carry weapons which you would no doubt use against our Wehrmacht forces. Where did you acquire these guns?"

Pierre, not being endowed with much common sense or intelligence replied sullenly, "They belong to my family and are only for shooting wild game so we can feed ourselves on the march."

" You are lying! Do you really think I'm stupid, you Belgian idiot?" shouted the Major. "Your entire family is implicated." He spoke to his three men standing by and they stood forward.

"Secure him and his family and then collect the weapons." Pierre looked directly at the Major and spat in his face. Rödl, wiped away the phlegm from his forehead and let it fall onto his shining black boots. With a deleterious, venomous smirk, he turned towards the crowd and using his megaphone shouted, "I warned you all that the German army would not tolerate any resistance or evidence of aggression. I was prepared to believe that you are all harmless evacuees and let you move on, but it's obvious there are those amongst you who wish to express their feelings. We must use this opportunity to set an example so you will realise that it is futile to carry arms and resist. You will not succeed."

"Hauptmann! Take them away!"

With the patrol unit watching, the crowd dispersed, some crying, sobbing and muttering. Fernand and Laure held hands with Odette and returned to finish off-loading their cart.

"What will happen to them?" asked Odette.

"Who knows?" replied her father. "That stupid boy has now put his family and possibly all of us in danger."

The column slowly walked on. Many were hunched up pushing wagons and cycles, showing their anxiety as they passed the line of stern-looking Germans. They dared not look up in case they were picked on. Suddenly, they heard shouting in German followed by dreadful screaming and the staccato sounds of machine gun fire and pistol shots.

As the crowd approached a clearing in the trees, less than two hundred metres from where they had set up camp, they came across a stone wall and saw four German soldiers holding smoking machine guns with the Major standing on the verge with a smoking Luger pistol still in his right hand. Lying on the ground, in front of the wall and no more than ten metres from the road, were several bodies. Pierre, his twin brother, their sister Monique, their mother, father and two uncles had been shot in the back of the head. There was a great deal of blood pooling on the ground and spattered across the stone wall. Those able to see the shocking evidence of Rödl's repulsive actions screamed and pushed forward with outstretched hands. Some fell on their knees and prayed fearing the guns would be turned on them. German soldiers beat them away using the butts of their rifles as clubs.

At the head of the column, Monsieur Ferrage urged everyone to move quickly and not to look as they passed, but he could not stop those who surged forward in grief and shock. Nor could he silence the screams and the crying particularly from those who knew the Delvaux family. They had tasted their first experience of brutal German occupation, one they would never forget. Nobody was left with illusions that this war would be any less cruel and devastating than the last one that ended twenty-two years ago.

The Major ordered his troops back into the waiting transporters while he and his driver climbed into their car before driving on. When they were out of site, the column stopped. Only then did everyone gather together to draw some comfort from each other and express their revulsion and fright.

"Now we know what to expect from these bastards," yelled someone deep in the crowd.

Monsieur le Curé raised his voice. "Please, everyone, God is still here amongst you all and will give us strength. Let us pray for those poor souls who are at peace and have ascended to heaven."

After a few moments of silence, he turned with outstretched hands and pleaded with the crowd. "They deserve to be buried. We can't just leave them there."

"I agree, it's the decent Christian thing to do," responded Fernand as he stepped forward. Five other men quickly joined him whilst everyone nodded in agreement.

Odette and Jacqueline were still in deep shock and weeping as Fernand and some of the other men walked back with an assortment of spades and shovels to where the bodies lay. They returned an hour later having completed their grisly work. Fernand sat on the grass verge. It was the first time that his daughter had seen him weep. Laure went to him and put her arm around his shoulders. She reassured him that he was their rock and that she and Odette loved him very much. Jean-Baptiste, Julia, Jacqueline and Aunt Hélène joined them as they declared their love and support for each other, but also their determination to carry on.

"Maybe, one day we will be given a chance to seek justice for what has happened," said Fernand. "We have put up a cross where they are buried so they can be located later and moved to a cemetery. For now let's move on since Tournai is only an hour away and we will find enough accommodation to rest a while and clean up."

An old dwarf of a man recognised as the 'Croque Mort' from Valenciennes, still dressed in his undertaker's outfit, was sitting on a rusty Peugeot cycle with a couple of punctures. He extracted a half bottle of cognac.

"I'm going to get pissed tonight, it's all been too much and besides, I wasn't asked to help bury the dead."

A few smiled at his pique and the irony, but a large woman, sweating profusely, dressed in a dark coat and carrying a large stick shouted, "Show respect you disgusting old man." She then stepped forward and poked the old man so that he fell off his bike. Those nearest laughed but the rest were still too shocked to express anything but anxiety or revulsion.

Slowly but surely, the crowd moved on. Footwear was already causing problems, not least with Odette who now complained that walking was really painful. She had developed blisters and, to alleviate the discomfort, used cotton pads soaked in surgical spirits. Later when supplies had dried up, she was told that the first urine of the day would be just as effective, if not better. It proved to be correct, even if the odour was a little indelicate.

Chapter 4: The Early RAF Years

"Alan Granville White!" The man behind the desk shouted his name. Alan had been sitting waiting in line on hard wooden benches for over two hours with nineteen other recruits. On hearing his name, he walked over to the Desk Sergeant and as he passed the line he heard others whisper, "Good luck mate," or in one case, "Ask them to hurry up, my arse is hurting!" Alan smiled and carried on.

"Please sit down. My name is Flight Sergeant Thompson and from now on you'll address me using my rank and name. Is that clear?" He waited for an acknowledgement and then carried on.

"I'm here to find out if you and any of those other scruffy apes over there can be knocked into shape and can be of some use to the RAF. Alan nodded in agreement.

"OK, I have your name, your age, your education and where you come from but that's all. Before you become a privileged addition to His Majesty's Royal Air force, I'd like to know why you are here? Why have you chosen the RAF?"

Alan thought about this carefully.

"Well man, speak up!" he said brusquely and loudly.

Alan answered nervously, "I'd like to fly Sir and try to help the war effort. I've always been interested in aircraft."

The large office suddenly seemed very small as Alan waited for a reply but none came whilst the sergeant set about writing notes. Alan gazed out of one of the tall windows adorned with black rolled up night blinds. He was transfixed by the lines of hopeful recruits waiting outside two enormous newly restored wooden sheds reserved for the Army and the Navy.

"Are you paying attention Mr White or are you day dreaming?" the Sergeant bellowed. "You seem more interested in what's going on outside rather than inside." Just at that moment and to everyone's great amusement, a pigeon flew in through one of the open windows and settled on a coat stand at the far end of the room where it proceeded to flutter around noisily and splatter the officer's coats with droppings. Someone giggled.

"Quiet, you horrible rabble!" bellowed Sergeant Thompson.

He turned to Alan. "So you'd like to fly would you? Well let me tell you this. The RAF is not just for flyers. There are many other vital jobs to do in the days and months ahead if we are going to stop the Jerries. In addition, His Majesty's Air Force is not for those who prefer to wear a nice uniform or a flying helmet and feel they belong to an elite service."

He shuffled amongst his papers and handed Alan a form and then added, "The fight ahead will not be easy and some of you may not return to your families."

"OK, fill in this form and take it to the large building behind this one. There you'll find the medical centre and others who will provide you with instructions on where and when you'll be posted. Good luck!" He dismissed Alan with a wave of his hand before shouting, "Next please!"

Alan pondered on what he'd just been told about the possibility of not returning as he filled in the form, before walking sixty yards to a large dark camouflaged building with blacked out windows. Somewhere in one of the adjacent streets, a couple of fire engines raced along ringing their bells loudly. As he neared the entrance steps to the ominous corrugated building, he heard a familiar voice.

"Hey! Wait for me." Alan turned to see Bill Bennett running furiously towards him and smiled.

"I'm late but was wondering if you were still here. Have you had the medical yet?"

Bill had emerged from another large building over half a mile away carrying a heavy raincoat and a leather briefcase containing all his papers and, after a long sprint, was now out of breath.

"I can't breathe," he said and, whilst taking in deep gulps of air, held on to Alan's arm for a couple of minutes.

28

Alan, with an amused expression, replied, "You'll never pass a medical in that condition. Your heart and lungs must be working overtime. I'm due in there too and I'm dreading it. I hate needles and probing fingers."

The two lads smiled at each other and entered the dark building via two heavy oak creaking doors, which Bill nicknamed 'The Cave'. They walked over to a grumpy looking middle-aged woman standing behind an open sliding glass partition. After glancing at their papers she directed them along a corridor towards two swing doors at the side of which the words 'RAF Medical Centre' were inscribed in red. Someone using the name 'Bugs Bunny' had written in crayon 'What's up Doc?'.

The Medical Centre was heaving. A flight Sergeant beckoned them and asked them to join the twin queue. All along one long wall there were over a dozen badly curtained pale green cubicles that hid very little. Alan and Bill could easily see various undignified scenes played out including Alan's premonition of probing fingers. A few nurses and medical staff walked to and fro as they joined the other men patiently waiting.

"Hope you've had a wash, mate." Alan recognised the man as Thomas Bingham who used to work as a cleaner for his father back in 1938 at the Scala Cinema. George White had been forced to sack him but not before tearing a strip off him so loudly that most shoppers in Abbey Street heard more than a few unsavoury words. He'd been caught making inappropriate advances towards one of the two usherettes who doubled up as an ice cream girl during the intervals. Whatever he had done, the girl had screamed, dropped her tray of ice creams and ran out in the middle of a matinée showing of 'The Hunchback of Notre Dame'.

"Maybe best if you just shut up pal," responded Alan. Bill looked at him with a grin that somehow combined amusement and dread.

"So, Mr 'la-di-da', you think you are above the rest of us, eh?" Bill was right to show concern. After all, Alan's reply was hardly subtle and the last thing either wanted was confrontation with a malcontent. Alan ignored him but the man's voice rose in anger.

"You're the son of George White ain't ya? You're just as snotty and pompous as he is. God help the country if your type joins the service. We'd all be better off if you stayed at home."

That was enough for Bill who grabbed the man's coat lapels and pushed him against one of the iron radiators. The man's breath smelled strongly of ale. "That's enough you deplorable little man. I'm his friend and we look after each other. Do you get it, idiot?" Thomas Bingham brushed himself down and quickly realised he was on a losing wicket, particularly as several others in the line were starting to get impatient and utter threats too.

"OK, OK, no offence meant," he mumbled. A tall, senior looking doctor with a stethoscope dangling around his neck had heard the dispute and walked over, accompanied by a security officer. He was clearly in no mood to argue with.

"If I hear anymore nonsense, I'll eject the lot of you," he said in a deep gruff voice. "Do I make myself clear?"

The three of them replied, "Yes Sir!" just as a pretty nurse approached and asked the doctor to follow her to one of the cubicles where a man had fallen over or fainted. Alan looked at her and caught her staring back before she disappeared.

"Wow! She's so pretty," ventured Alan, but Bill was indifferent and was looking very reflective.

"Listen Al, let's just agree to try and not find trouble, OK?"

"I didn't start it," Alan replied. "And, I will not be pushed around. You didn't have to join in, I could have sorted it."

"Oh right, I'm sure you would have," Bill replied sarcastically.

The two of them remained silent and slowly edged forward as the queue neared the cubicles.

"Next!" Alan moved forward as Bill disappeared into cubicle three with poor fitting curtains.

"Good luck Bill!" shouted Alan, but his friend had already disappeared inside the green-curtained booth. After a twenty-minute wait, it was Alan's turn. He walked towards cubicle eight.

"Take off your shoes, socks, shirt, vest and trousers, leaving your underpants on." The nurse's back was turned away from him as she collated a large pile of forms and paperwork on a rickety old wooden table. She turned to face him and Alan let out a soft murmur and turned red. It was the pretty nurse he'd taken a shine to earlier on.

"Can I have your name and address please?" she asked. Alan gave her the information before she looked up and smiled.

"OK Mr White, if I'm not mistaken, you're one of the chaps who was involved in some trouble earlier on. Am I right?"

"Yes Ma'am," Alan replied, trying to remain calm and dignified.

"Well, let's hope you are not a trouble maker shall we?" She smiled sweetly and asked him to take a seat.

"I'm going to do a few routine tests and then ask some questions before one of the doctors sees you and works out whether you are fit enough to serve in the Royal Airforce, or any other force for that matter."

She smiled whilst reading through Alan's papers, documents and reports charting his background and education. He could not help take in her features; she reminded him of Joan Fontaine with an hourglass figure and a flawless complexion rarely seen amongst the women in Nuneaton or the industrial Midlands.

"It seems you have an aptitude for mechanical and technical things but your school reports say you are also creative with a talent for drawing. I don't want to sound negative but you'll have very few opportunities to use your creative talents."

She was studying him with her deep blue eyes for what seemed to him to be an eternity. With a cheeky smile, she quickly added, "Quite the opposite in fact; you'll have to become more destructive if you want to survive when flying against the enemy."

Alan reflected on what she had said. She picked up her stethoscope and approached him. He was trying to relax but in her presence he failed dismally.

31

"You seem tense!" She listened to his breathing and heart beat and then took a blood pressure reading, before taking his height and weight measurements. "Well that all seems to be in very good order," she said.

"Your heartbeat is a little fast and you seem to be quite fit but need to put on a few extra pounds. I'm sure that after a few months in the RAF, you'll gain a few extra muscles." She smiled sweetly at him before writing a few notes.

Alan noticed she was wearing a wedding ring and suddenly asked whether her husband was serving in the armed forces.

She frowned and pondered for a minute and said, "I wear his ring but my husband died in a plane crash whilst training for night time operations last year. We'd only been married for five weeks. Why did you ask me?" she enquired.

She was looking straight at Alan. Her big blue eyes looked sad and he detected grief in her voice and realised that she was more than likely reticent to discuss matters further.

"Because I think you are extraordinarily beautiful," he replied, taking his time, "and you should not have had to face such sadness. I'm so sorry."

He immediately regretted asking such a personal question. Again he apologised but she smiled. None of the grief could hide her beauty and Alan was smitten. She waved her hand as if to brush away the past and said they'd better return to the business of the examination. However, she complimented Alan for his kindness whilst secretly realising that he might have to lose some of his sensitivity in the coming months. After many questions about his education, she concluded that he was bright, amusing and tenacious and would be a good team player. She stood up to go but Alan reached out and touched her arm as she walked away.

"I hope you don't mind but I'd like to think we will be able to meet again. I would be very sad if we didn't."

She quickly walked towards the curtain, paused and turned back, looking him straight in the eyes and replied.

"It's a little too soon for that but yes, I'd like to see you again. I doubt if we'll be able to meet before I'm posted elsewhere in the next few days so it have to wait until this awful war is over." Her reply made him smile. Before he left, he turned towards her and saw that she was watching him.

"I'll find you when it's over," said Alan.

The curtain opened and a rather short, tubby spectacled doctor with a white goatee and a pronounced stoop walked in unsteadily. He'd probably heard what Alan just said.

"I'm Doctor Trevor Jeffcoat and I won't keep you long. I just need to conduct a few standard tests."

He walked over to Alan and asked him to drop his pants. With cold hands, the sort that make any man wince, he felt Alan's scrotum to detect whether his testicles were in place and asked him to cough. He wrote down a few notes before reaching out and pressing his groins to establish whether hernias were present. Alan grimaced and was becoming increasingly hot and bothered. Various other tests followed to establish stamina, strength, and coordination as well as eye tests and dental checks. The only saving grace was that no needles were used and Alan's thoughts kept returning to the pretty nurse with no name. After hurriedly getting dressed, the doctor asked him to collect his reports before giving him instructions on where to go next.

"Try and find hut 22 where they'll process you and tell you where you'll be stationed. Oh and please button your flies and smarten yourself up. You don't want to give the chaps over there a bad impression do you eh? Good luck son."

Alan wanted to walk out quickly and find fresh air but before that, he spun round and asked for the name of the nurse. Doctor Jeffcoat slowly took off his glasses and placed them on the desk. He paused coughed and smiled before looking up at Alan.

"Her name is Nurse Kathleen McKenzie, but listen son, don't get your hopes up too much, she's off to France in a few days with the medical corps serving the BEF and she'll be up against it. She's a

33

lovely person and one of our best nurses. Kath has experienced much personal sadness so I'd hate to see her getting hurt again either because of war or in a hopeless romance." Alan shook his hand and thanked him but could not help feeling downcast.

An hour later he and Bill met and decided to walk into Coventry so they could catch a train back to Nuneaton via Bedworth. The dull grey streets were full of people wrapped up in heavy woollen coats, hats and chunky scarves. All this would soon be far away for both of them. They would be free from restrictions at home and this would be their greatest adventure. They walked rapidly, crossing the cobbled road and tramlines with their breath clouding the air in front as they chatted without pause. Passing the Cathedral and finding their way via a short cut along Greyfriars Lane to the railway station on the Warwick Road, they passed two drunks propped up outside the Hare and Squirrel pub, pointing at them and being abusive. A stomach-churning reek of urine permeated the air.

The talk was excited and animated at the prospect of wearing the distinctive RAF blue uniforms with unique 'Per Ardua Ad Astra' badges and actually being able to serve their country. It was May 6th 1940. Little did they know what lay ahead. In just under a month, British troops would be evacuated from Dunkirk. In less than 6 months, the Luftwaffe would be given a bloody nose by the RAF in the Battle of Britain, London would suffer during the first months of the Blitz and Coventry would be largely reduced to rubble by German bombs. Alan mentioned the nurse to Bill and he, trying to be like a more mature brother, advised Alan to forget about her and concentrate on what was to come in the RAF.

Bill's experience at the hands of the medical staff had also been disturbing as he recalled the horror of one very old doctor, suffering from the shakes with appalling halitosis, very bad eyes, and taking an age to locate his lower extremities.

Alan could not forget about Nurse McKenzie. He would be going to RAF Yatesbury in Wiltshire and she would be in France. It might have been on the other side of the world. He would soon be

34

an eager fresh-faced recruit in the newly formed Voluntary Reserve to train on radio detection systems, surveillance and navigation. There he would be allocated the grand rank of Aircraftman White. Much to his delight he would also have to take on some flying duties although he was unaware at this stage what that would entail. Bill, on the other hand, was posted to RAF Manston in Kent where he would also be an aircraftman and given a choice to train either as a pilot or as a navigation and radio operator. He chose the latter.

Chapter 5: The Road to Hell

Most of those in the column of travellers had now walked for over eighty kilometres and were feeling the first signs of physical exertion. It was May 22nd and several of them, apart from the strong in body and mind, had elected to stay in Tournai and risk their chances. Advanced columns of German infantry and mechanised vehicles including the Wehrmacht's 7th Infantry Division of which the 'Butcher' Major Reinhardt Rödl was attached, had been instructed to head North towards Antwerp in the hope of striking south and so they avoided entering Tournai. The German High Command were acutely aware that beyond Tournai and Hazebrouck, in a curved line between Calais and Ostend, French, Belgian and British forces were being deployed in a line that would cover a retreat to the coast. The column of evacuees was now, for the time being, in Flanders or Northern Belgium where the Dutch-influenced language sounded not dissimilar to German. The disparity between the Southern French-speaking Catholic Belgians or Walloons as they were known, and the Flemish Protestant north often boiled over into rows amongst the evacuees. Distrust, and intolerance emerged out of religion and politics. This would come to the surface in a dramatic way during the post war years.

Two nights in Tournai had helped to rest blistered feet, sore hands and allow time to forage or beg for food as well as sleep in deserted houses, cafés, hotels or farm buildings. The column had expanded to over one hundred refugees, many arriving from across the French border, pushing their prams, carts, bicycles and wagons but looking particularly miserable and badly clothed. They had suffered atrocities committed by various undisciplined Jäger scout reconnaissance units, trying to detect enemy movements. It became clear they were close to the allied front and German troops had received a battering from some entrenched French and British artillery positions, making them more belligerent than usual.

Once they had reached La Madeleine on the outskirts of Lille, a few dead Germans and French soldiers appeared in the ditches and on farmland. Some were already in advanced stages of putrefaction and covered with flies. In some places the smell was unbearable. There were also dead farm animals, including a few cattle and a decapitated horse, which horrified Odette as she thought tearfully of 'Hercule'. To make matters worse, German aircraft now patrolled the skies and occasionally in the distance they witnessed aerial combat between the Luftwaffe and RAF aircraft. Whenever a German aircraft crashed, the column cheered.

All of a sudden and without any warning, a lone ME109 circled above like a hawk and approached the column from a low altitude. Those at the front screamed and ran towards the ditches and fields. Bullets from the plane's twin cannons tore up the road and verges ricocheting off the hard stone road surface. Several unfortunate souls were caught and died immediately. Others not so lucky, were wounded and screamed for help as the German circled again for another killing spree. By this time most people had scattered including the Moreaus and their relatives or friends. Two small children remained terrified and transfixed in the middle of the road as the bullets came again. Their parents, with outstretched arms and pleading hands screamed. By some miracle, the twin lines of cannon fire passed alongside and missed them. Their parents and a few others shouting warnings, rushed onto the road and herded the two terrified children into a side culvert as the plane prepared to circle for a third time.

Suddenly, and out of nowhere, an RAF Spitfire came into view. The pilot had seen what was happening and although far from base, he decided to help out. This was despite knowing the German might soon be joined by his friends who would be more than willing to join in. The Spitfire half rolled and then climbed to over a thousand feet. He turned and came in above and behind the German who saw him too late. A long burst from the Spit's Browning cannons caught the ME9 along the fuselage and engine. Black smoke and flames poured from the engine as the pilot lost control and tried to steer towards the ground, hoping for a landing. There was a loud bang as the fuel tanks exploded and the Messerschmitt disintegrated in the air, no more than thirty metres above the ground and two hundred metres from the watching crowd. Loud cheers and frantic waving erupted from nearly everyone as the British pilot executed a victory roll and disappeared towards the West.

Odette turned to her father, shocked and trembling, her face as white as snow. She thanked the brave English pilot before begging her father to stop, as she was feeling faint and needed time to rest her feet.

"How long will it be before we reach the coast?" she asked. "My feet are hurting so much."

"I wish I knew the answer ma petite. It depends upon whatever circumstances and hazards we encounter up ahead."

"But Papa," she retorted with a cheeky grin, "How will we get there if our feet wear out and disappear?"

Odette's mother, suppressing a smile, joined in the conversation and said solemnly, "We had better try and help those poor people who have just lost relatives and friends."

Father Delage, the Curé, had already administered the last rights to an old husband and wife who had been shot, but were still holding hands as their lives ebbed away. Fernand, Laure, Jean-Baptiste and a tall ex-policeman who had once worked in Mons, helped carry eight bodies to the side of the road. They were now getting more used to the sight of blood and gore, but they were not prepared for a sepia photograph of a young handsome Belgian army captain and a child. The photograph was still clutched in the hand of a woman who had been shot in the chest. Odette and her mother started to cry. Odette's skirt hem had traces of blood on it, which made her shudder.

"When is it going to stop?" she wailed.

Fernand put his arm around her and her mother and responded, "When the allies knock the Boche back to where they belong."

"In hell you mean!" shouted cousin Julia, Jean-Baptiste's wife, who'd just joined them after the carnage. "That's where the Boche belong. Let's hope they will come up against the British and lose the war. Besides, and equally important, I've lost my dentures!"

Even in the midst of their fears and sadness, the gathered crowd could not help but laugh. It was nervous laughter, the sort that helps relieve tension.

It was now the 25th May as the slow-winding column dragged along its worldly possessions on wheels, bad backs, hand luggage and horses. The weary, the old, the sick and the young sat in carts and wagons as the stronger men sweated and toiled whilst they pulled and pushed. Medical attention was primitive and left in the capable hands of two former hospital sisters. Their work was increasingly concerned with healing blisters, splinters, sore hands, cuts and bruises. They had both helped when a man was badly wounded by shrapnel following the air attack. Sadly, he had died but not before he'd consumed a half bottle of Martel Cognac, the remains of their medicinal anaesthetic.

One family had taken possession of a nanny goat with a bad attitude, which they named 'Bertha'. She had a malevolent glare in both eyes and insisted on charging anyone she took a dislike to, which was nearly everyone. The family was eventually forced to tether her to their wagon. Somewhere else, three people were arguing over a couple of old dried loaves but apart from their angry shouts, the column walked on and made another 6 kilometres before they were approached by three vehicles, each with three soldiers.

It was a warm evening sky as the sun slid towards the horizon. Captain Lawrence Henderson of the 14th Battalion, Royal Fusiliers, stepped down from his Jeep. A short mop of blonde hair framed a weathered face as he raised his hand and brought the column to a halt. His expression was friendly as he introduced himself and addressed the crowd around him in badly pronounced French.

"We are on our way to St Omer. The road ahead around Lille is very dangerous. I'd consider taking the longer northern route to Kortrijk and avoid Lille altogether. Once there, take the route to Calais, which may prove to be your only chance. We are part of the British 10th army and with the French, we are retreating towards the coast and hoping to join the rest of our boys near Dunkirk."

The captain continued, "There are British and French Battalions protecting Calais so with a bit of luck you'll be alright. Just remember the Germans are advancing very rapidly but the good news is that Hitler, for unknown reasons, has issued orders for his forces to halt before the coast. You will encounter German troops if you do decide to carry on; that are inevitable, but I do believe they will be far more occupied with containing the allies at the coast. It's up you. I'm not here to tell you what to do, but simply willing to offer advice. My men and I will accompany you beyond Hazebrouck towards St Omer but from then on you'll have to manage on your own. Bonne chance!"

There was a lot of mumbling and a few louder comments as Captain Henderson climbed back into his Jeep and waited. Some of the people were clearly scared to carry on but hugely grateful.

"What shall we do?" asked Gaston Mendelier. "I mean, shall we go on, or go back?"

Fernand climbed up and stood on the floor of his cart, shouting for the crowd to gather around.

"You heard what the English Officer said. Those who wish to stay in Steenbecque, a village further back, or walk all the way back to their home town, raise your hands." Fourteen people sheepishly did so whilst looking around for approval. None was given.

"I'm assuming the rest of you who kept your hands down, wish to carry on to Calais?"

There was a resounding cry of "Yes!" with Gaston Mendelier shouting, "Vive La Belgique and Vive La France!"

The crowd broke into the Belgian National Anthem followed by the Marseillaise and then a brave couple started singing 'Run Rabbit

Run', amusingly trying to imitate Flanagan and Allen's song with pronounced accents. The fourteen, who had decided not to carry on, made up of three families along with a few friends, turned around and shuffled off in the opposite direction.

The main crowd now followed the three Jeeps, which were travelling at a very slow speed. A woman within the crowd ran towards the rear Jeep and called to the soldier sitting in the back.

"Monsieur, turn around! I want to show my thanks."

The soldier turned around as she caught up with the vehicle. Just as the driver stopped, she threw her arms around the startled man and planted a whopping big kiss on his right cheek leaving a large smudge of red lipstick.

The Lieutenant, sitting next to the driver displayed considerable surprise. He shouted back, "What the devil are you doing, Madame? Get down immediately and show some dignity!"

"I just want to show you how happy and safe I feel knowing you brave lads are escorting us to St Omer," said the woman.

The soldier in the rear, sporting a mop of black hair under his metal helmet, was smiling and red faced but clearly taken with this pretty girl. It was none other than Veronique, the pregnant lady from Mauberge. The Jeep stuttered back into life and set off again matching the slow marching speed of the travellers.

"What's your name soldier?" she asked him.

"Private John Lucas," he stuttered.

"Mine's Veronique," she said and hurriedly passed him a piece of paper on which she had scrawled 'Please meet me in St Omer'.

Veronique returned to the column, ignoring derisory comments expressing the indignity of it all, mainly from the older ladies.

A lively white-haired woman in her eighties dressed mainly in black and looking as though she was wearing traditional mourning clothes, yelled with a croaky voice, "Have you no shame? Nice Belgian women do not do such things."

Veronique replied, "I'm French and in France thank God, we are unlike you Belgians, we are not so stuffy."

41

The old woman's husband, who was even older and probably should never have attempted the journey, pointed at Veronique and shouted, "Typical French salope!"

There were a few muffled coughs and some laughter before the crowd settled down.

Veronique joined Odette, Jacqueline and the two other girls. Before they could say anything, Veronique said, "I told you I'd find someone. He's really rather much better than I had hoped and quite handsome. We are going to meet later in St Omer. I suppose my only concern is that he's English and people say that Englishmen are too reserved and backwards in matters of love. I'll just have to teach him a few things."

The other girls looked astonished.

"You don't waste any time do you?" said Suzanne.

Nothing else was said, so Veronique wandered back up to the front and stayed where she could wave occasionally at private John Lucas and coquettishly flash her long legs.

By now it was getting dark. The three Jeeps stopped up ahead and pulled into a wide entrance to a driveway belonging to an old partly dilapidated stone-built manor. The English Captain shouted back that he and his men would rest up in the manor until dawn before carrying on. He assured them that there were no Germans in the area. The three vehicles then disappeared along the tree-lined driveway into the dark.

Earlier, the column had met up with another influx of refugees at a large junction where the road from Tournai to St Omer met the old route to Arras. They numbered over 70 and had walked from Amiens, via Vimy, over 130 kilometres away and were clearly showing signs of exhaustion. The swollen ranks of homeless marchers merged and everyone did their best to help those less fortunate and shared what little food they possessed. It was now time to rest for the night before the final push to St Omer some 50 kilometres to the west. There were a few reproaches from the French mob, particularly those who had endured the longest march.

However, they did moan that the route would almost take them back in the same south westerly direction from where they had just come and some wanted to go in other directions.

Camp fires lit up the dark woodland next to the manor and the smell of cooking drifted on the back of a warm night breeze. Eerie shadows and drifting smoke created an unreal backdrop to the clearings in between dense birch and oak trees. The stone Manor was silhouetted against a dramatic red sky in a rapidly disappearing sunset. It was unusually quiet except for the occasional burst of laughter from the English inside.

John Lucas stepped outside and, in the darkness of the manor's canopied entrance, he lit a cigarette whilst glancing towards the busy encampment. People were moving around chatting or engaged in primitive cooking preparations. He suddenly heard a noise in the bushes and trees to his right. At the same time and from somewhere inside the manor, he heard Captain Henderson talking agitatedly on the field telephone.

"It's me." A familiar woman's voice whispered. "John it's me, Veronique." She slowly crept from out of her hiding place and beckoned him to her. He was startled but pleased to see her and walked a few feet to where she was half hidden beside a large overgrown and fragrant honeysuckle.

"Veronique, what are you doing here?" he asked. "You'll get us both into big trouble."

"I wanted to talk with you and explain a few things."

At that, she stepped right up close to him and took his hand whilst looking directly into his eyes. John said nothing. He was torn between his feelings and instincts for this pretty French girl and his concerns that his colleagues inside were likely to miss him and come looking for him.

"I thought we were going to meet up in St Omer," he said. "At least that's what you wrote in your note."

"I know," she said, "but back then, I had no idea where you and your friends would be staying for the night."

Somewhere close by on the old blue slate roof, a couple of white doves fluttered and cooed. He gently touched her face with trembling fingers and she responded by reaching up to kiss his open lips in a long passionate way that French girls do so well. At first, John was startled, but quickly complied with her intentions so clearly shown in her eyes and by her tactile manner. She pulled his hand, whilst putting a finger to his lips in a gesture of silence and then tried to guide him towards the trees where they'd be undisturbed.

"Private Lucas!" It was Captain Henderson on the steps of the entrance. He could see the private's cigarette glow and so shouted again loudly into the night. "We have new orders. Be so kind as to join us, if it's not too much bother - and jump to it man!"

John turned towards Veronique with downcast eyes, apologised quickly for the untimely interruption and then replied to his Commanding Officer "Coming Sir! Just finishing my fag."

He hurriedly kissed her again whilst looking intensely into her tear-stained dark brown eyes. Slowly caressing her cheek, he whispered, "So glad we met. I have a feeling that we are destined to be together."

Veronique remained hidden and wanted to tell him she was three months pregnant, but instead replied in very broken English with a husky French accent. "I will wait for you my darling," and blew him a kiss. She waited until he had disappeared inside before quickly hurrying back to the encamped travellers.

Odette and Jacqueline were chatting with the Curé as Veronique joined them. Just as they were about to relax over a mug of weak cocoa, Fernand walked up to Father Delage and asked him to accompany him to the manor.

"I've just been handed a note asking us to meet the English Officer immediately. There is no explanation."

Father Delage stood up and looking concerned, brushed his dirty black cassock and realigned his Cleric's inverted frying pan hat, before walking off briskly with Odette's father towards the Manor House. In his hands he clutched a rosary and a battered crucifix.

Veronique appeared pale and tears clouded her eyes. "Oh, I hope I haven't got Johnny into trouble," she said.

"What do you mean?" asked little Jacqueline.

Veronique pulled herself together. "We just met near the manor and I'm not sure if the English Captain saw us kissing. He is a nice man who feels the same for me as I feel for him. I never expected to fall for someone so quickly and now I've messed it all up."

She started sobbing, her shoulders jerking frantically. Odette crawled across the stony ground, bruising and dirtying her knees so she could sit beside her. Although still only young, she was mature enough to offer some words of consolation and kindness.

"It may not be too bad and, besides, it's surely not a crime to kiss a soldier and I don't think the English are unkind," said Odette.

Suzanne, who had just arrived but heard the conversation, interjected and with a childlike sneer asked, "Did you go further than a kiss or more importantly, did you tell him you are pregnant?"

"No, no no! I wanted to but didn't get a chance," replied Veronique. "We had no time at all before the English Officer called for Johnny."

"You should have told him, unless you intend to make him believe that he's the father! If so, it's not fair on him and it will be a shock when he finds out. You'll just have to let him know the next time you see him if you both still have the same feelings. For now let's hear no more about it and get some sleep."

At about 22:00 hours, Fernand and Father Delage appeared looking worried and agitated. They spoke loudly for a few moments causing others to gather around. Odette's father continuously fiddled with his hair before looking at the rapidly growing crowd.

"The Officer has received news that the Germans are closing in. He and his men have to reach their division before they are cut off at Dunkirk. It means they are leaving us in the next thirty minutes and although he regretted the situation, his orders are to find a way

45

through. In other words, they can no longer accompany us to St Omer. We shall have to find our own way through."

Someone at the back shouted, "Does that mean we cannot reach the coast at Calais?"

Fernand continued, "Captain Henderson said there's a good chance of us getting through St Omer since the French are still holding the German advance, but it will be risky. I think we should try to go on. After all the Boche are only interested in eliminating the allied forces and not us."

There was a great deal of uncomfortable shuffling and mumbling. The man at the back identified himself as Pierre Gautier, a respected artist from Liège.

"I agree, let's keep going. If we don't the journey up till now will have been in vain and if we do continue, we might reach England."

There was a general murmur of agreement although one or two morose types suggested they'd soon be big business for the Croque Mort. Veronique looked sorrowfully towards the other girls and wiped her eyes. They all knew what she was thinking.

"I may never see Johnny again," she blurted out. "Suppose he doesn't make it or is taken prisoner?"

At that, she turned around and ran through the dark trees, tripping over roots and debris before arriving at the manor just as the six Englishmen were climbing into their Jeeps.

Veronique shouted his name loudly. "My Johnny!"

John Lucas turned around along with the others, but the Jeeps were already moving out. She saw him wave furiously and heard him shout back, "I'll find you when it's all over!"

Suzanne had been told about the clandestine love match and, realising that Veronique might be devastated, caught up with her sitting on the steps of the now silent dark Manor.

"What am I going to do?" whispered Veronique. "How will I ever get to meet Johnny again? Next time, if there is a next time, I may well have a child with me. How will he respond to that?"

"Your first responsibility is to look after yourself and the baby inside you. There's every hope that your Johnny will come through all this and you'll find each other soon enough. If he's a good man as you say, he'll stand by you and the child. What will be will be."

The two girls walked back and on the way met Father Delage. He was a sympathetic man and after a few quotes from the bible and other comforting words, they all went their own ways to try and get some sleep. Veronique, trying to be calm, had taken up an invitation to bed down with Suzanne's family who had set up a rather grand double bivouac shelter next to the Moreau family.

A saffron and tangerine sunrise greeted the waking travellers as dawn broke on May 26th 1940. Shafts of sun gradually spread across the fields and woodland, gently warming the damp ground and fresh morning air. Heavy dew sparkled like diamonds on grasses and leaves. It was nature's way of revealing some brighter hope in the world, particularly to the many who were feeling anxious. They may have paused, looked and marvelled, even smiled during a few moments of respite. However, realism has a habit of bringing dreamers back down to earth. The realism of war and survival is a dream breaker.

Most people were bleary-eyed and busying themselves after a very disturbed anxious night and they were short of food. The journey ahead would be fraught with anxieties but their object was to reach Hazebrouck across the French border some 20 kilometres away before the evening. Somewhere in the distance they caught the soft thud of explosions and saw increasing aircraft activity. They had no idea that over three hundred thousand allied troops were now trapped by the German army and Luftwaffe on the beaches of Dunkirk and were engaged in a dramatic and heroic three-day evacuation.

The promise of a bright sunny day faded as grey skies rolled in from the coast. The air felt damp as the column slowly trundled on. Malnutrition was beginning to take hold although there was still plenty of water from the farms and houses they came across. They were desperate for somewhere to wash their sweating dirty bodies, find proper toilets and rest weary limbs, but also determined to carry on. This expanding band of untidy dishevelled travellers, now numbering over two hundred, were spread out for over a mile in small groups. Families, friends and neighbours had travelled over eighty miles since leaving Mons. Many from beyond Liège and across the French border had walked much further.

Amongst them, there were skilled men and women, able to serve the refugees or repair whatever came adrift or broke. From wheel rims that fell off, to farrier skills with the few horses and mules pulling wagons or trailers, someone would be available to help out.

After five hours feeling chilly under a depressing grey sky canopy, they could see the outskirts of Hazebrouck. The general mood lifted as they hoped to find more civilised accommodation, toilets, food and a comfortable bed. There was a shout from a deep male voice somewhere near the back of the column.

"The Boche are coming! We must get off the road!"

Bowed heads looked up with horror etched into their faces, people jumped and started to shout as they fled to the ditches and adjacent barley field. It was as if everyone had just touched an electrical circuit. They lay still with family and friends staying close together trying to make themselves invisible. A large column of heavily armed German troops numbering well over 500, quickly appeared, following tanks, gun carriages, rocket launchers, self-propelled guns and other armoured vehicles. They did not stop but carried on until they reached the hamlet of Borre and then turned towards Cassel. However, in the distance, a German black staff Mercedes stopped, turned around and retraced its journey back to the refugees.

After stopping, a heavily decorated senior German officer in the Field Grey of the Wehrmacht stood up and addressed the front of the crowd, most of them now having crawled out of the ditches and culverts. In word perfect French, Generaloberst Erich Hoepner of the

XVI Panzerkorps shouted that they must not obstruct German troops or resist in any way. Much to everyone's amazement, he surprised those within earshot that the occupying German forces would show respect towards the citizen refugees of Belgium and not molest them, or restrict their rights under occupation, or attempt to prevent their intentions to travel.

The impressively dressed and calmly mannered officer expressed geniality and dignity. He finished off by emphasising they must not show resistance or clog up the roads should they encounter any fighting ahead. All civilians ignoring these simple rules will be dealt with. There was silence before Gaston Mendelier, remembering the previous encounter with a German Officer and bravely risking retaliation, walked towards the Mercedes. The tall forty two year old Belgian engineer, a war hero from the previous 'war to end all wars', now carrying a long black beard and a worn out overcoat tied around his middle with string, looked strangely odd and slightly menacing as he prepared to speak. The German turned towards him with a hint of a smile, whilst in the background, mumblings of anxiety grew from those standing close by.

"How can we believe you when, a few days ago, we were stopped by a certain Major Reinhardt Rödl of the Wehrmacht 7th Infantry Division. He and his men murdered seven members of a family travelling with us. Their only crime was carrying a few weapons to kill game for food and to defend us all should we be confronted by thieves or dangerous intruders "

The German Officer looked around him but remained silent for some time before responding.

"I shall investigate this incident and if there has been any inappropriate action taken by this…err…Major Rödl." He paused, coughed, pulled his hat down and looking a little perturbed, continued, "If what you say is true, I shall personally see to it that he faces justice. The Wehrmacht does not tolerate unnecessary or excessive punishment against civilians." After a short pause, he finished addressing the crowd with click of his heels and a short half-hearted Heil Hitler salute.

Generaloberst Erich Hoepner and his driver disappeared rapidly and caught up with the rest of the German column, now just a cloud of dust on the horizon.

The long column of refugees appeared more optimistic and hopeful after the German Officer's words. "Maybe some Germans are human after all," said one gaunt looking woman, heavily wrapped up in wooden shawl and a dark dirty dress. She was obliged to secure her worn shoe soles with cords to prevent them parting company. Odette, her mother, father and the rest of the family along with a few friends chatted as they approached the outskirts of Hazebrouck and into the Pas de Calais of France.

Bertha, the nanny goat had broken free from her tether and caused much amusement as she repeatedly ran and butted Father Delage and Monsieur Haché. Both men had unsuccessfully tried to re-capture her for twenty minutes. The priest shocked Frédéric Haché by claiming the goat was in league with the devil and possessed of evil intentions. He intimated she should be slaughtered to provide food. He even blasphemed by employing a few choice expletives as he slipped in goat excrement, ending up on his backside. The Curé ashamedly apologising before murmuring about divine retribution and expressing concern that he might not reach the gates of heaven.

Hazebrouck was not quite what they expected. The town was deserted except for a few miserable confused people wandering around with no place to go. Many buildings had been destroyed and rubble, collapsed walls, house contents and the occasional dead body gave the place a morbid, depressing feel as well as unpleasant smells drifting on the evening air. They passed a damaged corner café advertising the remains of a large Orval Trappist beer poster. Two men in their early twenties, showing signs of sleep deprivation, wearing scruffy corduroy trousers and braces, walked over and addressed the leading people in the column with some grave news.

"The English have retreated towards the coast pursued by overwhelming Waffen SS and Panzer divisions. They bravely resisted German tanks, artillery and bombs for three days on the outskirts of Calais, but we understand the town has now fallen."

In the country villages around Hazebrouck, most of the inhabitants had fled for their lives with no option but to join the refugee lines. The majority headed towards St Omer and the coast, still hoping they would reach the coast and able to find a boat. Accommodation would be almost impossible but they might be lucky on the west side of the town and further out in the deserted countryside where they would find farmhouses.

The two men waved back as they ran off leaving the column in a fearful mood. Where would they go, where would they be able to rest and repair tired bodies? Overhead several German fighters and Stuka dive-bombers filled the sky with their ear-splitting engine noises. They were heading in the direction of Dunkirk.

Like so many around her, Odette's young feet were bleeding. Blisters had formed and burst causing excruciating pain. Despite strips of cotton and bandages held with string, she was getting worse. Her legs were swollen and she ached in her lower back, as well as both knee and hip joints. Her parents were horrified and felt helpless but knew they were also in grave danger if they tried to find somewhere in the town. Fernand lifted his daughter and wife onto the flat bed of his handcart. He too was suffering from pulling the heavy load but did not complain even though his hands were raw and his feet were almost insufferable. They came upon Hazebrouck residents huddled up as they walked slowly. Some were injured and crying. One old lady lying in a dirty, stationary, makeshift cart had lost a leg and despite attempts to repair the wound, she was still suffering. Her pale face was etched with pain as she clutched a small white dog to her. With her other bony hand, she reached towards Odette and Laure as Fernand passed by, muttering that it was the end of the world and we will all be going to heaven, except for the Germans who, with any justice, will be going the opposite way.

"We must keep going," said Fernand. "We must try and reach St Omer. There's a good chance we'll find an old farm just ahead where we can rest for a day, or maybe two."

The majority in the column had the same idea, particularly Odette's family and friends who looked up to Fernand, but there was now a growing number who wanted to turn back. Arguments broke out and tempers soared. The disappointment of not resting in Hazebrouck depressed many and they needed to cling to some hope. Going home was one option but it would involve accepting German occupation. On May 28th, King Leopold had surrendered without consulting his government, much to the displeasure of many Belgian people and Winston Churchill. In Dunkirk, the British BEF and French troops were being herded onto the beaches. The miracle evacuation of 350,000 men codenamed 'Operation Dynamo' had already begun.

Chapter 6: Surveillance, Radio and Radar

It was a sunny spring afternoon on May 29th 1940. A tall Flying Officer with a deep refined voice shouted at the twenty-four new recruits standing haphazardly on the tarmac in front of him.

"Look sharp you men! Welcome to RAF Yatesbury. Hopefully, after training, you will all be able to make much needed successful contributions towards Britain's war efforts in the air and on the ground. The last thing I or anyone else in the Royal Airforce wants to see is failure. Your country needs you at this time. Do you men understand what I'm saying?"

There was some coughing, very few 'Yes Sir' responses and several unclear mumblings.

He continued. "So there are those amongst you who can't or don't want to understand what I'm saying or prefer to ignore an Officer? Which one is it?"

He stood rigid and shouted at the top of his voice. "This RAF station has zero tolerance towards indiscipline. Unless I get a firm and loud "Yes Sir, understand Sir," you horrible lot will all be made to run around the two-mile perimeter of this camp until you drop. Do I make myself clear?"

The response from the men was a very vocal and very clear. "Yes I understand Sir!"

"That's more like it. My name is Flight Sergeant Bernard Osborne. I'll be meeting up with you men tomorrow at 7.00am, so get a good night's sleep. You'll soon be acquainted with the AOC and Station Commander who wants to officially welcome you. You'll also be introduced to your training officers who will show you where you'll stay, where you'll be learning how to operate a radio, Morse code and some new fangled detection apparatus. You'll also be taken on a tour of the station and shown the huts where you'll stay. Before that you'll need to collect your uniforms from the reception unit in that building over there and a word of advice. Always keep them in tip top condition."

He pointed to a long part brick building that had been mostly hurriedly coated in a dark olive grey render and upon which the words 'Stores' had been painted in pale blue letters.

"Once you've showered, preened yourselves and put on your uniforms, you'll reassemble on the parade ground over to your left. Just remember that here, discipline, hard work, loyalty, perseverance and respect are prime requirements. Have you chaps got all that?"

This time the 'yes sir' reply might well have startled the residents in the village of Compton Bassett just over two miles away. It certainly disturbed the rooks in an adjacent woodland and caused Alan to stop, pause and watch as the flock circled overhead cawing loudly and making their annoyance obvious.

"My name is Henry Silver but my friends call me Harry." Alan turned around to be confronted by one of the new recruits. Harry smiled and the two men shook hands.

"I'm Alan White but I'm usually called Al. It seems we may be heading in the same direction. Where are you from?"

"Bournemouth," said Harry, "but I was born in Manchester until my parents decided it was too wet and since my two sisters and I kept catching colds, Mother decided the climate was better down south."

Alan smiled and was about to reciprocate when the sky overhead filled with the sound of a low flying aircraft. Two new De Havilland Dominies and a single Percival Proctor came into view before banking over the twin hangers dominating the eastern side of the airfield.

"That's what it's all about," said Harry. "Being up there amongst the clouds and enjoying the view - I can't wait." The two men chatted excitedly and joined the others as they entered the accommodation block.

Alan and Harry stayed together as they strolled out to the

parade ground. They stood with the others all looking very dapper and pleased in their new uniforms. In front stood Flying Officer Richard Maxwell DFC, a tall impressive man with a soft Glaswegian accent and a drooping handle bar moustache, together with four very fit Personal Training Instructors. The Officer, who had already seen action over the skies of France with distinction, took one step forward before addressing the group.

"Men, you are here because the Royal Airforce needs surveillance, detection, radio and radar specialists. You have been chosen because someone, somewhere has rightly or wrongly assumed that you have enough intelligence to do these tasks well. We shall see! These key jobs are vital if we are going to help stop the German war machine from crossing the English Channel. If some of you hope to become pilots, I'm sorry to say that will not happen here. RAF Yatesbury is no longer designated as a flying school. Instead we will be at the forefront of new detection and surveillance developments and you will be trained to handle the necessary equipment over the next three months. Now, is there anyone who would like to ask a question?"

A man on the front row with a strong Scottish accent spoke out.

"What's 'Radar'?" he asked.

"Good question Sir! What is your name?"

"It's John McDonald," he replied. The Officer glared back.

"No! No! No! From now on you are Aircraftman John McDonald!" he yelled and barked out the word 'Aircraftman' before repeating it slowly and with greater emphasis.

He then paused and still red faced, shouted so loud that the rooks took to the air once again, clamouring with intense irritation.

"You will address me and all superior officers as 'SIR!' and when meeting or passing you will salute! Do I make myself abundantly clear, Aircraftmen McDonald?"

The embarrassed man quickly responded with a loud "Yes Sir!"

"That applies to you all and if you qualify in three months and are given your first commission, I may decide to return the salute.

Now, back to the question. Radar stands for 'Radio Detecting and Ranging'. It enables us to monitor and track incoming enemy aircraft. However, as I'm a pilot and not over familiar with the new detection equipment, I'm going to pass you over to my four able colleagues here who will induct you into the station's rules, protocols, expectations and your timetables. You'll be taken on a tour around the classrooms where you'll meet your teachers and fellow operators as well as seeing the new equipment. Flight Sergeant Bernard Osborne, who you met earlier, will see you at 7.00am for your first Physical Training session. He smiled ominously before saying "And good luck to those of you who are not fit."

"Christ!" said Harry to Alan, "it's going to be hell at 7.00am. We are going to die slowly even before we get a chance to handle those Radar gadgets. Must say though, the new detection thingies sound mighty exciting."

Alan was thinking much the same and dreaded the idea of PT. They spent the rest of the afternoon listening to their training schedules, touring the classes, taking in the numbers of dull inspiring wooden buildings, defence stations with anti-aircraft guns, and the airfield with its twin runways. A few of the older buildings were in a very poor state and had never been properly renovated after serving the Royal Flying Corps in World War One. There were three huge hangars housing Avro Ansons, lovingly called 'Annies', De Havilland Tiger Moths, Dominies, a Boulton Paul Defiant, a couple of Miles Masters and a much larger very impressive Bristol Blenheim Mk IV.

At 3.00 pm after four hours of induction, and much to their relief, they were finally allowed free time to try out the Mess canteen for NCOs where they enjoyed their first excellent meal and drinks. Over seventy others now joined the original twenty-four new recruits, including a few civilians on an apprenticeship course. Most had arrived a few days before by train, bus and taxi. It was not an easy place to locate, being out in the wilds of Wiltshire. The Mess was painted in drab duck egg blue paint, hidden in parts by pictures of aircraft, the King, Glen Miller, dancing girls in alluring poses and a few propaganda posters asking for volunteers, titled 'Victory in the Skies over Britain'. They were also confronted with an excellent catering service, bar and a dance floor. Here they finally found time to relax, make friends and listen to someone in the background playing ragtime tunes on an old piano, followed by a few communal cockney pub songs. Over the next few days, very little changed. In between training classes, most whiled away their time trying to familiarise themselves with their surroundings. There was also time enough to play darts, dominoes and table tennis as well as write home outlining responsibilities and a new way of life.

At 6.00pm on June 4th, a large dark walnut radio set crackled into life with an important announcement. It was Anthony Eden, Secretary of State for War. Everyone in the room stopped whatever they were doing. Apart from a few coughs and shoes scraping the linoleum, all was quiet.

"This is the BBC Home Service, broadcasting to the nation on June 4th 1940. In the past few days, I'm pleased to announce that over 300,000 troops from the BEF, as well as our French and Belgian allies, have been successfully evacuated from the beaches and harbour of Dunkirk in Northern France."

There was a pause as the transmission signal faded in and out causing an irritating humming noise, crackling and interference.

"After a week of brave resistance against insurmountable German forces and following the surrender of Belgium on the 28th May, Hitler's armies and airforce failed to extinguish our indomitable spirit. The evacuation was not conducted without losses. It is estimated that 68,000 men were either lost or taken prisoner. I wish to pay a special tribute to the Royal Navy, The Merchant Navy, The Royal Airforce and in particular the defenceless little ships that sailed from British harbours to help bring our troops back home. The Prime Minister will address the nation in the next few days. God bless the King." There was a long silence as the news and the implications sank in.

Smoke from cigarettes hung in the air as nearly ninety voices started to express euphoria. Before long the room echoed with whooping and cheering. Everyone stood up and shook hands or hugged the person next to them as the National Anthem played on the radio. Laughter broke out and the pianist rattled through 'Roll out the Barrel' accompanied by over forty happy voices.

It was past 8.00 pm and several beers later, when two orderlies walked in and a rather brusque mannered Sergeant called a halt to the evening's noisy gathering. Alan walked over to the wireless and turned it off after they'd been treated to Joe Loss's 'Moon Love' and 'Serenade in Blue'. He noted that the tuning knob was loose and promised himself that he'd repair it at the first opportunity.

The sergeant looked at the clock on the wall and ordered them to retire to their dormitories, as they would be woken at 6.00 am. This would give them time to shower and be ready for PT at 7.00 am. The two orderlies proceeded to herd people towards the stairs before tidying the room.

Just as the sun was beginning to warm the chilly dawn, a loud bell shattered the sleeping dormitories. Men rolled out of their beds in panic, but some took longer. Flight Sergeant Osborne had deployed six PTIs to bully the waking men into standing in lines at the foot of their beds before directing them towards the torture of cold water showers. Alan and Harry entered shower block A. At one end, the men were already dancing around uttering profanities as their bodies turned to quivering animated puppets under the jets of high-pressure cold water.

"Christ! This will kill us before we can make any contribution to the war effort," said Alan. Being skinny and without a lot of muscle, he struggled but survived by rapidly flapping his arms and jumping around like a demented duck. Harry was less vocal but shouted to the instructor to turn off the showers.

"You poncey bunch of petticoats! If you think this is bad, wait till you see what's coming next. The good news is that by the end of the month, most of you will get used to it. If not, you'll wish you were on a train home and believe me, you'll be taking feelings of guilt, failure and remorse with you. Now jump to it! Flight wants to see you on the parade ground promptly."

Two others joined Alan and Harry as they hurriedly made their way downstairs and out onto the parade ground where the other twenty men dressed in light vests and shorts were already assembled. The early morning chill seemed to cut through them like an arctic wind, despite being early June. Flight Sergeant Osborne and the PTIs were waiting patiently.

"So, you will now be fully awake and hopefully as bright as the morning dew. We will endeavour to make sure you are fit and ready to meet the challenges that you will inevitably face which may be terminal for some of you!"

The men were still shivering and shifting from foot to foot. A man standing three down from Alan was having some difficulties, which were noticed by the PTIs and the officer out in front.

"You Sir!" yelled Flt. Sgt Osborne. "Yes you! What is your name and what is your problem? Step forward man!" He was pointing at the unfortunate wretch doing his best to be inconspicuous.

Aircraftman Michael Allensby stepped to the front and gave his name in a broad Black Country accent.

"Sir, the 'lacky' band has bust in me shorts!" There was immediate restrained collection of guffaws and giggles as the desperately embarrassed man attempted to hide his dignity whilst his shorts slowly headed towards the ground.

One of the PTIs had already realised that replacement shorts would be needed by more than one man in the next two hours and had already acquired a few spares.

"Quiet!" The Flt. Sgt. yelled so loudly that once again the rooks took flight. He turned towards Michael Allenby and with a withering scowl remonstrated that he was a disgrace and had better pick his socks up as well as his shorts. The group smiled as the PTIs handed the man his replacement. He quickly exchanged the original ones causing him to momentarily expose his manhood in the process.

This caused a few giggles and smirks as well as some derogatory comments. Flt. Sgt. Osborne chose to ignore the gestures and comments believing that Aircraftman Michael Allenby would be feeling rather foolish. He dismissed the men, handing them over to the instructors ready for their first workout.

The nine-mile run took the men towards Compton Bassett, via Cherhill and along Park Lane. They passed two churches and The White Horse Inn, carefully monitored by the PTIs in case anyone was tempted to take a breather for 'medicinal purposes'. By 8.30 am, the sun was beginning to poke through although it remained cold due to a north wind. The men were beginning to struggle as they approached half way.

"Come on you lazy lot!" shouted Sergeant Frank Johnstone, the most senior PTI. "I've never seen such a bunch of pathetic lily-white men in all my life."

The twenty-four men, including stragglers who had been given the chance to catch up, were brought to a halt at a cross roads along a narrow lane that ran around the northwest perimeter of the airfield.

"Now listen up you poor excuses for men!" shouted Sgt. Johnstone. "I'm going to split you into two equal groups. I want twelve men in each group and I assume you can count." He paused waiting for a response before bellowing, "Jump to it!"

"From here the two groups, A and B, will race against each other. You will nominate a captain in each group, whose job it will be to guide their group across the fields using the shortest routes and to select the fittest and fastest member, who will then race the last leg towards the camp. The first group to reach the parade ground will be treated to a few pints at the White Horse pub this evening at 7.00 pm. "He spun round and pointed at the other PTIs standing close by. "The losers will clean the showers and the two washrooms. Do you understand?" There was a groan from someone in the bunch.

"Yes Sir!" they replied loudly. An Avro Anson distracted them as it flew close and low before disappearing beyond the trees

60

towards the airfield less than a mile away. They heard it splutter and throttle back before the thud as wheels slammed heavily into the concrete runway.

"I'm so tired and knackered," said Alan.

"Me too," gasped Harry, "but I can't wait to fly. It has to be much better than running!"

Alan was getting used to Harry's dry sense of humour and sarcasm. He liked it because it made him smile and, being a worrier by nature, helped him forget about the war.

One of the other men in Alan and Harry's group A had taken on the job of captain. He was a pugnacious little man whose name was Alistair who smelled strongly of 'At Ease' after shave, created by the makers of 'Listerine' mouth wash. He strolled up and asked if either of them would take on the last fast leg and bring glory to their group. He also stated that he had no intention of missing out on a hard earned trip to the Promised Land, a.k.a. 'The White Horse' in Compton Bassett.

"No chance," said Alan quickly, which was followed swiftly by Harry's adept sarcasm with "Do we look like athletes?"

A tall fit-looking man from Kent, nicknamed 'Ash' stepped forward and said he had previous experience as a fast runner in his father's business.

"What sort of business?" asked Alistair with a dubious smirk.

"He managed an abattoir."

Alan and Harry looked at each and shrugged.

"Why were you a runner in an abattoir business?" asked Alistair with a deeply puzzled frown.

"I used to run after the bloody cattle when they escaped. Sometimes they'd leg it across the field and run for miles. They knewwhat was coming." Alistair laughed out loudly.

"OK mate, you can run the last leg and let's hope you'll beat the bastard in group B." He turned to Alan and Harry plus two other men who'd joined them.

"You lot can help our abattoir man win the race. That means

making sure he's in a good place at the right time and, if necessary, causing distractions for the other team, if you know what I mean."

"Cocky sod aren't you?" said Harry, "I do believe that you want us to cheat. Is that correct?"

"Not cheating pal, just taking advantage of opportunities!"

The last leg worked out as a victory for the A team. Abattoir man, Ash, arrived on the parade ground a good fifteen minutes before Team B's top runner, a Cornishman called Perran. He immediately objected to the tactics and tricks employed by Team A who he called cheats.

He addressed one of the PTIs. "He wor 'elped by them lads o'er there, who turned the foot path sign around along Juggler's Lane so it pointed towards Winterbourne Bassett. By the time we'd realised, it wor a blinkin' long way 'ome - Sir!"

He pointed to Alan, Harry and the other four culprits who had arrived with the rest of the runners as they staggered up to the parade ground. Most of them were breathing heavily, sweating and distressed. By now Flt. Sgt. Osborne had joined the PTIs and had heard the complaint. He twiddled his moustache, brushed his lapels and stood stiffly whilst glaring at the six accused.

"So, you four men moved the sign post?"

"Yes Sir," replied Alistair, stepping forward and taking full responsibility on the chin. The Officer paused before replying.

"I'm prepared to overlook this, err - slight oversight!" He held his hand to his mouth, coughed and carried on. "I'm going to forget any notions of foul play on this occasion because it showed something we're looking for; it's called 'enterprise'! He loudly emphasised the word 'enterprise'. "You other lot can learn from this. We are looking for enterprising men with leadership qualities who can think on their feet and make decisions on the spur of the moment, even if those decisions are - shall we say - not quite in the rule book!"

He finished by telling the six to make sure they turned the signpost back to its original position, maybe after their evening at the White Horse. He reminded the members of group B that the showers and changing rooms needed their prompt attention, which invited a few loud groans and expletives.

The rest of the morning and afternoon was spent with some excitement in the RDFC (Range and Direction Finding Class), later to be called the RWTS (Radar and Wireless Training School). In groups of six, the men chatted with the five tutors and saw the new radar equipment being demonstrated. They also watched simulated sequences, where a number of aircraft could be seen as feint blips on the oscilloscopes. Outside, two CH (Chain Home) tower masts reached over one hundred feet high. By rotating a receiver goniometer, amplified radio frequencies from the towers meant the operator could detect interrupted signals from incoming aircraft, as well as estimating their distance and height. The men were left in no doubt how important this new detection science would become. They were also told that in no circumstances were they to engage in loose talk about anything they saw. Failure to do so would ensure a rapid exit from the RAF in disgrace, following a court martial.

Later that evening on June 5th, most of the men were back in the mess canteen listening intently to a broadcast by the Prime Minister, Winston Churchill, with his rousing speech, 'We shall fight on the beaches, we shall fight on the landing grounds'. It was a sobering reminder of what was expected of them and no one had any doubts that the battle ahead would be hard and extreme.

"About time we spruced up for our evening out," said Alan, trying to raise the men's spirits.

The other eleven men, including the six who had engineered the cross-country victory, finished off their evening meals of liver and onions over boiled cabbage and watery mashed potato.

"We're on our way!" shouted Alistair with a beaming smile.

The six had become friends after the morning's exercise. Harry had organised an RAF Bedford 30cwt long wheelbase truck, covered by a blue tarpaulin that stunk of fish, to carry the men there and back. However, he constantly reminded them that he'd paid out five shillings to the driver for the privilege until, under protest, they all chipped in.

The White Horse Inn, a delightful English pub run by Tom Goring, welcomed the twelve RAF men. Tom was a friendly but no-nonsense landlord. His wife Betty, a loud Cockney epitomised the typical blonde buxom barmaid and was never afraid to tell it straight or indulge in teasing the men. Tom, standing with his arms folded and a bar towel draped across his left shoulder, spoke out.

"We've had instructions to keep an eye on you lot and report back to Sergeant Johnston if there's any trouble. You RAF types have been known to upset our regular customers. So if you keep it straight, we'll let you come again."

Tom smiled and said, "Now what can I get you men? Oh, I forgot to say that until 9.00 pm the drinks are on a slate to be paid for by the Sergeant. After that you pay up."

The twelve men collected their first pints and two Scrumpy Jacks before retiring to the rear bar room where there was more space and a disintegrating dartboard.

On the wall they gazed at a large board upon which there were signatures of various RAF men who had frequented the pub in the past, or who were still stationed at Yatesbury. While the others started a darts game, Alan, Harry and Ash, the Abattoir man, scrutinised the names on the board. Amongst them was Guy Gibson who had moved on two years previously after leaving his mark upon those who remembered his arrogance towards younger novices. In 1943 he would become a household name and receive a VC for his heroic leadership in the famous Dam Buster's raid.

"So what have you been up to then?"

It was Betty the barmaid and the landlord's wife. She was looking intently at Harry who was ready for his second pint of bitter. He responded with a beaming smile as she fixed him with her big dark eyes and briefly flashed her seamed dark stockings.

"Tell you what, why don't you get us another round in and I'll tell you exactly what I've been up to and maybe you'd like to know

64

what I'd love to do with you," said Harry.

There were a few wolf whistles and jeers from the other men standing nearby.

"Well aren't you the cheeky one, eh? Just hang on for a few minutes and wait here, I'll be back."

Tom poked his head around the door and asked if all was fine.

"Everything is tickety-boo old bean," replied one of the men, "but could we have some music?"

"I'll see if the old gramophone is working."

At that moment, a very hairy Irish wolfhound dog walked in lazily and settled his huge body across Alan's feet.

"Don't mind him," said Tom. "He's the pub's secret weapon. He likes to chew the legs of troublemakers, including anyone who doesn't pay and those who show an unhealthy interest in the barmaid. His name is Murphy and he likes to be patted gently and I mean gently. He's been known to help himself to the odd finger or two." Alan and Harry frowned at each other, avoiding eye-to-eye contact with the dog as Tom left the room.

A few moments later, a gramophone somewhere in the bar area sprung into life with a few Louis Armstrong and Andrews Sisters' tunes. Alan tried to move his legs to one side but Murphy uttered a low growl and licked his right shoe.

Betty and a trainee barmaid arrived carrying trays loaded with drinks. Betty sat down beside Harry while Murphy, still spread across Alan's feet, watched carefully with one ear cocked.

"So what was it you'd like to do with me then?" she asked flirtingly. Harry, having noticed the dog eyeing him and remembering the landlord's warnings, decided that on this occasion, discretion had better override any blatant flirting.

"I'd like to take you to a cricket match sometime," he said.

The dog closed his eyes and made a snorting noise. Alan again tried to move but Murphy growled again. He pleaded with someone watching the darts game to help move the dog which was making his foot numb and besides there was a distinct smell of canine halitosis. Nobody moved. Betty inched closer to Harry and with a very cheeky grin asked him what else he'd like to do. Harry, being an efficacious romantic, easily trapped by love, confessed he'd take her away from being a pub barmaid and treat her to a life in paradise, away from the war. He was already weak at the knees when discretion disappeared and he moved his hand to touch her leg, caressing it slowly and seductively. She pouted her red lips sensuously and smiled.

This was all too much for the hairy wolfhound, just six feet away. With a sudden explosion from under Alan's legs, Murphy launched himself at Harry, baring his teeth and growling like a devil dog in a horror movie.

"Jesus Christ!" shouted Harry just as the huge dog's jaws clamped around his right lower trouser leg, missing flesh by an inch. Murphy instinctively pulled backwards and managed to tear the trouser leg completely off at the knee and proceeded to shake his trophy violently from side to side. The others watched, bemused, as Tom, who had heard the commotion, leapt in and dragged the dog away. Betty quickly disappeared into a back room, sniggering until she considered it was safe to reappear with Tom. He asked what had caused the dog to react. Nobody spoke.

"Well, if it wasn't a bad payer and it wasn't a trouble maker, that leads me to only one conclusion." Pointing at Harry, he spoke loudly.

"Well Sir, judging by the look on your face and seeing the remains of your right trouser leg in Murphy's jaws, you must have been out of order with my wife."

Tom looked sternly at Harry who cast a pathetic appearance minus his right trouser leg and without warning, let out a huge laugh, startling the onlookers. "You, Sir, will apologise to my wife and to Murphy, is that clear? Then we'll forget all about the incident."

Tom was clearly amused by it all as he disappeared, but later they could hear him remonstrating with Betty somewhere in the depths of the White Horse.

Harry's exposed leg caused much laughter as the twelve aircraftmen enjoyed each other's company until just past 9:00 pm. They spoke endlessly about Harry's humiliation for apologising to Betty and, when terrified on all fours mumbling incoherently, he came eye to eye with Murphy. Alan was highly amused but also concerned because he wasn't too sure if Harry would get into big trouble back at base. As it turned out, there was no punishment and in fact Harry's reputation as a lady-killer had been enhanced.

The driver of the truck was waiting patiently outside. He urged the men to hurry as he had to make sure the Bedford was returned to its proper place on time and he had about twenty minutes left. Team A clambered on board despite most of them being in a state of disrepair. They arrived with about three minutes to spare after the driver skilfully negotiated his way around the perimeter road at speed, slowing for the defence gatehouse and inner entrance where he was well known by the Military Police and sentries. Fortunately, everyone managed to find the accommodation block without any serious problems. The blackout windows meant they had to rely on dim blue lights to see where they were going. This caused some merriment and irritation when two of the men managed to climb into the wrong beds, including one occupied by the Cornishman, Perran. His vexation and threats in broad Cornish reduced most of the men to laughter.

At 10.00am the next day, after another five mile run, brutal exercises on the parade ground and cold showers, the new recruits were instructed to attend their first class in the RDF School building, No 2 Camp, on the eastern side of the station, the site of the World War One RFC aerodrome. Several aircraft had already taken off and were circling within a twenty-mile radius. The students would use them as decoys for the purposes of detection training. Harry and Alan sat together. They were fast becoming close friends, each propped up by the other's sarcasm, cutting jibes and, in Alan's case, his infectious laugh. The pair were popular and often entertained the others with their stories about living at home, family and schooldays.

A thin-faced man with black horn-rimmed glasses hiding his bulging eyes, entered the long classroom. He stopped by a large black chalkboard near the workstation that Alan and Harry had been working at.

"I'm Terence Tyler-Jones from General Electric in Wembley. I'm here with my other colleagues from the Air Ministry, Bawdsley, to introduce you to the up to date wonders of radio navigation and Radio Direction Finders. There will be individual tests afterwards."

Alan and Harry joined other aircraftmen from their group, as well other civil students. Everyone seemed to fidget and chat endlessly as they waited patiently to be called by the men from the Ministry. They were easy to pick out being similarly dressed in white laboratory coats over pin striped baggy trousers with deep turn ups, conveniently situated where they could be used as receptacles for cigarette ash and butt-ends.

"Your first month will be taken up with the basics. You'll learn all about celestial, marine and pilot navigation, radio operations, detection systems and Morse code. At the same time you'll be shown how to operate our new Chain Home (CH) equipment. These are exciting new developments and whatever you learn needs to be kept secret, even from your wives and families. Failure to do this will be seriously dealt with. Simply put, CH enables us to detect the distance and height of enemy aircraft. By the time you leave here you'll all be competent operators. Do you have any questions?"

Harry raised his hand and asked if the system was effective at long distance and at any height.

"Not yet, we are still limited to a height of roughly eight thousand feet at distances closer than twenty miles range or twenty thousand feet at approximately forty miles, depending on weather conditions. We anticipate much more powerful devices coming through soon. You'll be pleased to know that the Ministry and the War Office have already installed a number of these detection towers around the east and south coasts. They have been enthusiastically endorsed by the Prime Minister to help detect

German airborne activity. Some of you will be sent from here to these coastal radar stations once you've qualified. You may also have a chance to fly as radio operators with Bomber Command or Coastal Command. Only time will tell if you have the brains to meet the high standards required."

At 3.00 pm they were summoned to three oscilloscopes where they watched for the blips on the green screens that denoted the aircraft that had taken off earlier. Each operating station was connected to a manual revolving receiver goniometer operated by the tutors from the ministry.

"There," said one of the men standing by Alistair. "There it is again. Can you see it clearly? It's a constant blip on the screen."

The weather had deteriorated slightly with grey clouds rolling in from the west, but they had at least experienced their first detection and it excited them.

The rest of the day was spent trying to look enthusiastic whilst listening to the six tutors explaining the intricacies of radio frequencies and radio components.

Life at RAF Yatesbury was relaxed but always extremely vigilant. Aircraft were moved to satellite hangars away from the airfield during the months of July and August just before the Battle of Britain intensified. Airfield defences were improved and added to, as German incursions by long-range bombers were becoming more frequent. Fortunately, the Germans seemed to ignore most of the airfields further west in Wiltshire.

Parade ground drills were almost as disliked as the early morning cross country runs and PT work. However, there was some excitement on the firing range. Every recruit had to master a .303 Lee Enfield rifle and took things seriously, just in case they were called upon to defend against a successful German invasion. Alan was particularly good and known as 'Crack Shot Whitey', something that was noted by his senior officers.

In September 1940, not long after Churchill's famous 'Never in the Field of Human Conflict' speech, Alan, Harry and three others were transferred to RAF Wattisham in Suffolk where No. 110 and 107 Squadrons were based. They had all received new commissions as Sergeants but were also given one week's home leave after saying farewell to RAF Yatesbury. In his quiet moments, Alan thought about Kathleen McKenzie and wondered if they would ever meet again, but in his heart of hearts, he knew it was unlikely.

Chapter 7: Going Home

Aunt Hélène stood in the middle of a crossroads where the Chemin des Loups and the Rue L'Equarissage joined. It was less than four kilometres from St Omer. She was stooped over but propped up on an old elm cane. Her tattered stockings had fallen around her ankles revealing swollen legs with sores and pronounced varicose veins. A vintage 30s pulp-noir mourning dress hung loosely around a once ample figure as she shook her fist defiantly at the explosions and smoke that almost hid St Omer from view.

Odette's parents walked over and hugged her in an attempt to calm her down. She was sobbing and at the same time cursing German ruthlessness and cruel indifference to the people deprived of their homes. Rain started to fall.

It was 09:00 hours on Saturday July 27th, Fernand's birthday. The previous day, the evacuees had decided to return home after a long heated meeting. A high-ranking German Officer leading a division of armoured vehicles and heading towards St Omer, had stopped them and made a decision for them. He advised them to return home where they would be treated well. Besides, the road ahead beyond St Omer and towards Calais was impossible as heavy fighting was taking place. He also told them not to obstruct any German troops they might encounter, as to do so would be met with severe consequences.

Jean-Baptiste, Fernand, Laure, Aunt Hélène and the rest of Moreau family and close friends knew there was no alternative and so, with heavy hearts, they agreed to return to Mons. The only couple that disagreed were Paul and Celine Delvaux. Paul, a cousin of Odette's mother decided that he and Celine would head north towards Ostend where they had relatives and friends. They could not face the difficult journey back to Mons only to find the Germans had occupied their home. It was a risk that the majority were prepared to take but they nevertheless sympathised with Paul's decision and wished him and Celine well.

A few people had gathered outside La Ferme des Moulins, an old deserted farm and manor. Many had slept here for the past three nights, where surprisingly they'd managed to feast well and fill their empty bellies with fruit and vegetables picked in the adjacent garden and orchard. They'd also found several hens and eggs. Outside, Curé Delage and more than twenty people shouted for Fernand. He appeared a few moments later, his face covered with shaving cream. He wiped his face with a towel and smiled, before being greeted by a loud chorus of 'Happy Birthday'.

"Oh my goodness me, what a lovely surprise!" Fernand was completely overwhelmed as the crowd broke into the *Doudou* song from the *Ducasse de Mons*. He was clearly popular and considered one of the leaders. By now Laure and Odette had joined him. They enthusiastically joined the crowd who were singing and dancing. Laure in particular, was a tour de force with her extravagant pirouettes and arm waving gestures.

"We have a small gift for you." It was little Jacqueline accompanied by Suzanne, Vivienne and Veronique who was now clearly showing her five months' pregnancy. Jacqueline approached and handed over a package in grey paper and a ribbon tied with string. Fernand opened it and discovered a beautifully carved wooden plaque showing the Cathedral of Sainte Waudru in Mons. It had been hand carved by an artisan in Mons over fifty years previously and had been carried amongst other personal possessions belonging to Jacqueline's parents, Jean-Baptiste and Julia.

Fernand looked at the girls and the crowd with tears in his eyes. He also gazed towards Jean-Baptiste, who was grinning broadly standing next to his wife and daughter.

"Thank you all for this wonderful gift. I shall keep it forever. I'll also do all I can to help you on the long journey home. May God be our guide and saviour." He raised his arms in the air and shouted, "Vive La Belgique!" The crowd yelled their approval. A friendly brown dog, found wandering a few days previously by Suzanne and given the name 'Hugo', joined in with some howling and loud persistent barking.

The crowd disappeared and Laure gave Fernand a kiss whilst Odette tried but failed to circumnavigate around his tummy with a hug. He patted her head gently and assured them both that they'd be fine. Both Laure and Odette would be obliged to travel in the cart, as he was capable of pulling with the help of Marcel van Bekerts, a friend, who managed a boulangerie in Mons. Marcel had lost most of his own possessions when his cart had lost a wheel. As a result, the cart had slewed across the road and tipped into a ditch full of stagnant water.

The procession moved out an hour later, retracing their steps to Hazebrouck, Tournai and beyond. They hadn't walked more than five kilometres in open countryside when they were spotted by a division of German Waffen SS soldiers and panzer grenadiers in half-track personnel carriers advancing towards them. A little further ahead, there was an old windmill with broken vanes and a canal bridge, which the lead party now headed towards. It meant lugging the heavy wheeled carts and wagons off the road and across shallow ditches so they would not hinder the Germans. One cart was not so lucky.

"Please help!" shouted someone close by. An elderly man and two women were struggling with an overloaded flatbed wagon that had tipped, lost its tailgate and discarded much of its contents on the road. A few people volunteered to lend a hand but the first Germans had quickly arrived and seemed overly aggressive. They kept shouting and pointing at the items in the road, kicking a number of them around and laughing. A particularly irritated German SS-Obersturmführer, dressed in black, approached the broken cart with his MP40 Siebmaschinen slung across his shoulder.

"Why are you blocking the road with your rubbish? My men will be coming along here at speed and this pile of shit will be in the way. Move it all now or else or you will be punished!"

"We need your help to move it all," said the elderly man.

"You insolent swine!" shouted the German and in an instant, levelled his MP40 Sub-machine gun and fired a short burst along the ground in front of the old man and the two women. They were startled into frantically doubling their efforts to clear everything off the road. More Germans arrived, anxious to carry on towards the coast but hampered by the cart and scattered possessions. They added to the shouting and confusion.

"Move that junk!" screamed the irritated officer again. They were transfixed to the spot with terror and this time he aimed and fired a quick burst at the old man who collapsed. One bullet entered his chest and exited from his left hip. Another caught him in the neck slicing through his jugular. Blood spurted from the wounds and the old man collapsed dying. The two women screamed and dropped to their knees. The German officer screamed at them to move but suddenly stopped when Hugo, Suzanne's dog ran at him growling and sank his teeth into the German's right-hand boot. The German used the butt of his gun to hit the dog twice on the head, shouting obscenities. Hugo whimpered and dropped on his side, blood oozing from his right ear. The officer kicked the dog and ordered four of his men to move the cart and contents off the road. When done, he and the four men fired continuous rounds into the cart and contents, destroying everything. He then joined the rest of his men as they marched onwards towards the fighting ahead. After ten minutes had passed, the Germans had disappeared leaving the travellers shocked and sobbing.

Some people had gathered around the old man lying in the road and tried to console the two women who turned out to be his daughters. In the space of fifteen minutes, they had lost their father and all their belongings. Curé Delage administered the last rites and a party of men helped bury the man at the rear of the mill under some trees. They returned with the old man's crucifix, wedding ring, a wallet containing five hundred Belgian francs and some photos of his wife holding the girls when they were babies.

Suzanne was devastated. Poor Hugo was still alive but was suffering badly. The poor dog's wounds were a dreadful sight as he lay in a pool of blood escaping from a shattered skull. He looked into her eyes licking her salty tears as they fell while she gently caressed his head. Fernand and Odette, white- faced and trembling, left Laure by the cart talking with Curé Delage and walked over to offer a few kind words and help. However, there was nothing anyone could do.

"Suzanne, go with Odette and clean up," said Fernand, seeing that their hands and skirt were smeared with blood. He helped Suzanne get up and patted her shoulder sympathetically. Hugo convulsed, several times and whimpered pitifully.

"I'll carry Hugo to the grass at the back of the mill so he will have a better place to rest," said Fernand. He came back later and confirmed he'd died and buried him, but neither of the girls knew that he'd put him out of his misery in an instant by breaking his neck. He convinced himself it was the most compassionate thing he could do in the circumstances. Fernand, hated doing it, and was troubled for a few days, adding to his growing and intense dislike of the Germans.

The Curé hobbled over looking distressed. He beckoned Fernand and two others to follow him. As they went he turned to them and said, "It's Gaston Mendelier. He's been badly hurt." Gaston, a well-liked distant cousin of Odette on her mother's side of the family, was a much respected and a decorated former soldier in the Belgian Army during World War One. He had single-handedly destroyed a German machine gun post, saving the lives of many soldiers in the battle for Dixmude in the latter stages of the 1914 - 1918 war.

"He's being looked after by the two nursing sisters from Louvain Hospital but he's in a bad way," said the Curé. Odette and Vivienne had joined them but were ordered to go back and wait.

There was a sense of foreboding. The sky was a strange flat grey colour with low misty clouds untypical for a July day. Even the sheaves of barley and wheat in an adjacent field seemed to slump and rattle their heads in sympathy as a cool wind increased from the east.Occasionally aircraft flew into view but thankfully ignored them.

Gaston Mendelier was lying on a makeshift wooden platform, basically a door and crates acquired from the mill. The two nurses, Angelique Valois and Hélène Van Diest were furiously attempting to stem a huge blood flow from Gaston's groin area. Their clothes were wet with blood as they skillfully brought things under control. Gaston had mercifully lapsed into unconsciousness but occasionally murmured in pain as they worked amongst damaged blood vessels and torn muscle.

"Whatever happened?" asked Fernand. The other three just stared in horror at what could only have been described as a butcher's slab.

Angelique, looking more like an abattoir worker than a nurse, tried to explain in simple terms.

"He's been hit in the groin by two stray bullets and shrapnel when the Germans fired on the carts and contents earlier. It's a serious wound in his groin and regretfully, his genitalia have been destroyed. Fortunately for him, the femoral artery has not been affected and it looks like one bullet has passed right through the upper leg missing anything vital."

Gaston groaned again. Fortunately for him Hélène Van Diest had packed medical essentials in her bag and so he'd been given a morphine injection to ease the pain. The two nurses had then managed to extract shrapnel lodged in his pelvis area. They also removed the remaining bullet before sewing up the wound with fishing line, donated by one of the men who had carried Gaston from the road.

"Our biggest concern is infection. We have no anti-septic so we'll have to make do with iodine, which we managed to bring along. We'll have to stay here with him for a day at least and then lift him onto a horse-drawn trailer." She pointed at a man standing nearby. "Henri has already kindly offered his farm trailer but we'll need volunteers to keep an eye on Monsieur Mendelier as we'll no doubt be busy attending to others on the march."

Twenty-four hours later the rest of the column had reached the road to Tournai without too many more horrors or hold-ups. Exertion and fatigue had almost depleted their resolve and they were always apprehensive when encountering German troops on the road. For the first time they had nervously mixed with the occupying forces. The streets of central Tournai around the Grand Place, unlike the outer districts, had escaped serious damage. A few shops, hotels and cafés were beginning to open up to serve the local inhabitants as well as Germans. The column had spread out, looking for accommodation and food after deciding to stay for five days. Some had found reasonable but basic facilities in boarding houses and inns adjacent to the Hotel d'Alcantara which itself had been taken over by noisy German officers, who, when not on duty, entertained themselves with singing, local girls, music and Schnapps.

Once past Tournai, Bertha the goat had broken free on a couple of occasions whilst on the road to Beloeil, causing concern and amusement. The second escape was against all expectations when she chewed through her hardened leather tether and took off. They eventually caught up with her but only after she'd head butted and toppled over an old man on a bicycle. She'd also managed to corner a terrified dog, desperately guarding a deserted house on the approaches to the village of Leuze en Hainault.

The evacuees re-formed and resumed their march on August 7th, one day before Odette's fifteenth birthday. The Renault Monaquatre tourer belonging to René Léonard, had miraculously survived despite a failing carburettor, two punctures and several occasions when it almost ran out of petrol. Luckily, René had managed to syphon petrol from several abandoned cars along the route and fill up using a collection of 'borrowed' jerry cans.

The piles of useless belongings that once filled the Renault had been discarded a long time back, including the bronze statuette of Leopold III. René had smashed it in a fit of pique with a hammer on hearing that the Belgian King had surrendered, after accepting Britain's offer to send the BEF for the defence of Belgium and Luxembourg. The Renault was now used to carry people, including Odette and Laure whose feet were dreadfully painful. The ugly wooden monkey which had taken up residence on the front radiator grill was no longer on view after it was discovered that someone had painted a Hitler moustache on it. After decapitating the ape, René had buried the remains in a ditch as a matter of common sense, just in case the Germans discovered it and took exception. He did keep his prize possession though, a set of bagpipes in immaculate condition, which he would occasionally play, subjecting the marchers to a cacophony of mournful Scottish tunes, much to the irritation of many.

The next day, August 8th, Laure and Fernand decided to try and celebrate Odette's fifteenth birthday but it would have to be a low-key affair. The column was nearing Beloeil when it was agreed to stay in the village of Ellignies-Saint-Anne, on the outskirts of Beloeil. Being remote, it had been largely unaffected by the ravages of war and best of all, there was no sign of German activity.

Their temporary abode, at least for a couple of days, was a very pleasant deserted cottage nestling amongst others on an estate belonging to the Ligne family, owners of the Château de Belœil less than two kilometres away. For the first time in a long time, the travellers could rest sore feet and make up for much needed sleep. The others had found and occupied a number of other cottages and three barns, adjacent to an impressive 18th century manor and chapel. The Ligne family, along with all the other estate residents, had reluctantly emigrated to England and America following news of the German advances into Belgium.

The party started off on a bright note. Laure had found several provisions in a larder and in the cellar. There were eggs and all the ingredients to make a simple cake that she decorated with a honey glaze and slices of apple and plums from the garden. Fernand had found some Jacquemotte coffee, chicory and sugar cubes. There was no tap water but they discovered a deep well, fed by the best crystal clear water from surrounding limestone hills. The gas mains had not been shut down so, after a few hours in the kitchen, Laure and some of her women friends, in between bouts of singing and laughter behind closed doors, secretly managed to perform culinary miracles for Odette.

"I have nothing nice to wear!" shouted Odette from an upstairs bedroom where she, Vivienne, Suzanne and Jacqueline had spent the afternoon reading and dancing to gramophone record songs by Judy Garland, Édith Piaf and Maurice Chevalier.

She called again, "Mama, I can't find a party dress! Please can you help?" The other girls were equally determined to find something to wear for the occasion and as Odette pleaded with her mother, the other girls slipped out of the back door to go and find a change of clothing. However, Laure was in the kitchen with the other mothers and failed to hear anything at all.

"What's wrong, my beautiful daughter? You look as though you are carrying the world's problems on your shoulders."

It was Odette's father who had just returned from a trip to Beloeil town centre and he was carrying a surprise. He raced upstairs just as Odette appeared in her bedroom doorway. The girls had spent some time using whatever cosmetics they could find and had done an excellent job pampering Odette so that she looked like a Hollywood film star. Fernand was struck dumb. He'd never seen his daughter looking so beautiful and grown up, even if she had just turned fifteen.

"I have something for you, a special present for your birthday party." He could hardly get the words out as Odette came towards him with her hands covering her cheeks.

"Oh Papa, what have you got, this is so exciting!"

She opened the package and there unfolding before her was the most beautiful dress she'd ever seen. It was a pale blue polka dot organza evening gown on a light cream background, designed by Balmain in Paris. A wide French blue silk waist sash embroidered with exotic flowers added the finishing touch.

"Oh oh oh!" exclaimed Odette. Her eyes welled up with tears as she carefully unfolded the gown. "It's beautiful, so beautiful! Thank you Papa. Where did you get it? It must have cost a fortune. Please let it fit!"

She threw herself at her startled father and gave him several wet kisses on his cheek.

"I must try it on immediately."

As he was leaving, half way through the door he replied. "It didn't cost me too much. I explained to a woman in a fashion shop that it was for my daughter's birthday. She said it had been there for a while but as there's no business, and she'd rather you had it than the Germans when they arrive. She asked me to give it you with her blessing and best wishes. I think it was a very lucky find but I was concerned in case it's the wrong size."

Odette spent the next twenty minutes trying on the gown. It was a perfect fit if not a little long. That minor problem was quickly resolved with higher heeled shoes she'd packed when leaving Mons back in April. Her still swollen feet only just fitted into the shoes. Minutes went by as Odette went to the window and looked outside, wobbling on her aching feet. The trees opposite waved at her in the evening breeze and she dreamed. She fantasised of meeting a handsome man in uniform and at that moment, blushed but knew instinctively she was ready for love. The pains in her aching body and feet disappeared as she experienced new and exciting sensual sensations that heralded the start of womanhood. She could smell the most delicious aromas coming from the kitchen and felt happy. Ten minutes passed as Odette day dreamed her way out of reality whilst sitting on the end of the bed. The dream disappeared suddenly when her mother knocked loudly on the door.

"Cherie, I'm dying to look at you. Your father said he'd bought you a new gown for the party."

Odette was sitting on her bed crying in deep sobs. Mascara ran down her cheeks. It was now 17:00 hours and the village church tolled its hourly peal. Laure entered and quickly sat next to her distraught daughter.

"Whatever is the matter, my darling? You look like a princess and princesses should never be sad. Tell your Mama whatever is causing you so much pain."

"I don't deserve all this, I'm not that special," she said. "So many people have suffered, and when I walk out there, I will feel awkward because I'll be dressed like a princess and they will be dressed like paupers. We've all shared the same hardships and witnessed horrors. Something tells me it's not right."

Laure put her arm around Odette's shoulders and said nothing for a few minutes. The other girls had just returned and were standing in the doorway listening.

"Odette, you're very special to me and your father. You are one of the youngest here and one of the bravest. For someone so young, you have seen too much. All the others out there who have come to know you would agree that you are a wonderful, caring young lady and deserve to celebrate your birthday. Besides, you cannot suddenly discard the hard work that has gone into your party and your father has made a supreme effort to find you a beautiful outfit. Let me tell you this, you look totally beautiful, so grown up and very elegant. Don't waste this opportunity. With this war, there may not be a tomorrow so try and enjoy today."

Suzanne, Vivienne and Jacqueline skipped into the room. Each spoke slowly and clearly. They too had managed to find some new outfits by combining various cotton and silk blouses and skirts they'd brought with them on the march.

"Look at us," said Jacqueline, "you will not be on your own. We've found the latest fashions too and we'll be with you."

The older girls laughed at their young friend and twirled around dancing in front of Odette. "We feel special too, so let's all try our best to be special together!"

Laure stood up and joined in dancing around the bedroom and singing loudly. The old mahogany wardrobe trembled as Odette's face broke into a smile and she clapped whilst they danced and pirouetted around.

"I'd better mend that sad face of yours," said Suzanne. "Your mascara and tears have made you look like a clown!"

"What on earth is going on up there?" Fernand was standing outside the front door with Jean-Baptiste whistling, trying to draw attention to themselves. They gave up and went inside, climbed the stairs, knocked on the bedroom door and walked in.

"Listen everyone, you'll have to get ready. The party will be in the hall next to the church over there in one hour at 19:00 hours." He pointed through the window to a long sandstone building in the distance. Odette, you must be standing outside over there, ready at 18:50 hours." He indicated the exact spot.

Jean-Baptiste whistled when he saw Odette.

"You really are as pretty as a picture." He then turned to his daughter, Jacqueline, and looking at her and the others, said, "You look so lovely too. I'm proud of you all."

Laure and Fernand smiled at each other and chatted in whispers while the girls ran out. Odette, now looking radiant, decided to help her mother change into her only spare outfit, a simple floral cotton dress that really needed ironing. However, with dark seamed stockings, shapely legs and an instinct to walk with poise, the style made Laure look rather elegant, despite being only 1.55m tall. The crowning glory was her wide brimmed hat in beige, adorned with a few red roses. The day had proved very hot, too hot for some, but Laure insisted on wearing her fox stole, the one with the beady glass eyes. Worse still, there were a few bees, which were attracted to the roses that needed constant flapping to discourage them. Despite all this, everyone managed to be ready on time.

It was a beautiful still evening. The smell of roses and jasmine that had climbed the front of the cottage for more than twenty years filled the air. Odette studied the ancient oak, yew and elm trees that surrounded the cottage and watched as two red squirrels scampered and played no more than thirty metres away. She stood with her mother as René Leonard's Renault suddenly lurched into view. It was decorated with flowers, picked from the Chateau's walled garden. René had also managed to locate a few lucky horseshoes linked together with bright red coloured tape between the flowers.

"You are going to be chauffeured to the party in style, just like a princess," said her mother.

"Oh Mama, it's so lovely." Odette held back the tears but clapped her hands in delight.

"Is Mademoiselle Moreau ready for the ball?" asked René using his best exaggerated chauffeur voice as he opened the side door of his Renault.

Laure had to move his bagpipes off the back seat before Odette could get in.

"Where shall I put this long-legged obscenity?" she said, holding the instrument aloft and laughing as they moved out.

"Pass it over, I'm going to play it later on at the party."

"Really? You'd better make sure that everyone is drunk first," said Laure, furiously trying to swat away some obstinate bees and other insects buzzing around her hat. Odette laughed and asked where they'd managed to get any alcohol. René drew up alongside the barn and turned to Odette and her mother.

"Don't say a word but some of the lads and I managed to find a way into the Manor's cellar and we found rows and rows of excellent Bordeaux wine. There were bottles of Chateaux Margaux, St Emilion Grand Cru, Pauillac and some excellent Sauternes. When the family return after the war, they'll hardly miss them, there's so many. We also found two-dozen crates of Bierre de Chimay. I think we will have a great time and the party will be just the thing to help us all find a little happiness and joy for a change."

Odette and Laure looked at each other a little perturbed as René opened the rear door. They stepped out, spending a few moments straightening their gowns, batted a few flies away and thanked René.

Laure took his hand, smiled broadly and whispered in his ear,

"In hard times we sometimes have to resort to unconventional things. You did well, my boy."

The front of the barn and the footpath that wound around the chapel were decorated with flowers and hand made-streamers, cut from old newspapers and coloured papers found abandoned in the farm cottages. A large crowd had gathered on a wide lawn surrounded by birch trees, cyprus, old oaks, laurel, magnolias, honeysuckle and various pine trees. Tables from the chapel and cottages were all laid out with pretty paper doilies, candles from the chapel store and floral decorations.

Suzanne supervised the old wind-up gramophone with a big selection of 78s. She treated the crowd to classics by Tino Rossi, Charles Aznavour, Edith Piaf, Charles Trenet, Bing Crosby, Tommy Dorsey, Glen Miller and Billy Holiday. Best of all, the weather was perfect. Not a cloud was to be seen on this warm August evening, graced by a gentle westerly breeze. Somewhere in the long distance, muffled noises should have been reminders that a war was still gripping the country, but nobody paid any attention. The heady smells of wine, beer, cordon bleu cooking, vanilla flavoured gateaux, coffee, cigarettes and the odd cigar that Fernand had secretly kept hidden, all helped everyone feel at home.

As Odette appeared, the crowd cheered, shouted and clapped. Many surrounded her with their happy faces making her feel that the entire affair was a perfect occasion.

"You look so pretty and grown up." It was Veronique, now close to giving birth and very large. Odette walked over, put her arms around her and kissed both cheeks.

"I'm so happy you are here. I thought you'd decided to go back to Mauberge. How are you feeling?"

"To be truthful, I think there may be problems with the baby. I haven't detected any movements over the last few days and I keep experiencing pains."

"I'm sure everything will be alright," said Odette.

"Maybe baby is taking time off and needs to rest just like we all sometimes have to," replied Veronique.

Odette smiled sympathetically but was not too sure what to say.

"You're right," responded Veronique. "There's only about three or four weeks to wait. I intend to have some fun tonight and enjoy the dancing."

With that, she browsed through the collection of records, nodding in approval. Laure and Fernand, Jacqueline, Vivienne and Suzanne, walked over and joined Odette. They had abandoned the HMV phono on Fernand's request.

"Everyone! Here's hoping you can all hear me?" Fernand's strong voice carried easily across the seventy strong crowds.

"As most of you know, today is my beautiful daughter's 15th birthday. Her mother and I are so proud of her and have used the occasion to hopefully bring some happiness, hope and joy back into her life as well as all your lives. We have travelled many kilometres together, experienced hardships and now can expect the difficulties that will come with occupation. But we are strong; we are Belgians and can look forward to the time when we'll be liberated.

The crowd nodded and murmured its approval.

"I would like to thank you all for your time, help and incredible resourcefulness. Without it none of this would have been possible."

"Let's forget about the future at least just for now," continued Fernand, "and try to enjoy the evening in the only way that we know how, with laughter in our eyes rather than tears or anxiety. Let's dance and sing our fears away. Please take your seats. I know there's some delicious food about to be served, thanks to the wonderful efforts of my wife and her friends who performed miracles, so please enjoy the evening ."

There was a huge cheer. Laure could not resist the occasion. She grabbed hold of an awkward Curé Delage and tried very hard to persuade him to dance, but he was horrified. Instead, she started singing Josephine Baker's "J'ai deux amours" with great gusto. She'd already managed a few glasses of excellent red wine, which seemed to add fuel to her abundant energy and expressive gesticulations, albeit in a slightly unstable manner. Fortunately she found her way to the head table, alongside Fernand and Odette, without falling over. She was still bothered by black flies as well as a wasp attracted to her beige hat and its red roses.

The party finished in the small hours and people slowly made their way back to where they were staying. Some stayed to help clear up and remove the tables. A few, overcome with alcohol, had fallen into the shrubbery or rolled down into a dry culvert that ran alongside the chapel. One or two even snored loudly while they slept. Odette had spent an hour thanking everyone personally Gaston Mendelier, sitting in a wicker bath chair had given Odette a gold necklace that once belonged to his sister who had died of meningitis in 1939. Gaston had made a miraculous recovery in less than two weeks since the shooting but the wounds had damaged more than his body. Odette reserved her biggest thanks for her parents when they reached the cottage. René Leonard, very much the worse for drink had managed to drive them there but on his way back, became confused and collided with an oak tree. Fortunately the only reminder, apart from his bruised pride, was a broken headlight, dented front bumper and a re-shaped radiator grill.

"It's time to move on again!" shouted Fernand early the next morning. With sore heads and much flatulence from indulging in too many rich foods and drink they were no longer used to, the column slowly and wearily trudged towards the entrance of the grounds carrying their belongings.

Jean-Baptiste, Julia and Jacqueline joined the crowd. They had been delayed when Jacqueline found Veronique bent over by a tree vomiting in spasms. Her swollen belly pains were causing concern and becoming more frequent.

"We must find a doctor or the nurses Angelique Valois and Hélène Van Diest. They will surely know what to do."

"The two nurses said goodbye two days ago," said Gaston who was lying on a pile of coats laid out on an old farm trailer pulled by two men who constantly kept him smiling with their Borinage chat.

"What are we going to do?" whispered Jacqueline to her parents. Being so young, she was mystified but also curious, although most of her questions went unanswered.

It was decided to hoist Veronique carefully onto the same trailer as Gaston. "We shall just have to find a doctor in Beloeil," replied Albert Decours, Suzanne's father, who was occupied with adjusting the harnesses. He turned to Gaston and with a reassuring smile confirmed that it was only about four kilometres away.

The crowd moved out. Most were smiling and happy to be on the last leg of the journey. They had travelled nearly three hundred kilometres and although they had no idea what life would be like under German occupation, going home encouraged an outpouring of rare optimism and happiness.

In Beloeil, it took the men very little time to locate a doctor, Dr Francois Lamotte, a large genial man in his fifties who wore a monocle. His wife was equally large and fussed over Veronique who was quickly transferred to their care.

"I'm sure she'll be fine," said the kind doctor, "but you must be aware that life is no longer straight forward. Since the Germans occupied the town, it's near impossible obtaining medical supplies and medicines and one has to be careful what to say."

As they spoke and almost on cue, a detail of German soldiers with rifles hitched across their shoulders drew level, staring at Gaston still lying in the trailer. They walked past chatting animatedly and disappeared into the distance as Fernand handed over a healthy amount of Francs to the doctor. Despite having little cash, he'd set about collecting donations from most people in the group and they had responded with generosity.

"Look after her well," said Odette with tears in her eyes. She hugged and kissed Veronique, who was also tearful, before bidding her goodbye.

Suzanne, Jacqueline and Vivienne waved as the column slowly moved on. They were sad to leave their friend behind even if certain elders were not so sentimentally motivated.

"We'll catch up with you and the baby before too long! Good luck!" shouted Odette.

"If it's a girl, I'll call her Odette and if it's a boy, I'll call him John." Veronique smiled and waved as the crowd walked away.

Beloeil seemed to be quite normal apart from German patrols and soldiers sitting outside cafés. Some shops had reopened including a boulangerie. Laure disappeared inside and bought two large pain de campagne, some croissants and three fruit tartlets using a bag of loose change she'd kept hidden away. It was almost impossible to find other basics such as butter, but someone had acquired a large pack of 'Alma' margarine, which was shared out eagerly. An unwritten, rule meant children were always a priority.

They had travelled less than a kilometre when the leading people in the column shouted back that there were a number of Germans ahead congregating around what looked like a guard post. As they approached, two people walked towards them, dressed in military uniforms not unlike those worn by the Waffen SS except these bore insignia of the Légion Wallonie and they carried rifles. Less than fifty metres away, German soldiers were watching the marchers intensely. They had lowered a red and white pole across the road intending to stop anyone travelling on.

Initially, the two men addressed the crowd asking them where they were heading but someone in the crowd recognised them. Whispers and notes started to circulate.

"It's Jean Pierre Thielemans and Luc Van de Velde. They are Rexists, German sympathisers."

"Traitors!" exclaimed an elderly woman standing in the crowd, indignantly pointing at the two men.

The black uniformed Rexists stiffened and one of them called back to the Germans asking for assistance. They'd dropped their initial friendliness and shouted for everyone to be quiet. Odette clung to her mother's skirt, trembling with fear.

"You stupid woman," hissed Fernand.

Three German soldiers and an officer joined the two men. After a brief animated discussion the officer ordered the woman who had shouted to step forward. Terrified, she took four steps towards the officer and the two Rexists grabbed her arms brusquely and marched her off to an open bomb damaged courtyard near the guard post less than a hundred metres away. Moments later, the sound of two pistol shots sounded and many in the crowd screamed.

The German Officer shouted even louder. "This is what happens to anyone failing to show respect to the occupying soldiers of the Reich and their allies!"

He made the Nazi salute and marched off with the others to stand at the entrance to the courtyard.

After some harsh bullying and shoving by the German soldiers, the crowd moved forwards, many crying, others praying. They saw the woman on her back with her arms outstretched, lying in a pool of blood, as they filed past. She'd been shot twice. Nobody dared stop as the Germans continually and menacingly threatened them to move on quickly.

"It's Marie Leclerc from Hyon," said someone. "Poor woman, she lost her husband to tuberculosis two years ago and her two sons are in the army. Nobody knows where they are or if they are alive."

"Maybe, but she put us all in grave danger," said Fernand. "We are fortunate the Germans did not shoot more of us. We cannot and must not show our anger. It will only cause retributions."

Parents were shielding their children's eyes from the gruesome sight in the courtyard but they were just as concerned about the prospects of occupation and increasing numbers of traitors turning against their own people.

"I'm so scared," said Odette to her father. "We can't trust anyone anymore can we?"

"I know ma cherie," said Fernand. "We face very difficult times but we must not give up. I'm sure the Boche will just get on with their war and we'll just have to get on with our lives."

Two days later, on the 16th August 1940, after passing through

St Ghislain, and Ghlin, the crowd reached the outskirts of Mons. They had returned after a brutal three hundred kilometres and nearly six months on the road and looked forward to going home, so long as their homes were habitable. Suzanne Decours and Vivienne Van Damme along with their parents had shed many tears as they said their goodbyes in St Ghislain. Gradually, people left the column as they entered Mons. It was often tearful and emotional as each person spent time hugging his or her long-suffering companions. Most were hopeful that their homes were still unscathed by indurate German occupation.

Fernand, Laure and Odette circled around the town centre to avoid the risk of meeting German patrols. They walked through Jemappes and circled around near the cement works in Obourg, eventually following the Chemin de Mourdrieux towards La Bascule. They were now on their own apart from the Haché family who lived opposite the Moreaus.

René Leonard and his now battered Renault had disappeared with much waving and shouts of "Bonne Chance" for he lived just a stone's throw away. Fernand held up his hand and they paused by the memorial for a moment. They stared for ages and gradually smiles and grins replaced anxieties traced on their faces. Houses along the roads opposite appeared to be untouched and empty. As they stared, a number 90 tram suddenly appeared and stopped at La Bascule. It brought reassurance that maybe things were not quite as bad as they had imagined.

The Moreaus picked up the pace as they crossed the road and once more stood outside their home at 10, Chaussée de Beaumont. Odette skipped with happiness despite seeing German soldiers walking along the Chaussée de Binche towards Mons in the distance. They wept and hugged each other. It was a defining moment of joy, a moment they thought would never happen. It was also the start of a new dramatic phase and a complete change in their lives.

Chapter 8: Airborne at Last

Alan thanked the taxi driver and handed over one shilling and threepence for the ten-minute drive from Nuneaton Trent Valley Railway Station. He was desperate to get home and leave behind the putrid stink from crates of old dried fish that hung like a dark cloud throughout the station and surrounding area. He could not help notice how dirty and squalid the platforms looked. He stood outside his home in Higham Lane, also known as 'Elmentita', and took in the familiar stone lions adorning the driveway. The house name and the lions were George White's way of remembering the two years he'd spent in East Africa during the 1st World War. There were no signs of life but somebody passing by on a cycle broke the silence.

"Hello Al! Good to see you back OK." It was Bill Hawley who lived further up the lane. He had decided not to volunteer for the armed forces on the grounds of ill health. Instead, he'd joined the Warwickshire Home Guard where he was responsible for uniforms. Alan waved but Bill seemed to be in too much of a hurry to stop.

"I wonder where they all are? I'm sure I mentioned my arrival time in the last letter." Alan was speaking to himself loudly and frowning with a quizzical expression. He had a key but was a little disheartened not to be greeted with a welcoming party.

"Alan! Alan! Over here!" It was his sister Barbara. She was next door peering over a five-foot fence that divided the White's house from next door, owned by Francis and Nellie Cross. Helen, the Cross's daughter and her younger brother Johnny saw them and joined Barbara.

"Everyone's here, please come on over. We're dying to see you. We are celebrating Johnny's birthday - he's fourteen today."

Alan slung his kit bag over his shoulder and leaped over the fence where it dropped short to three feet. He was in uniform, trying to be careful not to snag anything. Barbara rushed up to him and gave him a big affectionate kiss on the cheek and lots of hugs. The other three smiled and clapped just as the front door opened. It was Francis Cross accompanied by two Siamese cats that immediately attached themselves to Alan's serge wool trousers, pulling a number of threads with their claws. Alan muttered a few expletives under his breath and gave them a sideways swipe with his boot.

"Come in my boy! It's good to see you looking so healthy and bright eyed. The RAF must be doing something right with our boys!"

"Thanks," said Alan, keeping a wary eye on the cats. He walked down the hallway and into the sitting room by which time the two feline pests had been disposed of with a quick deft foot action. Alice, his mother, jumped up and threw her arms around him.

"Why didn't you write?" she asked. "We only had one letter, but it doesn't matter, you've probably had no time at all. Come and sit next to your mother and tell us all about it."

Helen was standing next to Barbara listening attentively. She was a good-looking girl who'd always taken a shine to Alan. However, he had never shown much interest, considering her not be his type. He still thought of Kathleen Mackenzie in Coventry.

Across the room in the corner by a standard lamp and sitting in a large armchair, Alan's father George, fingering *The Birmingham Daily Post*, coughed loudly.

"Have you been up in the clouds yet?" said George. "And have they decided to let you loose in bombers or fighters?"

Alan moved closer. He was used to his father being unwilling to express emotions with his sons and daughter, so it was no surprise to him to be regarded almost as a stranger.

"Good to see you Dad."

There was no reply, just a grunt, even after Alice poked his leg and reprimanded him for not being happier to see his youngest son and willing to listen.

"It's a little too soon for flying," said Alan. "I've only just passed my surveillance and detection tests with flying colours, by the way." He smiled and apologised for the pun but it went unnoticed. "I guess it won't be too long now and I'm looking forward to it."

Nellie Cross entered with a large tray, bringing glasses of sherry and snacks decorated with a few cat hairs.

"Oh Alan, you do look very smart in uniform. Let's drink to all you brave lads who are fighting those horrible Germans."

"Hear, hear!" said Francis who suddenly stepped backwards and fell heavily over Johnny, banging his head on a piano stool. The boy was on his hands and knees playing with his new Dinky toy cars, a birthday present from his sister. There was a heavy crash as two very alarmed Siamese cats attempted to scale the curtains but their combined weight managed to bring down the entire curtain pole just missing Nellie's treasured glass figurine of a ballet dancer.

"Are you alright, Dad?" asked Helen, slightly concerned. At eighteen, she was a week away from starting a nursing career.

"Yes, yes, yes!" said Francis, trying to hide his embarrassment. "It was only a knock and a bruise, don't fuss!"

"Nellie, why not play some good old songs on the piano. I'll retrieve the curtains and then fetch the jelly, cake and a cup of tea.

Nellie Cross was an accomplished concert pianist able to play most things so long as it was classical. She kept the party spirit alive with some bright extracts from Strauss's Blue Danube and surprised everyone with a few jazzy tunes by George Gershwin.

Alan enjoyed himself bringing everyone up to date with his RAF experiences whilst relaxing over a weak cup of tea and a large slice of Johnny's birthday cake. He asked if anyone had seen Bill Bennett across the road but Francis, who was a reporter with the Nuneaton Tribune, volunteered the only news. Apparently, Bill had returned for a week's leave two weeks previously before being transferred to RAF Swanton Morley, near Norwich. He was already applying his radio navigation training in Bristol Blenheims with 105 Squadron.

The week passed too quickly. Alan had helped his father with odd jobs at the Scala Cinema and his mother in the garden. He had also repaired the greenhouse and destroyed a wasp's nest beyond the old pear tree. News filtered through that in a week's time, Graham would be home on compassionate leave, following the birth of his son Geoffrey. His wife Florence had not had an easy time of things during the pregnancy. Alice and George White were over the moon and Alan was disappointed that he would not be there. As for Gordon, Barbara had received a rare letter in which he described the horrors of war. It later turned out that he had not yet been directly involved in any action but was, for now at any rate, employed as a driver, engaged in training operations in Ireland.

By November 1940, RAF Wattisham in Suffolk, under C.O Robert 'Pussy' Foster and Wing Commander Lawrence Sinclair, was home to No. 110 and 107 Squadrons, under 82 wing and bomber command. It was one of the first RAF stations to see action. Blenheim light bombers had already flown missions over German occupied harbours but the cost had been excessive. The Battle of Britain had ensured that German ambitions to destroy the RAF prior to invasion had been thwarted, but the Luftwaffe still mounted bomber attacks against British cities and industry. In addition, it became increasingly obvious that Blenheims were far too vulnerable when confronting heavily defended targets.

Alan and his four companions, Harry Silver, Johnny Caxton, Robert (Bunny) Peters and William (Willy) Pendleton, arrived at the station on November 12th 1940. They were attached to the Radio and Navigation section under Flight Lieutenant Roland (Rollo) Bradford. Over the next three weeks, they remained ground-based whilst updating radio and navigational skills. They would soon be taking those skills into the air and having to grow accustomed to operating from the cramped conditions in Avro Ansons. Bunny Peters managed to survive a crash landing and spent eight weeks in hospital recovering from concussion and a broken femur before being transferred to RAF Scampton. By December, Johnny and Willy had been transferred to RAF Watton. It was the last time that Alan and Bill would see their two friends. Willy died over Holland in

94

1941 when his Blenheim crashed after it was hit by Flak and Johnny died in late 1942 from wounds sustained when he was attacked by ME 109s and crashed near Amiens in France.

"Where's the best place to grab a steak?" Alan and Harry turned around to be confronted by a man in a full flying outfit, including the best looking fur-lined Irvin jacket they had ever seen.

"From the accent, I take it you are American," said Harry.

"Canadian actually, and my name is Flying Officer Jean-Luc Bouvier, but you can call me 'Bo' - most of my friends do. Anyway, it's good to meet you guys."

Alan and Harry introduced themselves and the three men shook hands just as a very noisy misfiring staff car drove past.

"Good to meet you too," said Alan. "How come you're here? Where have you parked the kite?"

"Oh, that's quite a story," said Bo. "After I tangled with a couple of Dorniers and an ME109 over the sea, my Spit developed a problem. I was given permission to land here so your guys can sort it out. Looks like tracer may have hit the fuel tank. I should be off tomorrow back to Hornchurch. In the meantime, I need to eat. Are there any good pubs around here where a Canadian flyer can find steak and fries?"

The three of them smiled.

"There's a great place in Lavenham. It's called 'The Swan' and is very much Olde Worlde England. It's famous for good food and the best ales in Suffolk and it's only about thirty minutes away. Let's go! I'll drive," said Harry.

The Canadian stood chatting with Alan while Harry fetched his newly acquired red Midget TA Roadster, thanks to a generous contribution from his father, who wanted to learn to drive when Harry was on leave. The three of them jumped in and exited number 2 gate at some speed, hooting and waving at the sentries as they shot away into the inky darkness of the Suffolk lanes.

'The Swan' in Lavenham had a reputation for being rowdy and a second home to many airman from the local Suffolk airfields. Alan,

Harry and Bo arrived at 7.00 p.m. to be greeted by loud ale drinking bomber boys, holding sway on one side of the bar. Keeping to themselves on the other side, several fighter pilots from as far away as RAF Martlesham and Coltishall were chatting quietly. As soon as the word was out that a Canadian was amongst them, everyone wanted to hear about his experiences and details of life in Canada. Bo was a brilliant raconteur until the darts came out and someone suggested a match between the best three from the bomber crews and similarly from the fighter lads.

Alan decided he was by far the best darts player and so took on the role of captain for the bomber lads. A tall-dignified Flight Lieutenant with a moustache, who seemed to command attention with few words, captained the other team.

Harry turned to Alan and whispered in his ear. "That's Bob Stanford Tuck D.F.C. from 92 Squadron. Surely, you've heard of him? He's the chap that people say has shot down more ME109s than anyone! Good luck Al, he's already proved he's a damned good aimer with a three second burst from eight Browning 303s."

Alan gulped as the man, brushing his moustache, walked over to shake hands.

"May the best crew win," he said with an endearing smile. "As is our tradition, the losing team will have to buy a round for the winners and the captain will kiss my arse before he leaves." Everyone fell about laughing. They tossed a coin and Alan stepped up to the oche.

His first two darts hit treble twenty, the third bounced off the wire much to the bomber crews' anguish and the fighter boys' delight along with caustic comments.

Next up, Bob Stamford Tuck took aim. His first dart scored a one, the second a treble eighteen and the third a treble twenty. He cast a withering look towards Alan and Harry.

Harry's three darts scored low as did the second man's attempt for the fighter team. There were twenty points in favour of the Bomber team when Alan patted his third team member's shoulders, a man called Terry, and encouraged him to go for the bull and at least a treble twenty. The man's first dart hit the sixteen accompanied by some tasty expletives from the men in his team. His second hit treble twenty. They now needed just thirty-six with a double eighteen for the win. Terry stood calm and just as he was about to launch his last dart, somebody in the room broke wind, disturbing his concentration and he missed.

"Oh dear old chap, really bad luck" said Bob Stamford Tuck stroking his moustache and smiling broadly. "Let's put this one to bed, shall we?"

Alan and Harry looked at each other. They were convinced that the honourable Flight Lieutenant had purposely distracted Terry and was therefore a cheat.

Harry being the more direct, stared at Stamford Tuck and his smiling team, and loudly shouted "Cheats! You farted on purpose to put our man off. That's not playing by the rules is it?"

Stamford Tuck puckered up his nose in distaste, ignored it and motioned for his third man to step up. It was Bo, who needed two treble twenties and a double ten to win. Taking careful aim he hit all the required targets followed by some wild whooping and yells. The Fighter team were jubilant, clapping each other on the back whilst the bomber team grumbled and objected.

Stamford Tuck asked Alan and Harry to join him.

"Dear boys, I believe you called us cheats. I think we all deserve an apology, don't you?"

"Well, what else could it have been?" said Alan. "You put off our third man! It's you who should apologise."

Stanford Tuck scratched his chin and then bellowed across the room so that everyone could hear him.

"Seems we are all cheats, lads so I think we need to teach these heathens some good old-fashioned manners. What do you say?"

There was a shout of "Get 'em!"

At that, a burley Pilot Officer grabbed hold of Harry's hair and punched him so that he fell over a table. Alan warded off another punch but was caught by a glancing blow. Terry, still incensed, picked up a chair and swung it at two antagonists, breaking two of its legs. Within minutes, the room was filled with flailing arms and fists. The sound of breaking glass and shouting brought in the landlord who immediately made a phone call. He was used to this type of thing. Stamford Tuck, Bo and a couple of others escaped out of a rear window, brushed themselves down and walked into the pub's garden for a smoke.

"Terrible business, you know. Those bomber boys do not know how to play nicely. They're just so unrefined," said Bob Tuck.

The men laughed just as a squeal of brakes announced the arrival of the RAF Police, who showed little sympathy as they bundled the dishevelled complaining rabble into the back of their very uncomfortable truck.

Back at base, they discovered the CO wanted to see them early the next morning. It was going to be a very long night.

"Christ almighty! What in all that's holy do you think you were doing?" boomed a loud refined voice that echoed across the Mess.

Alan, Harry and the others were standing trying to look remorseful. They showed obvious signs of the previous evening's debacle with black eyes, scuffs and bruises. Before them, Wing Commander Lawrence Sinclair bristled with indignation and moved from side to side with his hands clenched firmly behind his back.

"So, what the hell do you think you were playing at, brawling in public and bringing shame on the RAF? What excuses are you going to offer me before I pronounce judgement?" Harry stepped forward and, looking straight at the officer, recalled the entire story. The Wing Commander coughed twice and spoke.

"You silly buggers! Do you mean to say you let those jumped up arrogant excuses for fighter pilots get the better of you?"

"Yes Sir, we certainly did," said Harry, trying to hide a smile.

"OK, I'm inclined to treat this as a prank where hopefully you chaps will have learnt a valuable lesson. Is that clear?"

Everyone replied with a loud "Yes Sir!" He was about to say

something else when a Sergeant walked in and mentioned that a couple of men outside wanted to speak with the CO.

"Who are they?" enquired the Wing Commander.

"Flight Lieutenant Robert Stamford Tuck and Flying Officer, Jean-Luc Bouvier, the Canadian chappie who landed here yesterday with a damaged Spit... Sir!

"Very well Sergeant, tell them the CO is away until tomorrow." He rubbed his chin and muttered under his breath, "Oh Christ, not Stanford-Tuck." He then ordered the Sergeant to send them in.

"Good day gentlemen." Bob Stanford Tuck stood stiffly and saluted the Wing Commander. The salute was returned.

"What brings you here Flight Lieutenant?"

"I've returned the Sergeant's motor car along with this Canadian gentleman here, Sir!"

He half turned, nodding towards Bo. "And I'd like to offer an explanation for the unfortunate incident last night."

Bob Stanford Tuck postulated for a minute or two and twiddled his moustache but mentioned that all those present had to share the blame for the altercation.

"Your chaps were provoked, but defended themselves very well against, shall we say, superior forces? Even though we were accused of cheating! But I'm prepared to forget about that. Also, out of my meagre pay, I have compensated the landlord enough to replace one table, two chairs and three pint glasses. Finally, I'd like to invite all you fine fellows to another show at 'The Swan' next month with a couple of rounds on us." He saluted again and stepped back.

"Very well Flight, I'll put this entire episode down to just one of those unfortunate things that seems to happen to RAF chaps every now again." He turned to Alan, Harry and the others.

"We need you men to be fit and ready for ops whenever required but should it happen again, I'll come down on you so hard you'll wish the Jerries had caught you first. Do I make myself absolutely clear?"

"Yes Sir," came back the response. Alan cleared his throat,

stepped forward and saluted.

"Permission to speak Sir?"

"OK, get on with it man!" Alan turned and addressed Bob Tuck.

"Speaking on behalf of the men as their captain last night, I'd like to thank you for your generous explanation of events as well as returning the car and our Canadian friend. I'd also like to ask you if the penalty for losing the dart's match still holds? As the losing captain of our team Sir, am I still required to lick your arse?"

There was a stunned silence.

"Sergeant, you'll show this gentlemen some respect," said the Wing Commander.

There was a short pause before the senior officer suddenly broke into a long deep chested spluttering laugh, startling every one present. He wiped his brow on a starched white handkerchief

"Dismissed!" he shouted, still smiling like a grinning bulldog.

The men gathered outside on a dull, cold morning, shaking hands and laughing aloud with Flt Lieutenant Bob Stanford Tuck, thanking him personally. While Harry re-fuelled his car, Bob Stamford Tuck chatted with Alan, assuring him there was no need to follow up with the infamous punishment. He looked Alan in the eyes for a few moments.

"I'll say one thing young man, you have enough guts to speak your mind. Good luck in the coming months, but above all let's show those Jerries what RAF boys can do and give the buggers a taste of hell.

He waved goodbye and jumped into a waiting taxi.

"Hope to see you all next month. Stay alive and show Jerry how the RAF boys play the game. "

Early next morning, Alan and Harry, in their flying kit, were each instructed to follow the other crew members as they headed towards two Ansons or 'Annies', parked about two hundred yards away on grass next to one of the two concrete runways. Both aircraft were ready to go and fully fuelled. Alan waved to Harry as he climbed on board the nearest one. Both aircraft were cramped and modified to take two radio/navigation operators, a gunner managing a single Browning .303 machine gun in the front fuselage and the pilot. The pilots in both aircraft received instructions to taxi into position. The entire fuselage was shaking as the twin engines gathered revs, making a deafening noise. After a couple of minutes the control tower issued permission to take off and once the brakes had been disengaged, they started to pick up speed. Once in the air, the sounds of banging and rattling subsided after bumping across the uneven grass and all crew members checked out their oxygen as well as on-board and out-board radio comms. Alan was sitting at the side of Flight Sergeant Stan Mitchell when he received a crackling message from the pilot.

"Welcome aboard Sergeant White. Just sit back, watch Stan, learn from his experience and enjoy the ride"

Both aircraft flew out over the east coast, south of Hull and onwards over the North Sea. It was a dull very cold day with limited visibility. Alan was thankful he'd dressed in two long johns under his trousers. His fur lined boots and jacket kept out much of the cold but he soon started shivering. Without warning, the pilots voice crackled in his headset and interrupted any thoughts about the cold.

"Pay attention chaps, we are dropping to a thousand feet."

"Alan, old chap, can you communicate with the other Anson. Let them know all's well at this end."

"OK skipper," replied Alan. He'd already picked up quite a lot of RAF parlance.

"Nothing to report so far, except it's bloody freezing." Harry's voice came through loud and clear. "Can't wait for breakfast with fresh coffee in a warm Mess."

Suddenly, the pilot's voice calmly came through again, "OK you lot, we've been asked to look for a U-Boat that's been reported in our area. Keep your eyes peeled and less of the chit chat if it's not too much trouble."

Alan looked through the port window. They were flying so low he could see the waves breaking. Spotting a periscope would prove difficult. Stan motioned to Alan with two outstretched fingers in front of his eyes, to concentrate. Alan was feeling slightly queasy but there was worse to come; he had developed a painful headache above his eyes. However, he convinced himself that it was a temporary problem and carried on spotting.

Without any warning the pilot banked the Anson to starboard and descended to six hundred feet. At this height it would be easier to spot anything unusual. Alan could see the second Anson doing the same when he heard Harry's co-radio operator say he'd spotted a long dark shape moving in and out of the low grey mist on the port side. Annie number two banked heavily and came down to three hundred feet.

"There it is!" shouted Harry.

The pilot had also spotted U-271 on the surface, heading in a south-easterly direction. He banked sharply so he could approach from the bow end and avoid the U-Boat's 20mm turret gun.

"Come in 'Annie two', this is Jimmy Anderson in 'Annie one'. Billy, I'm going to approach from his bow and shake him up a bit before he dives. Can you follow me in?"

"Understood and ready to follow you in Jimmy," replied Billy, the pilot of the second Annie.

Pilot Officer Anderson seemed totally calm and reassuring as he levelled at seven hundred yards to the rear of the U-Boat.

His voice cackled again, "Gunner, make sure you're ready. She's not diving yet but there's some activity in the tower and there's a few of them on deck."

"Understood skipper," said Gareth Morgan, a Welsh gunner from Tonnypandy. "Looking forward to some fine sport Skip."

'Annie One's' twin Brownings stuttered into action. The loud clatter from the front of the Anson reminded Alan of the noise from a kid's toy drum only more regular. He could see tracer lashing around the boats hull flicking up white spume and spray. Two men on the U-Boat were manning a twin machine gun on the conning tower and attempting to return fire. He saw them duck and disappear down a hatch. 'Annie Two' followed behind repeating the attack but the German boat was now rapidly submerging. Within five minutes, the time it took to circle round, there was little trace of the U-Boat other than a feint outline below the surface

"Good show, Taffy." Pilot officer Anderson, imitating a Welsh accent, praised Sergeant Morgan. The reply made them all smile.

"You may be a good pilot, sir, but you're a lousy Welshman."

At that moment, Billy's voice from 'Annie Two' came through in Alan's headphones. "Looks like we've been hit in the rear end but it's not serious."

"OK, take it easy Billy, we'll keep an eye on things, over and out." said Jimmy Anderson. Both planes returned to base and landed at 4.30 p.m. without any mishaps. Alan and Harry jumped out and stood looking at the tracer damage on Annie Two.

"Bit lucky there, Harry," said Alan.

Billy Mackinnon joined them along with the skipper of 'Annie One', Jimmy Anderson.

"That's nothing old bean," said Billy. "These 'Annies' will take a lot worse. Still, it was a good opportunity to see some action. You'll see much more of that I'm sure. By the way, you did well but get used to switching your radio off after each message chaps. I could hear you both chatting to each other and I'm not interested in your social lives. Don't forget, the radio speaks to the crew and the tower." He grinned at them both and clapped them on their shoulders. Alan and Harry looked at each other and smiled.

Alan, Harry and their friends spent the next two months, except for three days Christmas leave, gaining more experience in the 'Annies' and were both looking forward to transferring to Blenheims. In March 1941, Harry received news that he would be transferred to RAF North Coates in Lincolnshire where he was required for radio and detection work with Coastal Command. Alan was sad to lose his friend although he could not have known that in time, they would be reunited at RAF Stenigot in Lincolnshire, one of the growing number of Home Chain Radar stations.

It was at this time that Alan and Harry received the sad news that Bo, their Canadian friend had ditched in the English Channel after an altercation with an ME109 and was reported to have drowned after his Spitfire's canopy had jammed shut. The two of them took the news badly but had to return rapidly to the daily realities of conflict and the business of fighting the war. They were becoming more hardened to the daily loss of life amongst their peers and friends but were now more determined to pour retribution on the Luftwaffe.

Alan had become more concerned about his headaches and on one occasion when flying at high altitude, he suffered a very bad nose bleed. The medics indicated he had sinus issues, advising him to apply warm compresses and take Bromelin, an enzyme extract from pineapples. Unfortunately, in July 1941, whilst serving as a radio navigator during a long high altitude-bombing raid in a Blenheim, his mask almost filled with blood and mucus. It was an incredibly painful experience requiring three days supervision under the watchful eyes of the medical staff at Wattisham. With uncomfortable swabs filling his nostrils, he spent the time writing letters to his parents and sister, but received few replies. The constant drone of aircraft taking off and landing, sometimes in trouble after combat damage, kept him alert but also tired. Eventually, he was grateful for the odd visit to 'The Swan' at Lavenham as well as nearer pubs where the banter helped him forget about the growing mortality rates amongst his friends.

In early September 1942, following more nose bleeds and issues at high altitudes, six days before his twentieth birthday, Alan was deemed to be unsuitable for any further flying duties on medical advice. The past two years had taken its toll and he looked more pale and gaunt than at any other time. After two weeks of home leave, he was transferred to Chain Home Station CHL28A, Dunwich on the Suffolk coast. Here, he and ten others, including a few WAAFs, were constantly kept on their toes, communicating with staff in the very busy Opps. Room at Duxford with news of defence of Britain, he developed a deep interest incoming aircraft. Alan was devastated to be withdrawn from flying duties but after realising just how vital these roles in RADAR communications were becoming in the and skill that served him well during his future time in the RAF.

Chapter 9: Occupation and Resistance

It was Saturday morning on the 24th August 1940 and the sun was hot and bright in a cloudless sky. Odette woke later than usual, still trying to recover from the long walk. It had been over a week since she, her mother and father had returned to their home on the Chaussée De Beaumont.

The German occupiers had left the place unmarked apart from some damage to a door leading to the cellar. They had not even touched any linen. It was in the same secret hiding place behind a wall panel in the attic, where it had been hidden before taking to the road. Scrubbing the place clean took Laure three days even though it was hardly necessary. She hated the idea that the Boche had tainted the place and so all the repetitive scrubbing was essentially therapeutic. Fernand had already been into Mons twice to find basic essentials and food, but it was dismal. There were many German soldiers and officers hanging around, mainly in the Grand Place and the streets leading to it. All food was in short supply and he had to be content with poor quality vegetables, a couple of rabbits and some pork, which he managed to acquire from an old friend called Gérard who owned a Charcuterie on the Rue D'Hautbois. There was precious little of anything including coffee, sugar and milk and other essentials. Money was also difficult to withdraw. Banks, were controlled mainly by unhelpful German administrators and manned by staff trying to cope with long queues. More often than not, they were closed.

On the 27th August, Laure hosted Frédéric and Marie-Agnès Haché from across the road, along with Jean-Baptiste, Julia and Jacqueline, sharing out what little food they could find. Fernand was delighted to discover that the Germans had not found his cache of Bordeaux wines buried in the back garden. He retrieved them and as a treat, opened two bottles of Château Cheval Blanc St Emilion

Premier Grand Cru Classé A, dated 1938.

They discussed and decided how they would cope with rationing and the curfews imposed by the Germans. The three men decided they would have to find work in order to earn some money, even if it meant fraternising with German bosses. Fernand agreed to ask his former employers at the Waterworks, where he had supervised the filtration plant before their walk to the coast. It was agreed that the three women would stay at home, at least for the time being, as it was too unsafe in the town. Odette and Jacqueline would return to school and resume their studies in different year groups at the *Ecole Normale* but they would be taken there and collected by their fathers every day by tram.

Odette spent the next two weeks doing little other than helping her mother and reading several books. She did venture out on a couple of occasions with her parents to visit family and friends, but the day she returned to school at the start of the new autumn term was one that would be forever engraved in her memory.

September 16th 1940 was an unusually cold, miserable Monday. Heavy rain, driven by strong winds lashed at the tall windows of the *Ecole Normale*. Odette and a few friends were sitting towards the back of class 3A watching and listening to Madame Bervoets, the Head Teacher from La Louviere. They were enjoying stories of Belgian history when the door opened abruptly and two German soldiers carrying rifles entered without knocking. An officer wearing a full-length black leather coat and polished boots followed them. He looked around with dark cold menacing eyes, stood stiffly and clicked his heels before slowly removing and shaking his wet hat. The officer opened his coat after shaking off the rain and revealed the feared double SS symbols on the lapels of his jacket.

"I'm Sturmbannführer Heindrich Strichmann, Madame," he said, addressing Madame Bervoets.

"I have received information that you have a Jew in one of your classes by the name of Jan Stalienski, originally from Poland."

The teacher looked directly at the officer and calmly said, "I do not recognise the name and cannot help you as I do not believe we have such a person in this school."

The rest of the class were becoming nervous and some started to fidget and whimper.

"Very well Madame, then you will not mind if my men and I search the other classrooms."

The three Germans disappeared and after a few minutes, everyone could hear loud shouting and banging coming from another classroom along the corridor. Madame Bervoets tried to calm everyone down without showing her own fear. Odette, like most of the others became very anxious and frightened. She chatted to the girl next to her who put her finger to her lips as a warning to be quiet. Sounds of Jackboots on black and white marble floor tiles grew stronger. The Germans were coming back. They pushed a young man from one of the two senior classes into the room. There was blood on his face and a swollen lip where he'd been struck hard.

"So, Madame, you claim to be unaware of this Jew?"

"He's a new boy who I believe comes from Jemappes. He's not in my class and cannot remember his name," she said.

"Do not lie to me," said the officer who was becoming angry, slapping his gloves against his thighs. "A professor in the senior class confirmed that this man's father was from Poland. That's all I need," he barked, "and I have my orders."

Madame Bervoets, with tears in her eyes pleaded with the officer to be easy on the seventeen year old.

"I'm sorry I misled you," she said. "I beg you, please do not harm the boy, he's a very talented violinist with a bright future."

"That is of no concern of mine. We will take him for questioning and you will come too." He motioned to one of the soldiers to march the teacher out along with Jan Stalienski who had turned deathly white and was visibly shaking. Madame Bervoets asked the officer where they were being taken.

"To our headquarters in Rue d'Enghien, where you will both be made to answer questions."

The school's Principal, Monsieur Henri Delacourt, was summoned and took over the class as Madame Bervoets and the seventeen year old were escorted out of the building. They were rough handled into a waiting truck as a few onlookers gathered. The three Germans climbed in and they drove off.

At 16:00 hours, Odette walked out of the school holding Jacqueline's hand and joined their waiting fathers. Odette burst into tears, alarming Fernand and Jean-Baptiste. They could see that her other classmates were also upset as they hurried past. Jacqueline who had attended a junior class was anxious, but not fully aware of the earlier drama.

"Whatever has happened?" asked Fernand anxiously. Odette poured out her story in between sobs whilst tightly gripping her father's hands.

The two men looked at each other and, with a reassuring hug, quickly escorted the two girls towards the tram stop on the corner of Rue d'Havré and the Grand Place. They waited patiently, watching Germans marching towards the Hotel de Ville. The 90 tram destined for Binche came into view with a heavy clanging sound and a second linked coach. Its pantograph sparked randomly on the overhead cables and the clamouring of a shrill bell sounded as heavy metal wheels squealed on the mirror-bright rails. They all climbed on board as a German military car with two SS Officers overtook the tram and sped off towards the Rue de Nimy. It eventually turned left into the Rue Roland de Lassus where it stopped before a former theology college and the new location for the town's prison and Gestapo offices.

Fernand turned towards Jean-Baptiste and without alerting the girls, asked him to drop by later that evening. He had some news about a job, which he might want to think about. He also hinted that they should discuss the day's events at the school and ways to help resistance movements against the Boche and Rexist traitors.

Jean-Baptiste arrived at 18:30 hours. He rang the front door bell just as an old farmer suddenly appeared alongside him with a large

Landrace pig on a string lead. Fernand opened the door and smiled at Jean-Baptiste.

"Hello Emile, thank you for bringing the pig. Please come this way."

Fernand disappeared through a grilled entrance to the garden with the farmer and pig, while Laure welcomed Jean-Baptiste.

"Mama, what is that squealing noise in the garden?" said Odette with a puzzled look on her face.

"I'm not sure," said her mother.

Jean-Baptiste sat down at the dining room table with a glass of Picon prepared by Laure. "It's a pig," he said. Both Laure and Odette looked at each other bemused.

While delicious cooking odours wafted from the kitchen, Odette and her mother rushed into the garden via the laundry annexe. They were just in time to see Fernand pushing the rear end of a rather obstinate pale pig into Hercule's old stable. Moments later, a scruffy looking farmer emerged and shook hands with Fernand.

"What is going on?" asked Laure. She was clearly agitated.

"Do must remember Emile Bosquet, son of Jules, the farmer near St Symphorien? He's going to move in with his lady friend in Binche next week and she wants him to get rid of most things including his pig".

"Yes, I know the family but that pig is ridiculous." Laure was now seeing the funny side of it. "How are we going to feed it and keep it clean?" Emile Bosquet looked uncomfortable, rocking back and forth whilst rubbing his hands.

Fernand stood next to Jean-Baptiste who had joined them by the courtyard well.

"Things are going to be hard before much longer. That pig is our insurance. It may well provide us with food should supplies dry up and it becomes impossible to find anything else ."

"Where's that daughter of ours?" asked Laure.

They heard a grunt and walked over to the stable, opened the door and saw Odette sitting cross-legged in front of the pig. It had

110

its head in her lap as she stroked its ears.

"Oh Papa, let's keep him. He's very gentle. It's no different from keeping a large dog."

Emile Bosquets smiled and interrupted. "He's the gentlest pig you'll ever come across and as soft as butter in the sun. He seems to like your daughter too."

Jean-Baptiste mentioned that the latest addition to the Moreau household could hardly become a pet if he was going to be eaten one day. Fernand agreed but being a soft touch with his daughter agreed to let her look after the pig until the time was right. They locked the stable door and walked back.

"Come in and have a drink with us, Emile." The farmer was a patriot. He hated the Germans, having suffered the loss of two sons during the First World War. The three men retired with their glasses of Picon and large slices of gooseberry tart to the vine-covered veranda where they sat on Fernand's pride and joy, his recently acquired wicker arm chairs.

Laure persuaded Odette to stay in the kitchen, away from the men's conversation. She showed her how to make an economic ratatouille with meagre amounts of food.

"Ok! What are we going to do?" asked Fernand. "We can't just sit here and let the German's trample all over us." He recalled the events of the day at the *Ecole Normale*. "I think we should make some sort of contribution towards the efforts being made by our resistance people. However, it would be stupid to engage in any form of fighting as we have family responsibilities."

"Count me out," said Emile. "I'm off to live with my sweetheart in Binche. I dislike the Boche as much as anyone and I'll probably help out when I'm there. However, you are welcome to use my farm and its buildings for whatever purpose you want. I intend to leave it empty and return there with Josephine after the war."

"That's very generous of you," said Jean-Baptiste. "Maybe it can be used for storage or hiding important items."

Emile decided it was time to leave. He bid farewell, wished them luck and offered thanks to Laure for the hospitality. As he left, the two men heard him shout out, "Au revoir, Adolf! Be good for your new owners. Bonne chance mon brave."

"A pig called Adolf," said Jean-Baptiste. "That's really funny." He and Fernand burst into long fits of laughter.

"I've managed to find you a job working alongside me at the Waterworks starting early tomorrow," said Fernand. "The boss, Marcel Martenot, is a fat lazy Rexist, put there by the Germans three months ago. If we just do the work and don't ruffle anyone's feathers, he'll ignore us and at least we'll be paid. You'll be keeping the water pump filters clean. It's boring but it's work."

"Ok," said Jean-Baptiste. "Julia probably won't like it. She'll worry like crazy that it will bring risks and trouble."

"Don't think you are on your own," said Fernand. "Laure hates the idea of taking risks. You know how nervous she gets. We must moderate our zeal to do too much. Our families have already suffered enough."

Fernand looked out of the veranda windows. The sky was becoming dramatically red as sunset approached.

"It's going to be very warm day tomorrow."

He paused, looked at Jean-Baptiste and lowered his voice.

"I know a man in Obourg who can put us in touch with The Légion Belge. He's a cousin of my brother's father-in-law called Maurice and he's reliable. We can trust him because he was with me in 1917 where we spent time in a German prison factory near Liège. He prints papers and pamphlets for the resistance. Let's set up a meeting with him."

Jean-Baptiste was a little nervous but agreed. He got up to leave for home, a fifteen-minute walk away. "See you tomorrow at work!"

As he walked away, Jean Baptiste heard 'Adolf' grunting and chuckled to himself.

On Thursday 19th September 1940, the Waterworks prepared

for a routine visit by senior engineers, only this time accompanied by German officials. Marcel Martenot, the works manager, had given his forty employees a day off. Fernand and Jean-Baptiste used the opportunity to set up a first meeting with Maurice Dufrêne, the affable old printer in Obourg.

"Come in Gentlemen," said Maurice.

From somewhere within the old house that had seen better days, a Westminster clock chimed twice at 14:00.

"Apologies for the mess but I've been incredibly busy this week and we've had problems with one of the Heidelbergs."

He led the other two past a noisy printing press in what used to be a large living room and into a back room where there were five chairs, a table, two old bureau cabinets on which there were a number of family photos. Monique, Maurice's wife, stood there in a grubby white blouse, black skirt and loose dark stockings hiding varicose veins in her lower legs. She smiled and excused herself while she disappeared into a small kitchen annexe to make coffee. The shutters to all the windows were partly shut with chinks of light seeping through a few broken slats so the room was quite dim.

"Please sit down, gentlemen."

In Maurice's hand was a leaflet headed 'If we do nothing, we only have ourselves to blame.' The background picture was a very graphic stylised illustration of German soldiers treading on crushed civilians. On the back the word's 'We are Belgium. We will never be conquered!' were printed in the national colours of black yellow and red. He showed Jean-Baptiste and Fernand. They whistled quietly and looked at each other in alarm.

"How can you get away with this?" asked Jean-Baptiste.

"By hiding references to where it came from and warning people to destroy it as soon as they've read it and before they are caught," replied Maurice.

"It's far too dangerous and risky," said Fernand. "I hope you do not expect us to distribute these leaflets?"

"No, no, not at all," said Maurice. "I just wanted to see your reactions. These are for the big boys in the resistance and their contacts, the ones who have nothing to lose. They are willing to take the risks involved and I trust them never to disclose where they were printed even if caught and interrogated."

He reached into a wooden chest and took out another white paper. It read 'To all the people of Mons, we need to stay calm and stay together. Please do not antagonise those who have occupied our town but try to work with them, not against them. To do otherwise will risk retribution. Good people, we have not surrendered but are strong and will wait until we are liberated.'

"If you want to help," said Maurice, "these leaflets will not anger the Boche so much because the wording asks for co-operation. You will not be in much danger if you distribute these."

"What is their purpose?" enquired Fernand.

"To bring hope for the future. Many Montois people are becoming depressed about restrictions under German occupation."

Monique entered with three large cups of coffee and a plate of stale Baudoin biscuits.

Fernand looked at Jean-Baptiste and turned to Maurice.

"I knew you were a brave man from the time we spent at that infernal prison factory in 1917, but this is beyond courage, my friend. I think we can help with these but there must be many other things we can do for the cause?"

Maurice pondered for a few moments before his wife added, "Provisions need to be fetched from farms near Givry, Beaumont and as far away as Mauberge. We are trying to supply essentials for 'friendly' shops in Mons and surrounding villages. Essentials like sugar, salt, flour, coffee, butter and ham. However, they are scrutinised by German patrols who take an exception to what they call black market produce. If you do help transport them, you will be helping the cause in a big way and bring some relief for our people."

At the mention of ham, Jean-Baptiste looked at Fernand and

smiled. They were both thinking of Adolf the pig!

"Yes, we can do that! We both have good bicycles and I'm sure we'll be able to adapt them to carry anything that can be hidden."

Maurice and Monique smiled and clapped their hands.

"That's wonderful. We can keep in touch through family. They are all aware of the work here and they'll deliver schedules and news personally." He paused and looked thoughtful.

"Regarding your daughters, Odette and Jacqueline. I'm sorry that they and their school friends had to face the unfortunate events at school last Monday. I have some relatively good news and also some very sad news."

"Madame Bervoets was released after a little roughing up by the Gestapo and I have it on good authority that the Mayor, that Rexist swine Emile Denis, did absolutely nothing to help her. It seems the German's believed her story. However, here's the bad news! The young Polish violinist was interrogated and tortured here in Mons. Those cruel insufferable Gestapo bastards cut off two middle fingers on his left hand. He will never play violin again. He has been deported but we are not too sure where to. His mother is devastated and his father has gone into hiding. Nobody yet knows if the Polish lad, under duress, gave them the names of other Jews and resistance people."

Fernand glanced up at Jean-Baptiste. Both were aghast and shocked. "It will be our pleasure to assist as soon as possible," said Fernand. "We can start by passing on information we get from conversations at work. We'll keep our ears and eyes open."

The two men left and thanked their hosts. It was nearly 16:00 hours and after a slow walk in pleasant sunshine along the Route d'Obourg, they shook hands and headed for home. Both agreed not to mention the news about Jan Stalienski, the Polish boy.

Over the following six months, life in Mons became more oppressive, mainly due to the lack of food, imposed rationing and the curfews. Christmas had been a low-key affair with minimal celebration and little opportunity to visit church. Services and transport had become compromised when fuel was in short supply and people only ventured out when necessary. They were fearful of German reprisals whenever incidents occurred involving acts of vandalism and sabotage against German property, or anyone showing support for the resistance movement. The Wehrmacht elite forces had mostly moved out and were replaced by more ruthless troops including members of the dreaded Waffen-SS. Jews in and around Mons were constantly sought, victimised and arrested before being transported to prison camps or factories. The majority did not survive the war.

Odette progressed well at school and her glowing reports made her parents very proud. She was popular with the other girls who loved her grown-up positive attitude, fairness and care for all around her. However, she and they were ever aware of the Germans, vigilant and extra cautious, in case they said too much or gave the wrong impressions. Occasionally, she and her parents would venture into town for coffees or beer at the Maiheux's Café on Rue des Capucins, a stone's throw away from the railway station. They always had a generous discount owing to Fernand and Raymond Maiheux being good friends and their daughters being at school together. It often meant that the three of them would sit at the café tables, either inside or outside and often in the company of German officers taking time out. These were nervous days, but under her father's calm influence, Odette was able to relax. Laure was less able to do so and preferred to let off steam with friends at home.

Odette spent much of her time studying, playing records on the old gramophone rescued from the long march or looking after Adolf. She scrubbed him clean and kept his quarters spotless, claiming he was the cleanest pig in Belgium.

The distribution of the 'Hope' leaflets continued and both Fernand and Jean-Baptiste undertook several bicycle trips to fetch essential foods, which were then stored in the farm that Emile Bosquets had donated. On one occasion, Fernand had cycled near to

Mauberge with his specially adapted bike for carrying various foods. He managed to hide a few kilos of sugar in the two tyres, using waterproof bags carefully distributed between the rim and inner tubes. Once the saddle was removed, long bags of salt could be pushed into the tubular frame and then the saddle replaced. A large pannier basket at the front carried some apples but underneath, a hidden cavity between a real and false base was used to carry butter and flour. On one occasion, it nearly went disastrously wrong.

"Halt!" A strong voice shouted at Fernand.

He dismounted and let the cycle lean against his left leg as the German walked towards him. Beyond was a frontier post between France and Belgium manned by German guards and a couple of men in civilian clothes. The German could speak a little French badly and managed to ask for Fernand's papers and visa. He studied them for a few moments and handed them back.

"What is your business in France, Monsieur?" he enquired.

"I visited my family and friends in Mauberge. My aunt is very sick with pneumonia."

"Where did you get these apples?" said the German. "Did you steal them? Answer me now."

"No, they were given to me by a neighbour of my aunt."

"A likely story, Monsieur."

He walked slowly around the cycle, with his hand tucked under a rifle that was slung over his shoulder. His eyes kept darting back and forth between Fernand and the bicycle.

"Tell me, Monsieur, what is the white powder on the edge of the basket." He unslung his rifle and poked the edge of the basket. Fernand started to sweat.

"I have no idea," he said.

Just then the sound of a telephone distracted the German. One of his colleagues appeared in the door of the hut and shouted.

"Josef, it's for you. It sounds urgent."

He turned to go, waving a casual dismissal at Fernand, took one of the apples from the pannier and shouted for him to be on his way.

During the hour's ride back to the farm at St Symphorien where he carefully hid the items, Fernand realised just how close he had come to being caught. It was a wake-up call and he needed to check everything more thoroughly. The flour had been the culprit on this occasion. It would not happen again. He mentioned the incident to Laure later on. She was horrified but, worse still, Odette overheard the conversation and burst into tears.

She ran out of the house and sat with Adolf for an hour until her father found her. Despite apologies and promises to be careful, it took a couple of days for Odette to get used to the idea that her father was running risks helping the resistance. She smiled when her mother emphasised how brave he was, doing all he could to help his family and the community.

"Besides, we are going to have a treat tomorrow," said Laure. "Your father managed to bring back some butter, sugar and flour for me to bake a cake. He's also found some sugared almonds and fruit bonbons for you."

Odette clapped her hands smiled and raced out to try and find her father. She desperately wanted to tell him she loved him and was very proud of what he was doing.

It was at about this time that a dog came into Odette's life. He was a black and white mongrel about the size of a large Jack Russell and a year old. He originally belonged to a neighbour of Jean-Baptiste but he was too ill to care for the dog. Fernand and Laure agreed to take him so long as Odette cared for him and he behaved himself with Adolf. They bonded from the moment Julia, Jacqueline and Jean-Baptiste dropped him at the house. Odette called him 'Misky,' a name that seemed to suit him very well. He was young, lively, inquisitive, but most importantly, it did not take long to train him into obedience. There remained one problem though.

"Papa, come quickly, Misky is scaring Adolf!" An almighty racket was coming from the garden.

"Who has left the stable door open?" yelled Fernand. "Quick, get me a bucket of water."

Laure, distracted by the noise, ran outside and was greeted by Adolf in a stand off with Misky in the middle of Fernand's treasured potato crop. Loud grunting and barking noises could be heard for some distance around. Monsieur Barralet from next door, intrigued by the commotion peered over the wall and burst into laughter. The two protagonists had no intention of backing off and it was hard to tell if they were angry or playing.

Fernand was so incensed by the damage to his potatoes that he tried to calm matters down by throwing water over Adolf and Misky. He missed and instead managed to soak himself when the bucket handle broke away. Odette, chuckling at the comic events, took it into her head to tie a cord around Adolf's head and simply lead him back to the stable. He did not object but Misky tried to follow, nipping at the pigs hind legs until Fernand held him back at the stable door. It was the first time Odette had ever heard her father swear after he snagged and ripped his trouser pocket on the door's latch. She hid her face so that he could not see her giggle.

1941 came and went without too many incidents. Limited income from Fernand's work at the Waterworks meant they were unable to enjoy anything other than essentials. Some of the contraband foods and items procured from farms and wholesalers, secretly transported by Fernand and Jean-Baptiste, supplemented their meagre rations. The German patrols and border guards were becoming ever more watchful and their reprisals when someone was caught with illegal goods became more brutal. The local population became more disenchanted when they realised that the German occupation forces were able to enjoy luxuries such as perfumed soap, chocolate, cheese, champagne, fresh vegetables, fruit and, irritatingly, fine haute couture fashions and stockings for the ladies in their lives.

Perhaps the biggest advantage in the months that came and went was to indulge their love of entertaining. The Moreaus had a very big circle of relations and friends and loved nothing more than hosting a friendly social gathering involving up to fifteen people.

They laughed, ate Laure's famous delicious tarts and drank cheap beer or Fernand's cache of excellent wines, now residing in the cellar. Laure was in her element, often breaking out into song and dancing with whoever was available. Sometimes they played cards and on other occasions listened to popular singers such as Caruso singing opera and Neapolitan songs on the old wind-up gramophone. A real treat was to hear Jean-Baptiste singing extracts from popular operas. His favourite, which caused the ladies to weep, was the aria 'E lucevan le stelle' from Puccini's Tosca.

At home, the Germans rarely bothered them. However, on one rainy afternoon at about 14:00 hours in April 1942, the front door bell rang, followed by a loud knocking. Fernand opened the door and standing there were two German Wehrmacht officers. They apologised for any disturbance and simply wanted to know where the Van de Bergh family lived on the Chaussée De Beaumont. Fernand knew them vaguely and was aware they were Dutch Jews and lived about half a kilometre away in the direction of Beaumont. He also realised it could be something sinister so he lied to the two men staring at him.

"I'm not too sure," he said. "Many new people have moved in over the last few months. However, I've heard people say there is a Dutch family living in Hyon about two kilometres away. They have a similar name - perhaps it's them."

The two Germans thanked Fernand and disappeared. He watched them climb into a black staff car parked at La Bascule about a hundred metres away. Just as he was about to shut the door, Adolf the pig suddenly started grunting and squealing which aroused Misky who then barked in response. Fernand waited to see if the Germans had heard anything and breathed a sigh of relief when their car drove away towards Mons town centre. It dawned on him that the pig might well become a dangerous embarrassment if the Boche learnt that he was named after their Führer!

"Laure, listen to me and do not mention this to Odette. We may well have to get rid of Adolf by having him slaughtered." He explained that it was a cat and mouse game and they would be in big trouble if any passing German patrols heard one of them shouting out the pig's name or the animal's grunting made them inquisitive.

Laure wiped her hands on a towel and with a concerned expression, looked Fernand in the eyes.

"Maybe we can try and be extra careful. I know you want to eliminate risks but it would make our girl very upset. Let's give it another few months and see how it works out. I'll talk to Odette I'm sure she will understand but I will not mention the other matter."

"Ok," said Fernand. "Let's wait and see but if there is any increased risk, he will have to go. In any case, if food becomes too difficult to find, Adolf may well end up being our saviour. I will not let us go hungry."

Laure smiled at him and offered no response. She was fully aware that her husband was a good man and would always try to do the right thing for his family.

The next two years past by slowly and proved mostly uneventful although there were constant unwelcome reminders of occupation. During 1943, Fernand spent more time preparing his garden and planting out vegetables. Movement around Mons was increasingly restricted and austerity meant there was little money and food was scarce or very expensive. In order to help out, Laure took on part time work in a local general store and it was decided that Odette, on reaching her seventeenth birthday in August, could try to find employment. Her father had stopped working for the resistance claiming that the risks were too great. German retribution, vigilance and aggression resulted in higher numbers of civilians punished, tortured, deported or even killed for the slightest indiscretion. There wasn't a week that passed without news that someone they knew had been arrested or worse.

One of Odette's saddest memories occurred after Adolf, 'her' pig, decided to become more vociferous. His grunting could be easily heard on the Chaussée De Beaumont where German patrols

121

sometimes walked or drove past. One day in July, Fernand announced that Adolf would have to be slaughtered. He was too much of a liability and besides, the pork would be a welcome relief from their meagre rations. Odette pleaded with her parents, but to no avail. A week later, one of the butchers from Mons, a friend of Fernand, came and took Adolf away, promising he would deliver the meat in two days' time. When the remains of Adolf arrived, the various joints were carefully preserved in brine and stored away in the cool environment of the cellar. Odette refused to enter there and could not bear to see or smell pork for well over a year.

In September 1943, Fernand was offered a chance to work as a Clerk in the Hotel de Ville. The opportunity came via a chance meeting with Hector Renson, related to his sister Stephanie. Hector was already working in the Finance Department and they needed someone to help out. It meant that he would be working under a Rexist Mayor and probably other German sympathisers within the bureau. This irked him somewhat to the point that he could not sleep well for two nights prior to accepting the position. He also had to resign his permanent position at the Waterworks although they agreed to a retainer, allowing him to work one a day a week. It meant his income would be noticeably higher.

On 15th February 1944, a particularly cold day, Odette started work as an assistant to the Mayor's assistant Madame Marie Adélaïde Clotilde Fremont. She was a lady of noble birth who had tarnished her family name after a mourner reported her for indecently cavorting with a gravedigger in the cemetery of St. Waudru Cathedral.

Over the next few weeks, Odette discovered that some of the girls in the office were engaged in various acts of mischief against their German and Rexist employers at the Hotel de Ville. They were a friendly lot and took Odette into their confidence. She even helped them with such things as dropping sugar into the petrol tanks of the German staff cars and motorcycles. Many times she and the girls giggled after hearing loud shouting and German expletives as cars stuttered to a stop, but she and the girls were never caught.

"Odette Moreau." It was Madame Fremont. "Can you please come here, it's rather important."

Odette hurried across the office, bypassing three other older women who were busy typing or taking phone calls. One of them looked up and smiled. She whispered good luck and touched Odette's hand to reassure her as she passed her desk.

"Hello Mademoiselle Moreau, please take a seat." It was the Mayor of Mons, Monsieur Emile Denis and standing next to him was a rather important looking German with blond hair, smoking an American cigarette and dressed very smartly in a black full military uniform as worn by SS officers. The Mayor was short and fat with long slick black hair that kept falling over his round spectacles. He also sported a short moustache, which had been clearly influenced by either Charlie Chaplin or Adolf Hitler. Odette could not help notice that his waistcoat buttons were about to burst and his trousers were badly stained by food and cigarette ash. He addressed Odette.

"Mademoiselle Moreau, we have an urgent job for you which will involve working late here in the bureau for a couple of evenings and then delivering a number of reports to German Intelligence in Maurage. You are the only person here we can allow time to do this as the others are too busy. If you agree, you will be helping us to make sure your fellow citizens of Mons, currently held in detention, will not be held longer than is necessary. Naturally, your extra work will be generously compensated for with extra wages."

Odette turned and looked at the German Officer who smiled and introduced himself as Oberst Frederich von Roettig. The German was charming, well mannered and relaxed, but Odette detected a cold menace in his eyes that unsettled her. She was uncertain about the Mayor's promise to ease the pressure on suspects or anyone held in the town's prison.

"Well Mademoiselle, do you accept?" asked the German in a soft voice as he studied her.

Odette feeling somewhat uncomfortable and under pressure

was unsure of the German's mood or intentions so replied, "Yes Monsieur, I will do it."

She wondered why the Oberst could not take the reports himself until he told her he had been recalled to Berlin. He also said he'd be honoured if she would accept his invitation to accompany him to a restaurant in the evening, his last chance to enjoy the company of a pretty girl before leaving Mons. Odette blushed and thanked him but said it would not be possible, as she would be taking her stenographic diploma examination at college, an excuse the German flinched at. He expressed disappointment, but to her surprise and relief, he conceded.

The Mayor stood up and thanked Odette. She was asked to see Madame Fremont who would be collating the reports. Odette returned to her desk but it was not long before Madame Fremont came to her and said she would have to help her type out a few reports starting the next evening. She added that there were too many for one person to do. The reports had to be in Maurage two days later without fail.

That evening, when she eventually reached home after the class, Odette told her parents about the day's events and the job she'd reluctantly agreed to take on.

"You can't. How can you trust them and how do you know you are not being set up to do their dirty work?" responded her mother.

"I know it all sounds dubious" replied Odette. "It's hard to trust them, but in this case, I don't think there's any need to worry. After all, it's a simple task and they have too much to lose if it goes wrong."

Her father was not happy. He said he'd try and find out any other information that might be relevant before the next evening.

Odette slept badly that night. She kept turning over in her mind all the various scenarios and worrying in case the reports contained information that would condemn the prisoners rather than save them from any horrors they might face.

The next morning, a Friday, Odette and her father caught the number 90 tram at the Bascule and travelled to the Grand Place in

124

Mons. They spoke little apart from when Fernand reassured her he'd find out what was going on. He would not let her undertake anything too risky. They walked into the Hotel de Ville together before parting for their respective offices, having agreed to meet at mid-day for a coffee at the L'Excelsior.

At noon, Odette made her way across the Grand Place where her father was already seated outside the Café. He ordered her a Gueuze with Grenadine, her favourite drink and a special treat.

"I have discovered a little more, but it's all very hushed up and I nearly got into trouble with my boss for asking too many questions," said Fernand. "It seems that the poor people in that report have already been arrested and the authorities just need more information before carrying out further interrogation and probably torture. I don't know what they are supposed to have done. However, I can tell you that one of the men they want to interrogate is Jules Fraix, your uncle."

"Oh no, what can I do to help?" asked Odette. She looked around to make sure nobody could hear them. Fernand spoke quickly and quietly.

"You must not and don't even think about it, because if you try and get caught, you will be interrogated. Just think how it would affect your mother and me, knowing you were in so much danger?"

Odette thought about it and rather than cause concern simply agreed with her father. In her mind, she had already decided that she must try to do something but she had to make sure she could not be blamed and above all, her mother must not be made aware of her brother-in-law's predicament. She hugged her father before they both returned to work.

As she stepped through into her office, some of the girls tried to warn her that Madame Fremont was in a foul mood. Madame Marie Adélaïde Clotilde Fremont was a woman who liked the company of men rather than women and was starved of their company in the Hotel de Ville. The only exception was the short fat mayor who she disliked intensely. Seeing pretty girls, reminding her that she had

125

once been young and attractive enough to enjoy many lovers, despite being married. This often triggered her moods. She was still very attractive, but looked older than her thirty-eight years. Layers of foundation and powder along with bright red lipstick could not fully hide reality. Odette was a reminder of her younger years, not just because she was pretty but also because she was very clever.

"Let's get started then shall we?" said Madame Fremont to Odette. "You can use the middle table typewriter and I'll give you some notes which will need typing accurately and quickly on official report papers in front of you. I may have to dictate some that are not too clear."

It was very clear that the notes were nothing less than unsubstantiated evidence that the men and women held in detention by the Gestapo would be found guilty.

"Madame, these reports will not help the prisoners at all. It seems to me that they will all be found guilty. This is not what I was told by the Mayor and now I will have to deliver these reports to the Germans. I cannot do this Madame"

"Shut up you stupid girl," rasped Marie Fremont. "Someone might hear. If you want to keep your job and not displease the Mayor, you must be more discrete! Is that clear?" She looked at Odette sternly and whispered across the office, "These walls have ears you know and for your information, I do not want to be part of this conspiracy, set up by our fat Mayor. He disgusts me and simply wants to gain favours with his German friends. Like you, I do not want to see innocent people interrogated, tortured or deported."

Odette suddenly felt as though a weight had been lifted from her conscience. She smiled at Madame and carried on working although confused. The next two hours were spent in silence apart from the continuous clickety clack and carriage return bells of the two typewriters working at full speed.

At 20:00 hours, Marie Fremont stood up and collected all the reports on her desk as well as those completed by Odette. She walked over to Odette's desk and spoke softly.

"There are two versions of these reports. The ones you have completed which are the original incriminating ones and then there are those I have completed which are, let's call them, a variation of the facts. These also contain a signed affidavit from Oberst Frederich von Roettig and statements from four witnesses including two lawyers verifying the innocence of those in prison. You will deliver my reports tomorrow to Maurage, which will end the process and ensure the prisoners will no longer be needed for interrogation. This is possible because the Oberst carries a senior ranking and he's also a decorated respected officer who saw action in Russia. They will obey without question, as is the way with inferior ranks. You must then destroy your version as soon as you return from Maurage. I asked you to type out the original version simply to protect you should things go wrong."

"But I thought the Oberst was on his way to Berlin," said Odette.

"That's right Odette. Before he left, he telephoned the idiots in Maurage and told them the reports would be delivered by you and they were to act upon their contents."

"Why is he, a German, doing this?" asked Odette.

"Let me tell you something that you must promise to keep secret and never talk about in this office or with your family and friends. Frederich von Roettig is no ordinary German. He's kind, respectful, highly intelligent and above all very charming. He and I have been seeing a lot of each other and we have fallen in love. This is the real thing. It's never happened before and believe me I've known many men in the past. It also probably means that I will be considered a traitor, so my future here in Mons is uncertain."

Odette wiped a tear away, smiled and held out her hand to touch the other woman's arm in a gesture of sympathy. Nevertheless, she was thinking about the ruthless Germans she had encountered during and since her return trek to the coast. Forgiveness was not uppermost in her thoughts and besides she remembered the Oberst's invitation to dine with him. It was difficult for her to consider him as honourable or well intentioned although she did think he was a good looking man even if he was German.

Madame Fremont inserted her reports into a large stiff brown envelope and sealed it with red wax into which she stamped the Mayor's dragon symbol. On the front she attached an official label, addressed to Sturmbannfuhrer Jürgen Hanreich at the German regional HQ and Intelligence Offices in Maurage.

"Tomorrow morning take the number 17 tram to Maurage. I've drawn a map to show you directions from the station. Do not lose the envelope!"

That night, Odette retired to bed early, keeping all she'd discovered to herself. She slept badly again and in the morning, her mother was concerned about the dark circles under her eyes.

"She does not look well," she said to Fernand. "I hope she's not going down with something."

Fernand shrugged and said he suspected that their daughter was overdoing things at work.

The next morning, 25th April 1944, Odette walked from the Hotel de Ville to the station where she waited patiently for the number 17 tramcar that would take her to Maurage. It was a twenty-minute journey across town and during that time she was deep in thought about what lay in store. Had she been drawn into a potentially dangerous situation? What if Madame Fremont was planning to elope with her German lover? What if the Intelligence people in Maurage detected there had been some attempt to distort the truth? She would certainly be charged with being an accomplice and then what would happen? It was the wrong time to let her imagination take over.

Odette looked pale as she climbed the steps of the German Intelligence offices on the Rue de Boussoit in Maurage. Her long dark blue coat and fur collar wrapped tightly, kept out a cold easterly wind. In her hand she gripped the large brown envelope as she passed two SS Officers standing at the entrance.

One of them opened the door for her, clicked his heels and said in perfect French, "It's a pleasant change to welcome such a pretty girl. What is your name and are you looking for someone Mademoiselle?"

Odette cringed, gave her name and said she'd been asked to deliver her envelope to Sturmbannfuhrer Jürgen Hanreich, a colleague of Oberst Frederich von Roettig. The German bowed his head and motioned her inside. He escorted her to a large oak door and knocked. The pair entered into a well lit, newly decorated office where Odette's escort introduced her to an officer seated behind a large mahogany desk. On the wall behind him was a large picture of Adolf Hitler as well as an old etching showing the trial of Hippolyte Visart de Bocarmé, a Belgian noble found guilty of murder and executed by guillotine on 19th July 1851 in the Grand-Place in Mons.

"Good day Mademoiselle Moreau. My name is Sturmbannfuhrer Jürgen Hanreich. I understand you have something for me?"

Odette was nervous. She tried to blank out all the negatives that were racing through her mind. Would she be arrested or even interrogated?

"Yes, I have this envelope containing some papers for you," she said and tried to smile sweetly.

The German stood up and walked towards Odette. He placed his hand on her shoulder and called for his Offiziersbursche (batman) to bring coffee. Ten minutes later, a man in a white jacket and immaculately pressed black trousers entered, carrying a silver ornate tray. Upon it there was a cafetière émaillée, decorated with yellow flowers on a blue background. There were also two white porcelain cups and saucers, a matching milk jug and a small bowl containing sugar cubes. Odette's eyes lit up when she saw a plate of her favourite 'Speculoos' biscuits. The German noticed her expression. In silence, he served two coffees whilst bending over her so he could become closely acquainted with her cleavage. He replaced his hand on Odette's shoulder.

"Please help yourself to these delicious biscuits," he said. "I believe they are made in Hasselt and they remind me of the ones my mother used to buy for me and my brother when we were young. His name was Rolf and he died in Holland only two months ago."

His manner was kind enough but there was something sinister in his delivery. He was deliberately slow, measured and calculating so as to make one feel sympathetic but uneasy.

"I must thank you for bringing these important reports. We rely on co-operation in order to ensure the smooth running of our work in Belgium." He reached over and took the envelope before calling his Offiziersbursche again.

"Please take these to Commandant Heinz Dilscher on the first floor and make sure they reach him and nobody else." The man disappeared.

He turned to Odette, moved his hand and let it slowly slide down towards her breasts before asking her a few questions about her family and her work in Mons. She tried hard to be relaxed and answered brightly enough but under the surface she was petrified and anxiously trying hard not to say anything that would arouse too much interest or irritation. All of a sudden, the Officer retrieved his hand and thanked her again before ushering her out into the corridor. He gave her a military pass just in case she was asked to deliver any further correspondence and hoped she'd visit again soon.

Somewhere from within and below, she heard loud thuds followed by men and women shouting in anguish. She covered her ears and ran out. One hour after she'd entered the building, Odette stood at the tram stop waiting for the number 17. She was feeling tired, cold and slightly faint but above all, relieved it was all over. She no longer had to endure the sleazy German's clammy hand on her body or hear the sickening sounds of barbaric interrogation.

The tram came to a sudden grinding halt about two hundred metres from Mons station, just as the town's clarions in the Belfry started ringing in the distance. She waited patiently along with a dozen other passengers when two German soldiers with rifles boarded the tram and started shouting at those near the front. They were brusque, uncouth and aggressive, emptying bags and scattering personal possessions over the floor and seats. A women sitting in front of Odette received a smack in the face by one of the Germans because she was whimpering. Others started to protest, asking them what they were looking for. There was no answer. Then one of them saw Odette who was trying to make herself inconspicuous behind a seat.

"Ha ha, look at what we have here? A beautiful prize indeed." The German summoned his colleague and the pair of them walked up the tram and stood in front of Odette, smiling.

"What's in your bag, you Belgian schlampe?" said the older of the two, snatching Odette's handbag.

"Let's take a look shall we?"

He used the end of his rifle under the handbag straps and lifted it towards the other German who gleefully accepted it before tipping the contents all over the seat in front. Fortunately, Odette had hidden the Military pass, given to her by Sturmbannfuhrer Jürgen Hanreich, in the lining of the bag. They searched grim-faced through various cosmetics, identity cards, a diary and a purse with ten Francs, before discovering a pair of cream coloured silk knickers. Odette had packed a spare pair that morning. The two young soldiers kept laughing as they saw her embarrassment. They twirled the garment on the point of their rifles before flinging it at a smartly dressed man three seats in front.

While this was going on the tram driver sat patiently wondering what to do. He knew that another tram would soon be arriving on the same line and he would be obliged to move. Suddenly, a German Officer appeared at the door and shouted at the two soldiers to disembark. They quickly jumped down and saluted. It was fortunate that he'd arrived and was curious about the disturbance on the tram. The Officer signalled to the driver to move on to the station. Passengers could hear him yelling at the two soldiers as they passed by. Odette, unable to resist the moment, pressed her face against the window and smiled as they were given a dressing down.

That evening, after reaching home and having briefed Madame Fremont at work as well as destroying her reports, Odette was finally able to relax. She was exhausted with the day's stress and rather than hide the facts now that it was over, she decided to tell her parents but left out the German's lewd attempts to seduce her.

"You took many risks," said Fernand. "Not just for yourself, but there's a chance we may all have become implicated. Don't forget, I also work at the Hotel de Ville. However, in the circumstances, you were very brave."

Laure looked apprehensively at her daughter who was sitting with a bowed head. "It's obvious that Madame Fremont could easily deny she had no knowledge of the false reports and that you were the one who switched them."

"That woman has earned a bad reputation for immorality," said Laure. "What makes you believe she will suddenly change and do the honourable thing?"

Odette had promised not to tell anyone about the Madame's love interest and she kept her word.

"Mama, Papa, please trust me. I happen to know that Madame Fremont is not all bad. She's a good Belgian and wants to help make sure that our people are not condemned or deported. She's a patriot and, yes, it's a risk, but I believe it was a risk worth taking."

"Despite everything, we are incredibly proud of you. Many of our family and friends take risks when trying to help the resistance against the Boche," said Fernand. "I took risks and Jean-Baptiste is still taking them. I guess, what you have done is no worse than the rest of us. There is a difference though. You are our daughter and we love you very much. If anything happened to you we'd be inconsolable."

"Ma fille, I have some bad news that you need to know. This should make you realise just how dangerous it is for anyone caught spying or working with the Resistance. The Germans have executed Marguerite Bervoets, the daughter of your teacher Madame Bervoets last Friday. She was accused of spying and decapitated by those animals who do not belong in the human race."

Odette burst into tears. "Oh how can they do that? How could they do such an awful thing? How can they be so depraved? I hate Germans and I wish they could all be punished." Odette sobbed for a few minutes, turned and looked at the sky through the veranda roof glass and wiped her tears. Dark ominous clouds were rapidly forming into a long cascading pattern way off towards the horizon.

"Yes, it's appalling but there is some good news," said Fernand. "It seems that the Germans are losing the war at last. They've failed in Russia and the Americans are in England. There is a rumour that Churchill and Roosevelt are planning an invasion somewhere on the French Coast. If this is true, we can look forward to being liberated sooner rather than later. I'll listen to the radio later on."

Odette knew she'd come close to breaking her parents' hearts and she threw her arms around them sobbing. "I love you both so much. Let's hope the war ends soon. I will never willingly risk breaking your hearts again."

Little did she know that, within eighteen months, she would indeed break their hearts but in entirely different circumstances. Laure smiled and wiped away her tears. They were used to hearing tragic news but tried to remain stoic and positive particularly for Odette. In a moment, she'd left the bad news behind and broke away to sing and dance around the dining room table.

"I'll prepare something special to eat and we can open a bottle of wine to celebrate a brighter future and our clever brave, beautiful daughter who has become a woman before her 18th birthday."

Laure kissed her daughter on the forehead. Fernand decided that inspecting his potatoes was a far better bet than suffering his wife's energetic eccentricity.

Chapter 10: Grounded But Still Effective

One bright sunny morning on April 28th 1943, Alan received a letter from his sister Barbara. They were all worried because they'd heard little from him. Dad was poorly, suffering from high blood pressure and Gordon had suffered a broken arm after falling from his motorbike. Graham had apparently been sent to Italy and joined up with Montgomery's 8th Army after the invasion of Sicily.

Alan found little time to write home. His new work meant he undertook shifts operating the radar units and masts with twenty others and this sometimes meant working through the night. The Luftwaffe certainly did not stop coming in the small hours. In the first three years of the war, they had managed to infiltrate mainland Britain, bombing cities such as Liverpool, Manchester, Bristol, Coventry, Birmingham, Southampton and London. Now, with more advanced Radar units around the coast, enemy intrusions were easily detected. As a consequence, Hitler and Goering were discouraged from the sort of mass attacks and bombing seen in the early days of the Blitz.

"Time to go Al, the Kite is ready." It was Billy Marston, a Pilot Officer Alan had befriended a few weeks before. They and a few others were being transferred to RAF Stenigot in Lincolnshire where more updated Radar equipment and masts had been erected.

There was no leave and no chance of any in the near future. Rumours were circulating that Germany had a new secret weapon, a flying bomb propelled by rocket power that could be launched from France and reach London. This meant those responsible for detection had to be on their toes twenty-four hours a day.

"OK Billy, I'll be there in a couple of minutes." Alan finished packing his smallest kit bag and joined his friend along with three others as they walked out and boarded a scruffy looking Wellington that would take them the hundred and twenty miles to the next post in Lincolnshire. Two days previously, they had been driven to RAFHalesworth, seven miles from Southwold since the Chain Home Station at Dunwich had no runway. It gave them a chance to meet a few USAAF air and ground crew based there. The plan, which Alan thought was over complex, was to fly from Halesworth, land at RAF Ludford Magna and then on by RAF transport to the Home Chain station at Stenigot. It was a journey of only ten miles along narrow leafy lanes in the Lincolnshire Wolds.

They arrived at RAF Stenigot at 3.30pm where they were immediately introduced to their senior officers and a dozen other experienced operators including a New Zealander, a Frenchman and two WAAFs.

An Irish Flight Lieutenant by the name of Fergus O'Driscoll was the Officer in charge. He stood six feet six inches tall and, judging by his generous midriff and ruddy complexion, must have trusted his life to the power of the national drink. With his strong Connemara accent, he was heard to say on more than one occasion, "A wise man invented beer, a smart man drinks it, but a genius prefers Guinness!"

"Welcome to the country's coldest radar station here at Stenigot. It's taken me two months of hard labour, assisted by the odd pint of black gold at the *Black Horse* pub in Donington, to pronounce the word 'Stenigot'. In a few minutes, you'll be taken to our new facilities of which we have five. Some of you will be here at for some time and others will move on as required when needed by other stations. OK, I'll see you in the mess at 5.00pm if you need to ask any questions. Oh and there's a few of us going out to the *Black Horse* later on, that's if you'd like to drown your sorrows amongst friends."

Alan decided he'd miss out on the evening's social event and spend time writing a letter back home. That was until there was knock on his room door.

"Are you going to invite me in, you miserable anti-social excuse for a Sergeant."

"Harry, what on earth! Is that really you?" Alan opened the door and there stood Harry Silver with a big grin from ear to ear.

The two greeted each other and laughed loudly when Harry mentioned he'd only been there for three weeks after being press ganged by a Senior Officer into learning about advanced radar. He'd been told that it was because 'Serrate' Radar detection equipment was now being installed in Bristol Beaufighters with No. 236 Squadron stationed at RAF North Coates. The two men were so delighted to meet again that their laughing startled a passing orderly, who cautiously enquired if everything was all right.

"Let's try that pub tonight and celebrate," said Harry. "You'll love the barmaid. She's out of bounds old chap but there's no harm in a little sightseeing. Anyway, tomorrow you and I will be on the same long shift, rotating those damned mastheads. At some point I'll be whisked off to do more training with the flight radar units."

Alan changed his mind and decided to go. The letter would have to wait a little longer.

"The Irish Flt. Lieutenant," asked Alan, "is he OK? I mean, he seems a bit too keen on his Guinness and his humour is very err…'Irish'."

"He's fine Al. He's actually a nice guy. Fair and generous but yes, he loves a pint or two. There's a story going around that he flew Bolton Paul Defiants and was shot down over Northern France. Somehow, he managed to land in flames but his gunner was killed and he only just made it. It seems his legs were badly burnt and he walks with a slight limp. My guess is that he was grounded and sent here. I tried to chat with him but he just looked away. I guess he's still struggling and it's something he wants to forget."

That evening, Harry and Alan teamed up with six of the other radar operatives including a dark haired WAAF called Daisy. It became quickly obvious that Harry had a crush on Daisy and she seemed to like him too. They would have to be back by 10.00pm to relieve the eight shift workers left at base. Alan was not looking forward to the night-time shift work. Each shift schedule rotated on a weekly basis, which meant nobody missed out on the social gatherings every alternate week. The station's location was somewhat remote and lacking in social entertainment so the *Black Horse* in Donington on Bain, just two miles away, had become the entertainment hub for all servicemen and service women at Stenigot.

"Come on in you two!" shouted Flt. Lieutenant Fergus O'Driscoll. "Now let's see now - yes, you're the new chap, so you are. It's Alan I believe? Well who's the lucky one tonight then? Your first pint will be on us. But I must warn you and everyone too, that drunkenness or incapacity of any kind that obstructs the work back at base, will not be tolerated. If you can't take it, don't push it. If I catch anyone who falls down on the job tonight or at any time, they will be put on a charge. That does not mean we can't have some fun though. Barman, get this man a pint of the black magic!"

The Irishman spoke calmly. There was no hint of belligerence, arrogance or aggressiveness. However, Alan was no lover of Guinness but decided that it would be rude to refuse the free pint.

"He makes that speech every week," said Harry.

"You could have told me about the rules, pal," Argued Alan. "You know it takes little for me to end up horizontal and I don't want to be put on report."

"You're right, I should have briefed you, but hey ho, you'll be OK! Meet Daisy."

"Good evening, Miss," said Alan, his eyes magnetised by her intense blue eyes and full lips skilfully decorated with the latest fashionable glossy red lipstick.

"Why, hello Alan, I'm delighted to meet you. Harry has told me so much about you. You can call me Daisy, but if you'd rather use my real name, it's Dorothy."

Daisy was a pretty, well-heeled and well-spoken twenty two year old with an hourglass figure. Alan could see how Harry had been easily attracted to her but there was a big height difference. Harry was just over six feet tall and Daisy barely reached 5 feet 3 inches. The three of them engaged in amusing conversation for ten minutes when Alan's pint of Guinness arrived, delivered by the Irish Flt. Lieutenant.

"Compliments of the house to you Sergeant and may all your troubles be little ones. If there's anything you need to know, just ask and I'll amuse you with some good old blarney, honed to perfection by the little people of Connemara." Alan laughed and thanked him. The Irishman disappeared to join his friends at the bar.

"I'm beginning to like this place," said Alan. It's very friendly." Daisy smiled at Harry and sat on his lap. Alan decided playing gooseberry was not his thing so he went for a walk, taking his pint with him. The sky was turning into a darker RAF blue except for a few sunset coloured clouds, spread out across the horizon. Shafts of pale primrose light cast their searchlight beams like giant torches and towards the west, a blood orange sun shimmered in its dying moments before the oncoming night. Bird chatter in the fields beyond Main Street and the peaceful warm evening seemed unreal and so remote from the war in Europe, less than two hundred miles away in the east. Alan suddenly thought of Nurse McKenzie and his folks in Nuneaton. He wondered whether his brothers were all right and even alive and if his father was not too unwell. Although he felt happy, Alan also felt a strange loneliness.

Suddenly the quietness of the night sky was plundered by the sound of many aircraft flying eastwards. The steady droning of heavy bombers vibrated and invaded the peace of rural Lincolnshire. It was 09.15pm on May 16th 1943.

"Lancasters from 617 Squadron at Scampton." Harry had escaped the pub's claustrophobic smoky bar room to join Alan. He was holding hands with Daisy.

"How do you know that?" asked Alan.

"When I was in North Coates, I overheard one of the Officers saying that Scampton was planning a large bombing raid on some industrial centre in Germany and judging from their engine noise they are Lancs, so it must be them."

The others in the pub and a dozen or so locals disturbed in their homes by the noise had joined them. One of them, a bare-chested man in slippers and no socks, wearing braces to hold up a pair of very baggy paint-stained trousers, shouted "Good Luck! Give the Jerries a taste of their own medicine!"

Within a few days, news of the Dam Busters success over the Ruhr Valley and the destruction of the Möhne and Eder Dams had reached most people. It lifted morale and let the Nazis know that Britain was very capable of reaching and destroying Germany's industrial heartland.

Alan, Harry and Daisy decided to walk the two miles back to camp. The night was now very dark and, without a torch, they could only rely upon a hazy moon and using the hedgerows as a guide.

Laughing and giggling broke the silence. Alan turned round and saw Harry and Daisy disappear into a ditch. Fortunately it was dry but the nettles caused Daisy to yell loudly.

"Alan, can you find some dock leaves? These nettles are dreadful."

Alan walked on and tried but failed to see anything clearly in the poor light. He suddenly cried out.

"You two, come here quickly! There's a man in the ditch with a bicycle on top of him."

Daisy and Harry ran the 30 yards whilst patting their coats to get rid of grass and leaves. Alan was already down in the ditch, lifting the bicycle off the unfortunate man.

"He's wearing a dog collar. It must be the local vicar. Quick, you get hold of his feet. Let's lift him on to the verge."

"You're right," said Harry. "It's the Rev. Nichols from St Michael's. He lives in the Rectory, a few hundred yards away back in the village but hang on, he's coming round. Oh my giddy aunt, he's completely pissed and stinks of God knows what!"

The Vicar moved and groaned before turning towards Harry.

"Dear boy, I heard that! Kindly do not blaspheme in the presence of one of God's messengers. Can you tell me if my cycle is still intact?" His speech was very slurred.

"I think we'd better walk him back to his place," said Alan. The other two agreed.

"Now don't be telling my wife about any of this," said the Vicar. "She worries terribly, you know."

He attempted to stand up but his feet were not going where his brain said they should be. They reached the Rectory just as Mrs Nichols opened the door.

"Oh dear Lord, Gerald, what have you been up to, or do I need to ask? Look at your clothes, I'm never going to get rid of those stains." She smiled at her husband's rescuers and invited them in for a nightcap.

"We'd better be off as we have to be back for our next shift at Stenigot, but thanks anyway."

"Thank you very much, maybe see you in Church on Sunday," shouted the Vicar's wife as the three of them raced off. After avoiding any further falls in ditches, they arrived back at Stenigot with five minutes to spare. They hurried to R4 on the east side of the complex where Flt. Lieutenant O'Driscol was waiting.

"Good to see you all back on time and fully compos mentis. Ok chaps, we have a problem. It seems that telephones are down at RAF Bentley Priory and High Wycombe. Ops are playing funny games. You'll have to use the local telephone exchange to connect with RAF No 1 Group at Baltry Hall. They will then put you through as a priority. We need to move as quickly as we can, given the current delays. There are people working on the problem but so far, there are no clues when things will be up and running again."

After only ten minutes, Daisy called for Harry.

"I've got large unidentified signals in sector 4 bearing south west on my receiver. Distance approximately one hundred miles."

Harry, Alan and a French chap called Leon who smelled of garlic walked over to Daisy's station.

"It doesn't make sense," said Alan puckering his nose as he had an obsessional hatred of garlic aromas. "The transmitter is not showing pulses, yet the receiver is showing three echo blips."

Leon walked over to the radio goniometer and turned a knob. Suddenly, the transmitter burst into life.

"Excellent," said Harry. He was reading the data on the receiver whilst Leon kept the beam on target. "Aircraft approaching, altitude approximately fifteen thousand feet and heading in direction north by northwest."

Daisy studied the screen closely. "Please confirm that we have no incoming friendly aircraft with Bentley Priory or High Wycombe," requested Daisy.

Harry was already onto the local exchange and within four minutes was through to both Fighter and Bomber Command Centres. There was a further delay as the operators pushed switches and plugged in leads. Twice the operators said the lines were busy, but eventually Harry was able to confirm that no British aircraft were in the vicinity.

Flt. Lieutenant O'Driscoll heard Alan calling, "Enemy aircraft detected bearing Lat: 51° 13' 42.3948" N, Long: 2° 56' 4.0740" E. He immediately grabbed one of the three telephones and answered a call from RAF Stoke Holy Cross in Norfolk. They had also picked up the same pulses.

He shouted to the nine operators, "Co-ordinates confirmed. Enemy aircraft in three waves with twenty five heavies in each wave." Height now twelve thousand feet approaching Vector 3 approximately eighty miles from Ventnor. The Irishman then reached for the third telephone handed to him by Diane, the 2nd WAAF operator.

"Wycombe still on the line, Sir," she said, "but we've lost Bentley. I'll keep trying." O'Driscoll asked to be kept updated every three minutes but was expressing much frustration.

"Sir, it's O'Driscoll at Stenigot. We've detected over seventy enemy aircraft approaching the east coast and heading in our direction. I can't get through to Fighter Command at Bentley or Watnall, the lines are choked and we have other comms issues still to be resolved. Can you contact them from your place and warn the Control Opps people at Coltishall, Duxford and Wittering?"

"Of course, old chap. When this damned show is over, we must meet and catch up on things, if only to hear that magnificent accent of yours. Leave it with me, I'll contact them." It was Wing Commander James (Jimmy) Flint, an acquaintance from way back in 1936 when they learnt to fly. The Flt. Lieutenant felt relieved knowing that maybe the worst of the conflict was over. Later, when the radio and comms system had been sorted, an Officer at Bentley Priory phoned and confirmed that Spitfire pilots had been scrambled at Coltishall and Duxford.

The operators in building R4 continued their watch, monitoring the oncoming enemy aircraft and reporting their progress. Someone was heard to say, "It looks as though they are heading towards Manchester. They won't make it - our boys will sort them out!"

Harry walked over to Alan's station. "That drunk Rev. Nichols shoved a piece of paper in my pocket and I've only just found it." Harry began to read the note, becoming more choked and pausing often as he neared the end. Alan listened intently and was joined by Daisy. She held Harry's spare hand tightly.

'*Please can someone help? My wife and I are most anxious to know what has happened to our son who is a wireless operator stationed at RAF Scampton. His dog Winnie, who we look after, cries for him everyday. Please let one of us know. We pray to God to look after him. His name is Sergeant Richard (Dicky) Nichols.*'

After a few moments, Alan responded. "We must go as soon as we can and talk with them. In the meantime, I'll try to ring around to see if there's any news."

The next day, after a long sleep and some table tennis next to the canteen, Alan finally wrote a letter to his parents. As usual, he attempted to bolster their morale with optimism rather than reality. He told them about Harry and all the escapades but really could not say too much as he knew the censors might clamp down. He'd also telephoned Scampton to see if there was any news about the Vicar's son. It took two days of enquiries before he could reach the right people at RAF Scampton and even then he had to withstand a barrage of questions and checks.

The Church Bells rang just as the three of them knocked on the Vicar's door. It was 6.00pm on the third day after they'd fortuitously rescued the Vicar. On this occasion, he was perfectly sober and greeted them with a warm smile.

"Please come in. I hope you've managed to find out some information. We tried but could not get through to the right person."

They were ushered into a brightly decorated front room with many highly scented garden flowers. His wife came in followed by Winnie, a friendly Cocker Spaniel who took to Alan immediately. The three of them introduced themselves and they chatted briefly about the flowers and the many photographs of Richard and his family that were sitting on a dark oak sideboard. The Vicar's wife, a jolly lady with a generous figure, stood with her hands on her hips.

"Would you like some tea and cake? I've just finished baking a rather nice Madeira and it's still warm."

Alan looked at Harry and decided he'd better start the conversation.

"I wish we were the bearers of good news but it saddens me to say that your son will not be coming home." There was a long, painful pause and even the dog sensed what was happening as he stared atAlan with downcast, sad and watery eyes.

The Vicar hugged his wife Jill tightly as she quietly cried and rocked gently in his arms. Her sadness affected them all; even the Vicar wiped away his tears and shook uncontrollably. Alan continued as Harry comforted Daisy and with his spare hand passed Jill a white handkerchief and then reached out to hold her hand.

"Richard is a hero. He was one of a crew of seven in the first formation of Lancasters who successfully damaged the German war effort in the Ruhr Valley on the night of May 16th. They managed to breach two massive dams so that the floodwaters destroyed armaments factories and other industries vital to the Nazis. Unfortunately, nearly half the 18 aircraft were destroyed. The Lancaster carrying your son and the rest of the crew did not make it. Early reports say that his aircraft crashed after being hit by flak on

143

the way home over Holland. You'll be getting an official report any day soon with more detail. We are terribly sorry. Hopefully, and not before too long, once the shock and grief have subsided, I'm sure you be incredibly proud of your very brave son."

Daisy moved next to Jill, wiped her tears and hugged her. She headed off towards the kitchen saying everyone needed a cup of tea. Alan sat wondering if he'd said all the right words. Harry who had remained quiet throughout pointed at the dog. He had a cricket ball in his mouth.

"Richard gave Winnie that ball the day before he left five weeks ago," said the Vicar. "He used to go with him to cricket matches and sit patiently waiting for him. Laurie loved his cricket. He was a very good fast bowler, but he and Winnie, who he'd known from a pup, were inseparable and the best of friends."

Winnie dropped the ball at Alan's feet and licked his hand. There was a deep sadness in his eyes. It was as if he knew that life would never be the same again. Alan gently fondled the dog's head.

"He likes you," said Jill, just as Daisy came back with five cups of tea. Rev. Nichols stood up and walked over to the sideboard. He picked up a picture of Richard in his RAF uniform and sobbed.

"I'm so sorry that you had to find me in the ditch. I'd reached a point where my thoughts were all too negative. The war and where God stood in all of this. Jill is constantly anxious about Richard and then my own thoughts that aircrew do not seem to survive for very long." He looked forlorn and started to sob again, his tears falling on the framed photograph.

He paused without taking his eyes off the picture. "That night, I had a premonition. It was about Dicky inside one of those bombers. He kept calling out for both of us in the dark and I could see flames. I just could not take anymore so I spend two hours in the snug at the *Black Horse* drowning my sorrows." He walked back to his wife and they cuddled each other lovingly before she broke away and headed towards the kitchen.

"You must try my Madeira cake. It was Richard's favourite." Jill was trying hard not to appear too emotional, but it was to no avail. To stave off the pain, she started to ask questions and took an interest in Harry's mother's work as a teacher. She continued to ask the other two about family and their life in the RAF.

"Is Daisy your girl, Harry? Are you stepping out together?"

"Er, yes," said Harry slightly embarrassed, looking at Daisy for some kind of reassurance.

"And how about you Alan, are you courting yet? Do you have a young lady somewhere?"

"No, but I do have hopes of seeing a nurse I met back home before I joined up. Unfortunately, she was sent to France and we haven't corresponded." Daisy looked slightly disappointed when Harry said, "It's a little daft getting too serious when we know there's a good chance one of us may not make it."

"Quite right young man. I'm sure the good Lord will guide you into making the right decision at the right time," said the Vicar.

Alan looked at his watch and said they'd better be off. The three of them thanked the Vicar and his wife for their understanding, promising to attend church on Sunday. They also agreed to call in from time to time to see if they needed any help.

Jill hugged them tightly and the Vicar shook their hands. He thanked them for their kindness and help. Alan turned to Jill and said, "Would you mind if I take Winnie for walks every now and then, providing I can find the time?"

"Not at all, we'd be delighted to see you anytime." Winnie wagged his tail and watched Alan intensely until he'd disappeared down the lane with the other two.

The weeks and months went by. News came in on a few occasions that German bombers were still reaching a number of inland cities and airfields around London and along the east and south coasts. The raids were nothing like the earlier assaults back in 1940 during the Blitz. Goering, much to his frustration, had been ordered by Hitler to switch from airfields to key industrial cities. Due to radar and the increasing production of fighter aircraft, the

Luftwaffe had miscalculated the ability of The RAF to offer such strenuous resistance and they were concerned.

The chaps at Stenigot proved to be a real asset. Their improved detection and ranging skills along with the advanced radar units were more dependable than even the ones at RAF Martlesham, one of the key command centres in 11 Group Fighter Command.

Four weeks before the USAAF took over at Martlesham, Alan, Harry and Leon, the French operator, spent three days at the station updating some of the RAF and civilian operators on their Chain Home apparatus. It was here that they came across Squadron Leader 'Johnnie' Johnson and Flight Lieutenant Peter Townsend. They were normally stationed at either Tangmere or Hornchurch but Fighter Command often deployed pilots where they were most needed.

James Edgar Johnson ('Johnnie'), came from Leicestershire and spoke with a mild East Midland's accent. He came across as easy-going and relaxed, though his reputation as a Spitfire ace and master tactician had not been lost on the three of them. He was principled but approachable, willing to join in with stories from his missions.

Peter Wooldridge Townsend on the other hand, was the opposite. He was shy, charming, well mannered, distinguished and played the part of a perfect gentleman, even if those around him considered he was too reserved. He, too, was a Battle of Britain ace, but little did they know that in the years to follow, he would make newspaper headlines for his highly controversial relationship with the King and Queen's younger daughter, Princess Margaret.

In August 1943, Alan, Harry and three others including Leon were chosen to supervise a small Chain Low Radar Station recently installed near the village of Roghadel on the Isle of Harris in the Outer Hebrides. The Royal Observer Corps, who, like the Radar specialists and radio operators, kept an eye on Shipping and U-Boat activity in the North Atlantic, would also use it as a base. They were needed to help the limited RAF personnel track any aircraft approaching from the east.

It was a move that none of them looked forward to. Alan, like

Harry and Leon, had long conversations about the best way to dress so as to avoid the biting cold winds they would inevitably face when winter approached. Leon, from South West France near Toulouse, was particularly anxious. He was not hardy enough to withstand a bad Hebridean winter. Harry was more upset that Daisy would not be coming and, despite his requests, permission was denied. The good news was that their stay in the remote Western Isles would only be for about six months.

On September 4th 1943, at 2.00pm, the three friends stepped out of a Handley Page Halifax onto the grass at RAF Stornaway in Lewis. It was a warm, bright day with a cloudless blue sky. To the northeast, only a few hundred yards away, they could see twinkling lights on the waves of the 'Minch' and in the far distance a hazy outline of Scotland's rugged west coastline.

"Good afternoon, gentlemen." A tall well built man with a strong Gaelic accent and wearing the uniform of a Squadron Leader greeted them warmly.

"Welcome to Lewis and the friendliest laddies and lasses you'll ever meet. I'm Squadron Leader Dougie Macleod of Raasay, descended from Malcolm MacLeod, second son of the Laird of Lewis. I've arranged for you and a few others to be taken to Roghadel by Ghàidhlig. It's the only way we can get you there. It will be a long ride but you'll be treated to the most glorious scenery. Before you go, I'd be delighted if you'd join me for a wee dram in the Mess. "Bidh thu a 'feumachdainn aon airson an rathaid. In case you Sassenachs don't know what I'm on aboot, it means 'you'll be needing one for the road'."

"Excuse me Sir," said Alan, "you mentioned a 'Ghiddly' or something similar?'"

"Och aye laddie, the word is 'Ghàidhlig' - it means a motor coach!" He laughed and said "You'd better learn Western Isles Gaelic if you want to understand the locals!"

They followed the affable highlander to the mess.

"It was never going to be 'a few wee drams," said Alan, who

felt quite tipsy after sampling several twenty-five year old malt whiskies. They said goodbye to the kindly Dougie MacLeod and boarded the maroon and cream fifteen-year-old Leyland Tiger coach, along with a few locals and other RAF NCOs. Harry, Leon and Alan slept for much of the journey south. They woke up just as they approached West Tarbert, a small strip of land that connected Lewis with Harris. Either side of them, agitated seas rolled their white crests across the inlets. The blue sky had disappeared to be replaced by grey clouds rolling in from the Atlantic and it was starting to rain.

Leon perked up, excitingly pointing to dolphins breaking the surface less than 100 yards from shore. They drove into Tarbert, stopping to drop off a couple with their very smelly dog.

Alan thought of Winnie, the kindly Vicar and his wife Jill. He'dcalled in on several occasions, walked the dog and made sure they were all okay. Harry and Daisy had also visited and the three of them had attended Church on three occasions. Daisy, an accomplished cook, baked puddings and cakes while Harry helped in the garden. The Nichols found it difficult adjusting to life without their son but they had many friends in the village who supported them. They had received a wonderful citation from the RAF and discovered he'd been buried in a cemetery in Holland. They promised themselves they would visit as soon as the war was over. As for Winnie, the spaniel with the permanent wagging tail, he always looked forward to seeing Alan and, uncannily, always detected him at some distance even whilst still out of sight.

"Christ!" said Harry. "Is this what we've got to put up with for six months?" The three of them had walked from where the bus had dropped them off in the village and were now confronted by five small Nissen huts and wooden shacks that had been erected near a newly constructed brick building adjacent to twin Radar masts.

"Bit primitive, ain't it Harry, but you'll get used to it." The voice sounded familiar.

"Terry, good grief, what are you doing here?" Alan shook his hand and introduced him to Leon who was bemused by the man's

Black Country accent. Terry Wandsworth was the third member of the infamous darts team that had represented RAF Wattisham against Bob Stamford Tuck's fighter boys, two years previously.

"It's a long story Al," said Terry. "It all started when I was posted to Hornchurch, hoping they'd select me for pilot training. Unfortunately, I was turned down. They said I'd be best in radio and navigation so they packed me off to RAF Bawdsey. Not sure why but it's probably something to do with my powers of co-ordination and maybe my accent doesn't fit." He smiled and carried on. "Anyway, last year I was on a flight in a Halifax, heading east on a mission to Mannheim, with four others, escorted by three hurricanes. Several ME 109s near Ramsgate jumped us. They shot us to pieces, injured the pilot and killed the nose gunner. For my pains, I received a couple of wounds in my left leg. I'll never forget Tommy Brownwell, the pilot. Despite a mangled arm, he brought the kite down and landed in the sea. Tommy, the tail gunner, and myself managed to escape and we were picked up by an MTB two miles off the coast. I spent five weeks in hospital having shrapnel extracted from my leg and then six weeks recuperation down in Surrey. The Station Commander recommended me for a commission and a DFM. After that, they decided to send me to Benbecula and from there on to this useless piece of rock. I've been here for three weeks."

"So what's happened to you guys?" asked Terry. "I hope there were no more dart competitions?" Alan and Harry laughed.

The four of them decided to have a look at the facilities. Terry escorted them around as they chatted about the last two years. Leon had decided to go for a walk and let the three friends reminisce. He was taken back by the number of sheep in the adjacent fields and marvelled at the birds around him. A brief brisk trot took him to the coastal footpaths once trod by ancient Scottish warriors and clans. Here he could feel their presence in the walls of the stone buildings and hear them on the gentle breeze that softly caressed a breath-taking landscape. He wanted to walk down to the pretty harbour but thought he'd better be heading back.

The new Radar facilities were well known to the three of them and, after a week, Terry quickly picked up how to operate the transmitter and receiver units. Their main task was to teach the raw recruits, Coastal Defence chaps and the ROC how to use the apparatus. Terry's skills in the latest radio and communication advances paid off because using the island's telephone network was ponderous, inefficient and often out of order. He managed to set up direct links with both Benbecula and Stornaway, cutting down the delays and risk of errors.

For a week, Terry and Leon spent time at the local exchange, re-wiring some of the cabling. The female operators found them both entertaining and helpful. One local girl, Beatrice MacKenzie, betterknown as Birdie, took a shine to the man from Toulouse and the pair of them became close friends. It proved to be a relationship that lasted. After spending two years in France, the pair retuned to Rodel in 1946 and were married in the local church. They became very popular in the community, serving it well for over forty years

The sleeping, catering and toilet facilities were pretty crude. Alan especially hated the claustrophobic cramped quarters that offered little privacy. He slept badly and was permanently cold particularly during night shift work. There was a overall smell from the latrines next to their hut and the smokey wood burners needed greater ventilation.

"Harry, have you read our schedule for the next month?"

"Yes. It should to be very interesting," replied Harry in his usual optimistic way.

"We've been assigned to join the ROC boys for some observation work in return for teaching them how to decipher signals and twiddle a few knobs," said Alan.

Harry laughed. "Yes. It means we'll be camping out, boy scout style, in tents overlooking the Atlantic to watch out for passing convoys," said Harry.

Leon jumped in and enthusiastically mentioned they'd be able to watch animal and bird life in their spare time.

"Hang on Leon, I thought there was only one 'Birdie' in your life!" joked Alan. The other two laughed loudly. Leon was not amused, probably because he was still not au fait with Alan's humour. Instead, he mentioned that he'd seen a white-tailed eagle as well as buzzards. His growing love of ornithology kept him from being bored.

Alan, found time to draw and paint. His watercolour sketches were always greatly admired by the others.

Harry wrote endlessly to Daisy and spent his spare time walking to and from the Post Office to pick up her mail and post his own. Alan was beginning to see how much he missed her.

On one occasion six weeks after they'd arrived on Harris, they watched, monitored and reported three U-Boats heading out into the North Atlantic. All of them were on the surface probably keeping an eye on the occasional stray from regular convoys. They passed on the information to the Benbecula Control Centre who set in motion an interception by a couple of Catalina Flying Boats from Sullom Voe in the Shetlands and two Beaufighters temporarily stationed at RAF Leuchars in East Scotland. News came through that two of the U-Boats had been apprehended and sunk.

On September 20th 1943 it was decided to celebrate Alan's 22nd birthday in a special way.

"Come on you two!" shouted Harry. "They won't wait forever, you know." Harry had managed to hire a motorboat for the day and they were due to collect it at 9.00am.

The day before, Alan had managed to find and acquire a second hand Kodak Retina camera with some money sent from home. He was late after desperately trying to work out all the controls during breakfast and how to load a film.

All three of them were looking forward to the trip and then, afterwards, a nice social gathering at the Rodel Hotel Bar.

They reached the old harbour with minutes to spare. An old fisherman with skin like brown boot leather walked them down some stone steps and a landing ramp to where a white painted boat with a single outboard engine lay ready for them. It was named 'Kelpie', the Gaelic for a mythical sea creature.

"Now you'll be takin' it easy, lads," he said. "The forecast says the weather should stay fine until mid afternoon but don't risk the big waves. If it gets too choppy, she'll take some water but not a lot. The lass is a wee sook, broad in the beam, nah much draft and tends to rock away so ya might puke and get a little dreich!"

"Thanks for the tips. I'm sure we'll be okay," said Harry.

Alan helped Leon push the boat into the water and they bothclimbed in. Harry followed next, holding Alan's camera, then immediately set about starting the outboard.

"He's right, this damned thing does rock. I gather we may feel a little queasy and we have to watch out for high waves. Best if we stay close to the shore."

Harry was trying to put on a brave face as they exited the harbour and headed for the open sea. The sun was shining but a north-easterly breeze kept them wrapped up. Alan took several photographs of the rock promontories and Leon became quite excited when they spotted cormorants, puffins and a couple of seals. Above them, gulls and terns wheeled and dived whilst Harry skilfully steered them into open water. The waves were a little boisterous and, as they suspected, the boat's rocking motion and the spray made them feel uncomfortable.

They'd only travelled for twenty minutes when the outboard decided to splutter and die.

"Oh bugger," said Harry. "Now what's going to happen?"

Alan said he'd look at the engine, a 2-stroke TD20 16hp Johnson Seahorse. With a few primitive tools kept in an oily rag under his seat, he managed to strip off the cowling and lift off a cover revealing the carburettor. As he suspected, the unit's jets were very dirty so he spent ten minutes cleaning the parts and generally making sure all was well.

"OK, start her up," said Alan. The engine burst into life and actually sounded sweeter than before. "The tank is only half full so we'd better not go too far and besides, there's a leak in the stern."

"Cheers Al," said Harry. "Even if you are occasionally much too over cautious, you do know your engines, old bean."

The sea had calmed down as well as the rocking. They now started to enjoy the ride. Suddenly Alan shouted in alarm.

"What the hell is that?" he exclaimed, looking down from the side of the boat. The other two quickly looked, studying the dark water for anything unusual. They were about a mile off shore and keeping parallel with it.

"There, over there!" They looked to where Alan was pointing, their faces anxiously scanning the surface.

"Christ, it's a bloody huge shark," said Harry. "No, hang on it's two huge sharks," he stuttered.

Leon was excited and asked Alan to take some photographs.

"It's a sea monster and it's coming this way! Let's get out of here!" Harry reached over and hit the throttle so that the boat stood high in the bows as it scooted away.

They'd only travelled a hundred yards when their escape came to an abrupt stop as the engine died again. "Oh blast, not again." A feeling of panic rapidly hit them as a large dorsal fin broke the surface less than twenty feet away. The sea chopped up and down, making the boat sway around.

"Oh my God, we are going to die," said Harry. Leon started laughing as a huge dark shape glided under the boat.

"It's a basking shark you idiots! No more dangerous than a small whale. It does not eat humans"

The three of them watched as another dark shape slid slowly beneath them. It then surfaced and they watched its dorsal fin moving away. Alan tried to take a few photos but, by the time he'd set up the camera, the creatures had disappeared much to Leon's frustration.

"Mon Dieu, that was amazing!" exclaimed Leon.

Alan and Harry were still unsure, assuming that a shark's only objective was to include them on its menu.

Alan cleaned the carburettor jets three times before they headed back. The sea was becoming choppier and they still had about two miles to go. Leon and Alan were slowly turning pale shades of green as Harry tried hard to keep the boat from rocking in the swell. A few waves bounced off the top of the gunwale and swirled around in the bottom of the boat. Alan and Leon set about bailing out before it became too difficult. It was almost 11.30am when they finally arrived back at the quay ramp in Rodel. Birdie was waiting for Leon and theyall decided to walk to the Rodel Hotel bar, chatting excitedly to Birdie about their encounter with 'Moby Dick'.

The evening was spent in merry conversation. They were joined by a couple of Birdie's friends from the exchange. One of them, Doreen Kirkbride, tried hard to attract Alan's attention, but he was having none of it. After the evening's festivities, which involved Harry in a yard of ale dare and a contest to see who could balance a pint on their open palms, Harry asked Alan if he fancied Doreen.

"Not a chance in hell," he said, "the girl is not my type. She's too crude and besides, have you seen her arms? She's either a boxer, wrestler or a weight lifter!"

Harry laughed as they unsteadily sauntered out of the hotel and made their way back to base, a good ten minutes away. Leon walked Birdie back home, arriving back an hour later with lipstick on his face and collar. Harry remarked that to a Frenchman, affairs of the heart were second nature. Leon was not amused by such trivialities and refused to take the bait.

The weeks flew past as the weather turned colder and windy. However, it did not stop the men from persisting with their observation and surveillance duties. Camping out under canvas in a Hebridean early winter did have a detrimental physical effect on Alan. He carried little fat and bulk to protect against the cold and damp and blamed his growing aches and pains on the weather. Leon also found it difficult. Harry on the other hand, loved it. Alan was heard to say to him one morning, "You must have Eskimo blood in you!"

154

From January till the beginning of March 1944, the entire team including the ROC people remained indoors as the temperature dropped below freezing. On March 15th, Alan and Harry received a telegram transferring them from Rodel to RAF Bungay in Suffolk. They were to fly from Benbecular to RAF Banff where a Bristol Beaufighter would transport them to RAF Halesworth and then they would be driven on to Bungay. There was no explanation for the move other than a few days later when Harry telephoned Wattisham to try and extract more information. All he could glean from them was that several radio detection and radar guys had been handpicked to help the USAAF chaps at Bungay, Hardwick and Seething. "Seems the Yanks might be desperate to know about our operations and need us," he muttered.

On March 18th, Harry and Alan boarded an Avro Anson bound for Banff. They had already said their goodbyes to Leon and Terry over a few drinks the previous evening, not knowing if they'd ever meet up again. Like all those serving in the armed forces, they had come to terms with shortened life expectancy and were therefore fully aware that long term friendships rarely happened. No one had warned them that life would often be lonely during wartime.

The flight from Banff to Wattisham in the Beaufighter was not enjoyable. It was cramped, cold and they hit a number of bad storms flying over Newcastle and then Durham.

When they arrived at RAF Wattisham, Wing Commander Reggie Baker DFO, DSC and Bar, along with a USAAF Officer greeted them. Reggie Baker was already known as an ace fighter pilot in Hawker Typhoons and he was the archetypal RAF Officer. He was self assured, eccentric, well spoken and carrying half a handlebar moustache. The other half had been shaved off in some infamous New Years revelry in the mess. He was only here briefly at Wattisham after flying up from Harrowbeer in Devon to attend a high profile meeting with top brass RAF and USSAF Officers.

The American, Kyle Riddle, spoke to them in an accent they found intriguing. It turned out he was the station's future

Commanding Officer, a man who had spent much of his early life hunting in Texas. He was also an ace pilot who'd recently converted to Lockheed P-38 Lightnings for bomber escort missions.

"You guys must be the ace radar operators we've all been hearing about. We need guys like you two, here and at other USAAF stations, so we can hit those Luftwaffe laddies before they hit us. I hope you'll show us all you've got." Wing Commander Reggie Baker stepped forward, excused himself and took over.

"OK chaps, you'll be working in Bungay where our American friends have a few special units, on the ground and in some of their aircraft. It's all set up ready for you to play with. You may find some of their equipment rather primitive but don't let that get in your way."

Kyle Riddle coughed and looked somewhat embarrassed.

The Wing Co. continued, "There's every chance that the British and Americans are planning to undertake a major mission on mainland Europe. Obviously mum's the word eh! No tittle tattle if you please, gentlemen, rumours will not start here."

Alan and Harry saluted as 'Reg' as the men knew him, walked away. After a few feet, he turned and shouted back. "We've arranged for some lodgings for you both in Bungay. It's by the river. Someone will take you there. Oh and be good chaps, don't fall in!" He laughed out loudly.

The two Americans disappeared leaving Alan and Harry to wait for their transport. They looked around and took in the grey concrete buildings with their blackouts, the Officers' Mess, the canteen and accommodation blocks. Behind them were a number of parked aircraft including the Beaufighter they'd arrived in and, in the distance, a couple of hangars. There were also several dugout shelters scattered around and sandbagged anti-aircraft gun stations.

"This should be fun," remarked Harry. "I'm looking forward to 'playing' with those primitive Yankee toys."

Alan agreed and mentioned that when they managed to arrange a few days' leave, he would like to return to Donington to see the

Nichols and obviously Winnie. Harry didn't need to be encouraged. He could not wait to meet Daisy again. He planned to phone her the next day from the lodgings in Bungay.

"I guess we must soon be due for some home leave. I haven't seen my family or friends back home for ten months."

"That's true," said Harry. "I need to go back too. I miss my mother's dumplings."

Alan looked at Harry and burst into fits of laughter.

A shining black and maroon Austin 8 drew to a halt and an orderly jumped out.

"Are you the two chaps going to Bungay?"

"Yes, that's us," said Alan.

"OK jump in, shouldn't take more than an hour."

They threw their kit bags in the boot and Alan was about to get in when a shout attracted his attention. He turned towards a man running from the accommodation block, waving furiously. Harry was already sitting comfortably in the back of the car, but stepped out to see what all the fuss was about, leaving the driver to wait patiently.

"Alan, it's me, hang on!"

Alan stared and suddenly broke into a huge laugh. He walked towards the man who was dressed in a flying jacket and boots.

"Good grief, I can't believe it's you Bill! What on earth are you doing here? This is truly amazing and it's good to see you again"

Bill Bennett smiled broadly and chuckled at Alan's warm greeting. Before he could say anything, he was introduced to Harry. They shook hands as he tried to explain hurriedly all about the last three years.

"If you have a few hours, jump in with us - we're off to our digs in Bungay. We can catch up on things at one of the local pubs and indulge in some fine grub and a few beers," suggested Alan.

"Sounds like a good idea to me," said Harry.

Bill enthusiastically endorsed the idea. "I'm only here for four days," he said. "This is my second and I have this evening off."

The driver accelerated once they were all in the car. Harry and Bill were catapulted backwards into the leather seats, laughing, as they sped off down the lanes. Alan sitting in the front listened intently above the whining of the Austin's rear axle and engine noise as Bill explained he was a radio navigator in Blenheims, stationed at West Raynham. Harry took out a packet of Players and offered them around. All three of them gratefully took one and lit up using Alan's silver lighter given to him on his 20th birthday by his sister.

"They promoted me to Flight Sergeant in 1942 after my aircraft crash landed near Ashford in Kent. We'd been spooked by a lone ME109 over Dover. The bastard followed us down and strafed us when we were escaping and I caught one in the back. Fortunately it passed right through and missed the important bits. Left me with a couple of nice scars though. Sadly the skipper bought it. I spent a month in Canterbury recuperating and where I met a really nice girl working in the hospital."

Bill continued talking, despite the noise. He wistfully glanced out at farm workers, guiding large shire horses, dragging harrows over the land. In the grey broken sky he saw a couple of aircraft in the distance heading towards Wattisham.

"They posted me back to Raynham where I worked with AI Mk. IV air to air Radar units. Since then, I've flown on missions to Norway, Holland, Germany and more recently tried to disrupt Jerry's U-Boat pens and harbours along the French coast. Last week, Mosquitoes arrived which means I might be out of a job. I guess they'll post me somewhere I can be useful."

They drew up with a squeal of brakes outside a pretty whitewashed cottage adorned with a glorious display of honeysuckle and roses. A wooden name plaque bore the simple words 'Rose Cottage'. They all climbed out and Alan thanked the Adjutant. Harry knocked on the door of the cottage and waited.

"Hang on, I'll be there in a minute. There's a problem with the lock!" The voice trailed away and they waited patiently. Suddenly, a woman appeared from a side path. In her arms, she carried an aggressive looking Siamese cat that hissed and growled at Bill.

"You must be the RAF boys from the airfield up the road. They said there were only two of you, not three." She looked puzzled but quickly smiled and chuckled when Harry explained that Bill was only visiting for the evening.

"Oh that's alright then, I'll show you to your rooms. Please come in and don't mind Cleopatra, she's really quite friendly. She'll get used to you soon enough. My name is Mrs Brownlow but you can call me Ruth if you want. I hope you are better behaved than the last two men who left last week. They broke my lavatory seat and kept upsetting Cleo. On top of that, they regularly arrived late at night, completely puddled after spending too much time in the *Fleece Inn*. I had to have a stern word with them."

With Bill hovering around nervously, keeping an eye on Cleopatra, Ruth led Harry and Alan to their rooms, which were along a corridor with walls overcrowded with various old pictures of family members. The two bedrooms were adjacent to each other with a bathroom opposite. On the wall at the end of the corridor stood an ancient grandfather clock between two pictures of the King and Queen.

Before leaving for the Fleece Inn, Alan and Harry promised Ruth they would be back before 10.00pm. She gave them a key each and they waved goodbye. Alan fiddled with the lock and soon sorted out the sticky mechanism. He even dared to stroke the cat but Harry took a wide berth. The three of them sauntered up to the pub.

"Good grief, what have you smothered yourself in? You smell like a woman!" exclaimed Harry. He was looking at Alan and smiling in his boyish way.

Bill grinned and said that Alan had always shown a preference for a 'cissy' fragrance.

Alan ignored the comments and said, "It's called Aqua Velva shaving lotion by Williams."

"Wooooh wooooooh! Get you!" They both cooed in Alan's ear as he led the way into the bar at the Fleece.

There were only a few locals hunched up over a game of cribbage. They looked up and peered intently at Bill's outfit before muttering, "Look what's dropped in!" before asking him where he'd hidden his parachute. Ignoring the odd sense of humour, the three of them were delighted to spot a skittles alley.

Alan bought the first round and with a grin asked the barman if they could play if they conducted themselves according to the rules.

"No problem Sir, but please play nicely! I don't want any broken windows or any of you trying to be too damned clever with the balls." They fell about laughing when one of them promised they'd keep all their balls under strict control.

During the following two hours, over a couple more pints, Bill enlarged on his flying experiences and listened intently to Alan and Harry's adventures over the past three years. He also went into raptures over Victoria, the girl he'd met whilst in hospital.

"She worked as a secretary to one of the senior surgeons, the man who patched me up after Jerry had tried hard to stop me flying permanently."

"God knows where they'll send us next," said Harry, drawing on another cigarette. "Seems we'll only be here for a short time as we have to help out the Yanks."

At 9.30pm Bill telephoned for a taxi. His temporary lodgings were in Harleston about eight miles away.

"I guess we may not meet again for another year or more," said Bill. "I'll be back at West Raynham after a couple of days and then they will probably post me overseas. At least that was the last rumour but they change their minds on a daily basis."

Alan gave Bill a shoulder hug and said, "Maybe we'll see each other back in Nuneaton sooner than you think. I'm going to try and arrange some leave in the next few weeks."

They all shook hands and wished each other good luck before watching Bill walk out to his taxi.

"He's a really nice chap," said Harry. "Easy to get on with."

Alan agreed and mentioned they'd better be getting back and

then deciding they had enough time to take the long way back by following the river.

The sky looked ominous. Dark grey clouds were rapidly tearing in from the west and, although it was warm and there was some blue sky, it did not last long. They increased their pace along Castle Orchard and across the River Waveney at Earsham Dam before turning right along a footpath parallel with the river. They arrived just as the first heavy drops of rain bounced off the entrance porch.

"Welcome back boys. Would you like a mug of Ovaltine?" asked Ruth. Harry looked at Alan, saw him nod and answered with an enthusiastic "Thank you, that would be perfect!"

"How did you manage to find Ovaltine?" asked Alan. "I thought rationing meant most things were out of bounds?"

"They are," she replied. "But I have a few friends who see me right, if you know what I mean."

Alan and Harry spent an hour in the sitting room with their Ovaltine, reading various well-thumbed 'Life' magazines and 'The Illustrated London News', along with an incomplete 'Daily Sketch'. Their attention was suddenly drawn to Cleopatra carrying in a half chewed but live mouse, which she deposited on the carpet. The poor thing tried to make a run for it but was hauled back by the cat and tossed unceremoniously into the air.

"Oh you naughty girl!" shouted Ruth. "You are a bad Cleo."

She stooped down and picked up the mouse and carried it through to the kitchen, opened a window and threw it out.

"So sorry about that, she does hunt and has a habit of playing with mice and birds. I found half a sparrow in my bedroom the other day. I swear she's getting worse." Cleo sneaked under a sideboard making strange mewing noises.

"Breakfast will be served at 7.30am prompt in the dining room. I take it you'll have porridge and a good English fry up? Can't promise too much though. I'm waiting for my friend to call in with a few much needed essentials."

The two of them nodded enthusiastically.

"By the way, I should have warned you. We do have a resident ghost who pops in occasionally. He won't do you any harm apart from spook you a little. I'm off to bed. Don't be too late now."

They looked up, thanked her and smiled, caring little for what Harry later called exaggerated 'Old Wives' Tales'.

The next morning at 6.30am, Alan was the first to go into the bathroom while Harry was still fast asleep and snoring. After a quick toilet visit, he switched on the light and prepared his shaving items before testing out the hot water. Alan looked in the mirror above the basin and applied a generous layer of shaving foam around his face and was about to pick up his leather strop to sharpen his razor when he noticed a face dimly lit in the mirror reflecting someone in the corridor beyond the open bathroom door.

"Harry, is that you? I won't be a moment!"

There was no reply, but when he looked again in the mirror he could make out a shadowy outline of a man's figure in the corridor gliding past the door towards the grandfather clock.

"Harry, for goodness sake, what are you up to?" Again, there was no reply and Alan was becoming apprehensive.

He rushed to the door and looked down the corridor towards the end wall and the clock. There was nothing other than a strange musty smell. He knocked on Harry's door and waited for him to open it.

"Have you been sleep-walking along the corridor? Or has anyone barged into your room?" asked Alan.

"Of course not, I've only just woken up," said a very disgruntled Harry. He stood in his pyjamas looking at Alan's face still covered in saving cream, very much aware of his concerned expression.

"What's up, old chap? You look as if you've seen a ghost," smirked Harry peering at the white face before him.

"I have Harry," said Alan. "I've just seen that damned ghost, the one that Ruth warned us about. Look at it this way; I was standing at the wash basin looking into the mirror when I saw a

162

man's figure walk past the open door, heading down there." He pointed to the end wall and the grandfather clock.

"That's just not possible," said Harry. "Nobody opened my door and I have not stepped out of my bedroom. Moreover, whoever it was must have walked through a brick wall."

Alan wiped off the shaving cream and the two of them, suddenly looking pale, stood facing the clock when Ruth appeared behind them. Alan quickly explained what he'd witnessed but he was talking so fast that Ruth had to ask him to slow down.

She smiled. "Well don't say I didn't warn you. You must have encountered Albert. He was an old gardener who lived here and died twenty years ago from a broken heart. His wife and son disappeared and were never found. He still wanders around the house looking for them." She then turned around and shouted back, "Breakfast will be ready in about ten minutes!"

The two troubled men returned to their rooms and dressed quickly. Breakfast consisted of one rasher of bacon, a fried egg, half a slice of fried bread, something that resembled a piece of black pudding and a small shrivelled tomato.

"I'm sorry, it's not much," apologised Ruth. "Things should be better tomorrow when my friend pops in with fresh provisions."

Harry and Alan each responded with a "thank you" and said everything was fine, but clearly they were troubled and kept whispering about Albert. They came to the conclusion that Alan had experienced the inexplicable. Harry laughingly suggested they should get in touch with a priest and have the house exorcised.

The next day, Harry and Alan arrived at RAF Bungay via Flixton. An American Sergeant driving a Willys Jeep had picked them up. On arrival, they were met by a tall, attractive lady wearing the uniform of a WASP (Women's Airforce Service Pilot). They were immediately escorted to a large old and badly lit Nissan hut, temporarily converted to house the USAAF's detection, intercept and telecommunications units. Inside it was murky and the room was mainly lit by the glow from numerous oscilloscopes.

They were surprised to learn that the U.S. Navy's pulse radar system, the CXAM, was very similar to the British Chain Home technology. Although the U.S. boffins had developed a pulsed radar system, independently of the British, there were serious weaknesses in its operation. This came to light when it was realised there was no integration of radar into a unified air defence system. Here, the British were well ahead in the game.

Harry and Alan soon realised that their transmitter power was far too weak to be reliably effective beyond a few miles. They spent weeks upgrading both the transmitters and receivers with parts raided from unused new units earmarked for RAF bases too far from the coast. This entailed using clever and sometimes mischievous persuasion with a number of top brass officials.

Work came to a standstill for two weeks in early June 1944, when British and American forces mounted the biggest ever seaborne landings on the Normandy coast. D-Day on June 6th involved 150,000 allied troops and most of the British and American airbases in the south, south-east and eastern counties. Airborne radar and interception units were now installed in most US bombers, particularly the Flying Fortresses, based in Lincolnshire, Suffolk and Norfolk.

By the first week in August 1944, Alan and Harry had completed their work, much to the relief of the US Airforce. For their efforts and excellent work, they were both promoted to the rank of Flight Sergeants and told they would be posted somewhere overseas. However, before that, they had three weeks leave to look forward to. They decided that before going home they would visit RAF Stenigot and the Nichols. Harry looked forward to being with Daisy again for a few days. He did admit that he missed her

While on home leave back in Nuneaton, Alan received news that he and Harry had been specially selected to join a front line detection and surveillance unit attached to 109 Squadron and 72 (signals) Wing. Their destination would be Mons in Belgium. The German army was being gradually pushed back after the D-Day

164

landings. The allies co-ordinated a drive across Europe to reach Brussels, Paris and Berlin. At home, Alan finally caught up with his two brothers Graham and Gordon who'd returned from the army and their campaigns in Italy. Graham had seen action near Monte Casino and Gordon, still engaged as a driver, bragged he'd escorted Montgomery to meetings with US Lieutenant General Mark Clarke in Salermo. There was a growing feeling that the war would soon be over as more and more successes made headline news in the newspapers, on the radio, or with Pathe News at the cinema.

Alan's main concern was his father George who was not a well man. Scar tissue from his bouts of malaria, a legacy of his East Africa days in the army and later pneumonia, left him with breathing difficulties. In addition his heart was not very strong. Alice and Barbara looked after him very well and there were long periods when he seemed to recuperate. George being George, with his stubbornness, insisted on carrying on working at the Scala Cinema with Barbara now working as one of the two usherettes. Barbara's boyfriend Norman also lent a hand when George felt under the weather.

Two weeks later, on the 20th of September 1944, Alan and Harry, along with ten other men in 72 Signals, boarded a Dakota at RAF Blakehill near Cricklade. They were bound for Vitry-En-Artois, south of Lille and then on to Chièvres air base near Casteau, a suburb five kilometres from Mons.

"Alan, this kite's got a few issues. Have you heard the port engine? Sounds like a biscuit box full of nails!"

"I know, I think the pilot knows too. He's just communicated with the tower and warned them to prepare for a bumpy landing."

The port engine was spluttering and a trail of dark smoke trailed behind. Alan thought he could see flames. The Dakota was losing height but suddenly the airfield came into view. They descended rapidly from 9,000 feet and lined up for the landing. Harry saw a fire tender racing across the open ground towards the runway, recently repaired after allied bombing raids.

The pilot's voice came over the radio. "Prepare to evacuate rapidly on landing."

One of the others stood by the door and as soon as the Dakota came to a stop, he swung it open and threw out the extending steps. Flames and smoke billowed around the fuselage, showering them in sparks as Harry and Alan joined the others and exited without panic. A black tender arrived and quickly extinguished the fire with foam while the pilot, navigator and their fourteen passengers climbed into a large canvas-covered troop transporter and disappeared towards the main complex and control tower over a kilometre away. On the way, they passed the remains of a wrecked Focke-Wulf Fw 190s and a Junkers 88, reminders that this had been a busy German airfield just a few weeks previously. A group of over twenty people attracted by the sirens and fire on the stricken Dakota were waiting to greet them and check them out. Amongst them, a doctor and nurse enquired if anyone was hurt or needed attention. Alan recognised the nurse immediately but hardly dared to believe his own eyes. Harry turned to see Alan waving furiously.

"Kathleen McKenzie!" He shouted out her name twice. Harry, startled, turned with a puzzled expression. The nurse also turned and recognised Alan. She ran towards him and stopped a few feet away.

She stepped forward and took his hand in hers. "It's really you, isn't it? Oh my goodness, what a small world!"

To Alan, she was even more beautiful than his memory of her at their last meeting in Coventry.

"Let me introduce you to Jean Luc." The tall doctor behind her stepped forward and shook Alan's hand. "This is my fiancé, Jean Luc. We're getting married next June."

Alan did his best to hide his emotions and responded with a smile when she suggested they all go for a drink in one of the local bars.Harry, looking bemused, introduced himself as Alan's best friend and guardian angel.

"Sounds like a good plan to me," replied Harry enthusiastically.

As they walked towards the airfield gates, a young French officer approached and apologised that their flight to Chièvres had been delayed by two hours.

Harry joined Jean Luc, leaving Alan to chat with Kathleen.

"You looked disappointed when I introduced you to my fiancé."

"Yes, I cannot lie. Ever since we last saw each other, I have carried you in my heart and dreams. Don't get me wrong, I wish you both a very happy future. Your fiancé is an incredibly lucky man. I have to confess to being a little jealous."

"Alan, because of circumstances, timing and the uncertainty of knowing how things would turn out, we never had a chance to get to know each other. I quickly realised you were special, but it's been four years since we last saw each other. During that time I worked in various field hospitals for the army and saw far too much. All those young chaps in the forces who have been injured, some of them dying from dreadful wounds, left their impressions upon me. Two years ago, I had a breakdown and Jean Luc, a French doctor, helped me recover. He made me very happy and we saw a lot of each other. I also grew to love France and have met his family who live near Harfleur. I'm here right now to help Jean Luc with his work in one of the town's very busy hospitals. We attend allied as well as German patients."

Alan looked at her, smiled and realised he'd missed his chance. After a few drinks and a light meal, generously paid for by Jean Luc, the four of them walked back to the airfield. Once again, Alan said goodbye to Kathleen, only this time he knew he would never see her again. He shook Jean Luc's hand and asked him to take good care of her. Kathleen walked over to Alan and kissed him on both cheeks, leaving a smudge of lipstick on both. He smiled and wished them both good luck for the future before patting Harry on the shoulder and pointing towards a Lockheed Hudson with engines running.

"That must be ours," he said. "The other chaps are waiting patiently for us so we'd better hurry."

Harry looked at Alan and asked him about Kathleen. There was a distant vacant look in Alan's tearful eyes that made Harry wonder what had happened.

"She's very beautiful, old chap but I can't help feel there is an interesting story somewhere about the two of you. Jean Luc didn't give much away."

Alan was about to say something but could not easily express his thoughts without feeling sad. Eventually he reluctantly spoke up. "I'll tell you some other time, although it's not that exciting or interesting."

Harry detected a hurt in Alan's voice and decided that discretion was necessary for the moment. The two of them and the other twelve men from the 72 Signals, led by Captain Phillips, stepped out onto the grass runway at Chièvres air base after a very bumpy ride. It was unusually cold for September due to a brisk and cold easterly wind.

A well-dressed Flight Lieutenant met them and walked them over to a recently renovated dark green German transport wagon. It was still bearing various inscriptions and signs in German. One hour later, Alan and Harry arrived at the *Ecole Normale* in Mons, where they and other RAF personnel would stay for the foreseeable future. It was September 24th 1944 and for Alan as well as all the others, everything was about to change dramatically.

Chapter 11: A Most Agreeable Romance

By early September 1944, the 1st and 3rd US Armoured Divisions around Mons had confronted the retreating German army. Members of local resistance parties had already passed on valuable information to ensure the liberators faced few surprises. Between 60,000 and 70,000 men were trapped by the Americans who, for inexplicable reasons, did not completely finish the operation and let more than 30,000 Germans escape, most of them destined to play a role in the Battle for the Ardennes during the coming winter months.

Over four days, between September 1st and 4th, what became known as 'La Bataille pour la poche de Mons' (The Battle for the pocket of Mons), took place in the suburbs of Framerie, Jemappe and Cuesmes. During that period, many Belgian civilians were caught up in and suffered during intense street-to-street fighting. Fortunately the area around the crossroads at La Bascule and the roads to Binche and Charleroi were unaffected. Further afield, USAAF and RAF aircraft continually bombarded German infantry and Panzer units around Mauberge, Binche and Ath. By September 5th, Mons had been liberated. American troops, some riding their Sherman tanks, jeeps and personnel carriers, were mobbed by happy crowds throwing flowers.

The centre of Mons was largely left intact by the fighting but there were a number of Germans continuing to take advantage of Belgians sympathetic to the Reich. Some of these isolated Waffen SS troops left behind were snipers, hidden by their Rexist hosts in buildings around the town. Their objective was to confuse, slow down and disrupt the Americans as they liberated Mons.

"Bonjour Monsieur Licope."

"Bonjour Odette. I hope you and your parents are both well?"

"Very well thank you, except my father is not so good. He's at home with a lingering cold."

The genial Curator of the town's archives, Georges Licope, acknowledged her reply by tipping his hat and asking her to give Fernand his best wishes for a speedy recovery. His offices were opposite to where she worked in Les Jardins du Maire.

Odette arrived at work in the clerks' bureau in the Hotel de Ville as usual just as the Belfry bells and clarions indicated 8.30am.

The girls waved and greeted her as she walked in. Madame Fremont waved and called Odette into her office.

"Odette, please sit down and close the door." She looked apprehensive, even a little anxious. Her pale complexion and dark shadows indicated she'd had little sleep.

"What I'm about to tell you is important." She hesitated and continued. "I'm pleased to say that The Mayor, Monsieur Emile Denis, was arrested yesterday evening by military officers and senior resistance leaders. He stands accused of provided assistance and information to the Germans, as well as several counts of embezzlement." She stood up clearly anxious.

Odette sat patiently as Madame Fremont paced up and down.

"Under pressure, he will probably tell them all about my relationship with Oberst Frederich von Roettig. You know what that means don't you?" She took out a French cigarette from a silver case and lit up.

Odette knew exactly what would happen. "They'll regard you as a woman who fraternised with the Boche and accuse you of being an informant, maybe a traitor."

"That's right," she said. "They'll cut off my hair, paint me with tar and put me on public display by tying me to a lamp post. At worst they'll hang me from it."

"It hasn't happened yet," said Odette. "In any case, I'll stand by you. I know what you did and how you saved the lives of many people including one of my relatives."

"Oh thank you, lovely girl." Madame Fremont reached over and hugged Odette. "Let's hope that your evidence will help, should

170

they ever come for me. In a way, my future is in your hands."

Two days later, Odette discovered that Emile Denis had died of a heart attack whilst in prison. It seemed that Madame Marie Adélaïde Clotilde Fremont, by a stroke of luck, had managed to avoid the humility she'd imagined might happen.

The arrival of American troops, USAAF airmen and the RAF in Mons brought a feeling of optimism to the people of Mons, known as Montois. They clapped them, fêted them, threw kisses and enjoyed their willingness to join in with any festivities. Singing and dancing broke out spontaneously in the streets whenever the military arrived. On the downside, there were reports of shootings by snipers, causing several fatalities mainly to Americans. Commanders, well aware of the sniper presence, ordered searches on several occasions and many were eventually flushed out, including their Rexist hosts. Most were taken away for interrogation and later imprisoned, but a few remained undiscovered. Some of the Belgian traitors were executed by hanging or by a firing squad.

Amidst all the chaos that liberation brought to Mons, the RAF surveillance and radio detection boys, including Alan and Harry, arrived at the *Ecole Normale*. They had already been briefed that they would be needed for setting up and helping operate smaller radar units for detecting German aircraft whilst the allies pushed rapidly towards Germany, the Rhine and Berlin.

"Alan, come over here quick!"

Harry called his friend over to some papers that had just been handed to him by a sergeant in the Ops room.

"Intelligence and Signals have intercepted radio messages that indicate the Jerries may try to counter attack somewhere in the South of Belgium, maybe in the Ardennes. They must be stark raving mad!"

Alan agreed, but reminded Harry the morning shift had finished at mid-day. It was now 12.30pm so, along with a couple of radio operators from Signals, Larry and Tom, they headed towards

171

the town centre. Dressed in uniforms they reached the Grand Place and settled in around an outside table at 'Chez Saey', a high-class café, restaurant and patisserie. There wasn't much on offer due to rationing but at least they were open for business.

"You know what," said Harry, "I really miss Daisy. We've written every week and most letters get through but it seems that absence does make the heart grow fonder!"

Alan combed his hair just as a waiter arrived. Larry, a Yorkshireman, spoke first. Despite the waiter being confused by his accent, he ordered Pernod with water followed by Tom asking for a Duvel lager and Harry choosing a Stella Artois. Alan decided to order a Biere de Chimay out of curiosity. They asked the waiter if there was any food.

"Yes, I can offer you a plate of Boulettes de Porc à La Chef and legumes, Monsieur. I apologise for the lack of choice but as you know, everyone is rationed."

"OK, let's go for that," said Alan. "I'm starving."

They were joined by a couple of USAAF radio navigators who Larry seemed to know. They ordered beers but declined any food.

They introduced themselves as George Rydell and Zac Wilenski, both from Chicago. It turned out they had been sent to Mons to update their knowledge by liaising with the RAF radar specialists. They got on well with Alan and Harry. The smell of Camel, Lucky Strike cigarettes and cigars filled the air.

After an hour it was time to return to The *Ecole Normale* on the Avenue Dolez. It had been decided that the RAF chaps and the USAAF would organise a dance evening at the earliest possible opportunity.

As they were leaving, Alan spotted what he described as the most beautiful long haired brunette he'd ever seen. She was tall, elegant, self-assured and carried an hour glass figure as she crossed the Grand Place. He watched her until she met up with an older man who guided her towards a café on the corner by the Rue D'Havre.

Harry noticed his gaze, snapped his fingers and pulled his arm. "We're going to be late. Let's get a move on."

They all caught a tram and, as it moved on, Alan saw the girl again. She happened to glance up and smiled as she saw him gazing through the tram window.

"Papa, I hope you are feeling better?" said Odette. "Yes my child, it was important for me to work. I've had too many days off with this cold and we need the money. What have you been up to today?"

"Oh, nothing very important."

She looked up as a tram passed slowly by and saw a man in an RAF uniform smiling at her. She smiled back and mentioned that the English flyers are really quite handsome in their uniforms. Fernand looked at his daughter with a grin.

"You need to find a wealthy young Belgian friend, not a foreigner." He drew on his Upmann half corona cigar, fiddled with a beer mat and smiled.

"Papa! Really! I'll make up my own mind should I ever be lucky enough to find a man who I fall in love with."

Her father chuckled softly, knowing he was never going to change her mind.

Fernand spotted Georges Licope, striding across the Grand Place and called him over.

"Come and join us for a drink."

Georges greeted Odette with a kiss on each cheek before sitting down. Fernand attracted the waiter and ordered three filter coffees.

"I've got some good news," said Georges. "I'm going to be made curator of the Museum, once the town is fully back on its feet. It's a job I've always wanted to do."

"Congratulations!" said Odette and her father.

"I hope it's a well paid job," said Fernand.

"Oh it will be," Georges said. "The other good news is that the Mayor, Victor Maistriau, will be back tomorrow."

"That's excellent news," said Fernand. "Now we'll see things moving for the better. The man is a genius."

"That's for certain," said Georges, "but Victor experienced bad times including imprisonment and I believe the Gestapo tortured him. It is rumoured that Emile Denis, the Rexist pig who had a lot to do with it, has died under strange circumstances." Odette looked down and could not resist smiling.

Six days later, on Tuesday September 26th, George Rydell handed a note to one of the WAAFs working in the advanced Ops room where Alan and Harry were supposed to be. The message ended up on Harry's desk. The note stated that the two of them had been ordered to travel out towards forests near La Roche en Ardenne near Bastogne with three American observers, where they had to set up a TRU (transportable radio unit). The outfit consisted of two vans for the electronic equipment and a generator van. It used a 105-ft portable tower to support a transmitting antenna and two receiving antennas. It was now almost October and the weather was turning colder. Alan and Harry couldn't wait to get back to the warmth of their quarters at The *Ecole Normale*.

"Hey, Alan, the Yanks have organised a dance evening on Saturday 30th at a place called the Waux-Hall. They've asked if we can bring along our chaps and provide booze and music. Food will be down to them and some local volunteers."

"Doesn't leave us much time," said Alan. "It's already Tuesday, but it's good news. We need a break. Besides, it was my 23rd birthday five days ago so it's time to celebrate in style!" Harry agreed and said he'd make sure of it.

They spent that evening after the late shift making sure everyone had bought a ticket for the dance. By visiting a market stall in the Grand Place, Harry had managed to find over twenty 78s and a Collaro electric gramophone with an HMV turntable.

The next day, Alan persuaded a friendly requisitions officer to let them have beer and wine at a very discounted price. By Friday, everything was ready. Zac Wilenski dropped in and reassured them that food had been organised and he'd persuaded a dozen local women volunteers to help as hostesses and with the catering. He added that since the Americans had done most of the work, they would be in charge of the bar. Harry shouted an obscenity at Zac and threw a glove at him but missed and hit an inkpot instead. Zac laughed and quickly escaped.

It was Thursday morning and Odette had arrived home from work after a short day. She decided to use the afternoon to check out Misky at a local veterinary. The dog had somehow managed to get a small sharp bone stuck in his left paw.

"Hello, is that you ma cherie?" Odette walked in, acknowledged her mother and gave her a hug before picking up Misky.

"I'm off to the vet. Earlier, an American airman who was asking for volunteers to help out at a dance on Saturday stopped me in the Grand Place. I hope you don't mind but I said you and I could go. He gave me two passes. I think it will be a really good idea to show our appreciation for all they've done for us." Her mother was going to say something but hesitated and then said she'd have to put it to her father.

"Odette, your mother has said you've agreed to help out at a dance on Saturday." Fernand was standing in the kitchen doorway. He had just spent an afternoon in the garden and was looking somewhat dishevelled in his baggy corduroy trousers, braces, black beret and stained shirt.

"Yes Papa. I thought it would be a way of showing our gratitude. After all the Americans and the English have liberated us."

"Quite right and I think it's a good idea, but you'll have to follow your mother's advice. I'd like to know where this dance will take place and what do they want you and your mother to do?"

"Mama and I will work behind the catering tables and I'll also look after the music. The American said I'd be given a list of favourites. I think they and the English will contribute many records

175

but they may have different ideas on what are favourites. It's taking place in the *Waux-Hall* and it starts at 20:00 hours." She grinned and waited for her father's response.

"I really don't have a problem with it but only on two conditions. Firstly, I will take you both and I'll return to pick you up at 22.00 hours. Secondly, do not leave your mother's side without her permission even for a moment."

"Thank you Papa. This will be my first chance to thank the Americans and the English. Mama will no doubt enjoy it - you know how she loves dancing and music. It will be hard to stop her joining in!" They both laughed and hugged.

On Saturday morning, Harry, Alan, Zac and George were walking along the Boulevard Dolez when a convoy of American jeeps and field guns drove into view. Harry saw an old lady who was totally oblivious to the oncoming column. She suddenly walked out into road. The column stopped abruptly but right at the back there was a loud thud followed by shouting and chaos. Zac and George ran towards the column and as they drew close to the rear jeep, George suddenly kneeled down and started to vomit.

Zac looked distraught, holding his head with two hands and looking towards the sky. He shouted to Alan and Harry to stay back. US army medics arrived quickly and joined several personnel who had already surrounded the end Jeep with tarpaulins.

Zac and George spoke briefly with an officer and shaking their heads, walked back to Harry and Alan who were patiently and anxiously waiting for news.

"Oh Jeez, that was goddamned awful," said Zac, who was supporting George. "The driver of the last Jeep did not stop and ran into the barrel of the gun in front. The barrel burst through the screen and took his head off. It was carnage. Never seen so much blood."

"Oh my god," said Alan turning pale and looking like he might vomit too. Harry was visibly shaken.

"Is there anything we can do to help? We can't just stand around."

"It's pointless," said George. "They told us to stay away."

Traffic had built up to the rear of the column and a few onlookers, curious about the accident, had started to gather.

The four of them walked back towards a café in the Marché aux Poissons off the Avenue d'Hyon. They sat down and when the waiter arrived he said they all looked like they needed a stiff drink.

Harry was the first to speak. "Yes we do, please bring us a bottle of something strong."

A few minutes later, he reappeared with a bottle of Croizet Bonaparte 1928 Fine Champagne Cognac and four glasses.

"Christ, that looks good." said Harry.

"And expensive," replied Alan. They sat in silence obviously deep in thought and affected by what they'd just witnessed.

"It's a shame," said George. "Almost at the end of the war and that poor sod gets taken out. I bet he came across with the 3rd Army and survived the landing. Now this."

The Cognac was beginning to have its effect and they loosened up a little. Harry mentioned he'd received a letter from Daisy. She was sad because the Nichols' dog, Winnie, had died. Alan looked at Harry.

"Christ! Can it get any worse today? I'm not sure I'm in the right mood to go out socialising tonight."

Zac, who overheard Harry, jumped in. "We must all go. It will help us forget and besides I'd bet that the dog's owners wouldn't want you to miss out."

With half a bottle of Cognac consumed, they headed back. It was now 14.00 hours and Alan wanted to write a couple of letters to his parents and to the Nichols family. He sat on his bed and wrote for an hour before falling asleep. Clearly, the Cognac had worked too well.

At 17.00 hours there was a knock on Alan's room door. It was

Harry. He called out to Alan saying he would be in the canteen downstairs in twenty minutes and the coffees were on him.

"OK, I'll be there," replied Alan rather grumpily. He was carrying a nagging hangover headache.

The *Ecole Normale* was a large imposing building, one of the better schools in Mons until the RAF had acquired it on a temporary basis. However, it was cold and austere with tall windows. The walls were painted a pale eau de nil colour and the blackboards were still in place. One of the two halls had been converted into a restaurant and canteen area. The other hall was used as a keep fit and games room for billiards and table tennis. Most of the downstairs classrooms were now offices or storerooms for radio detection and surveillance kit. Upstairs, served by a wide winding staircase decorated with an Art Nouveau style balustrade, were the other rooms that served as sleeping quarters. It was from one of these that Alan emerged, walking quickly and skipping down the marble stairwell to meet Harry in the canteen. Two aspirins had solved the headache. Harry was sitting with a WAAF already drinking coffee.

"Meet Assistant Leader Kate Harrison. She's attached to 72 Signals. She comes from a place called Fenny something or other near Nuneaton." The young fresh-faced blonde smiled and said, "Fenny Drayton", quickly correcting Harry. Alan grinned and said he knew the place but only because it was on the road to Sibson and *the Cock Inn* where he'd been a few times with his family after Sunday afternoon rides in the country. It's the place where legend has it that Dick Turpin used to frequent the place and hide his horse Black Bess when he was wanted by the law.

Harry had already told Kate about the awful incident in the morning. She expressed her shock and sorrow and hoped they would not be too upset by the tragedy.

"I've invited Kate to the bash tonight. She's agreed to be my escort," said Harry. Alan winked at Harry and smiled.

"I guess I'll be the one on my own then," said Alan. Kate touched Alan's hand and said she'd be more than happy for the pair of them to escort her. Harry gave Alan a slightly disapproving glance, so Alan said he'd prefer not to play gooseberry. However, Kate insisted.

George and Zac appeared and strolled across the canteen shouting, "It's time to get spruced up guys; it'll soon be party time!" They waved and disappeared.

"I guess we should be doing the same," said Alan. Kate got up to leave, agreeing to meet the two of them at 19.30 hours. Harry checked that the records and the gramophone had been collected and deposited in the Waux-Hall. Alan darted over to the stores and made sure that the wine and beer had been transported and received without delay.

Odette's eyes lit up as she and her parents walked into the *Parc du Waux-Hall* off the Avenue Reine Astrid. It was a large imposing faux manor that offered a dance hall, theatre and offices. It was partly decorated to the exterior in dark red, reminiscent of 19th century French Parisienne style. The two women arrived just after 19:00 hours as a few staff were busy preparing tables and hanging balloons and streamers. Above the entrance someone had hung a huge banner with the words 'Happy Days are back'.

Fernand hung around for a few minutes after hugging Laure and Odette. He then disappeared and walked home which was less than twenty minutes away. He was not in the best of moods when he arrived, having trod in something very smelly whilst taking a short cut across the grass lawns in the *Parc du Waux-Hall*.

Mother and daughter entered the building and were delighted to see young Jacqueline and her mother Julia.

"What a lovely surprise, and so good to meet you both. How come you managed to get an invitation?" asked Laure.

"We were 'recruited' by one of our neighbours. I think you know her, Madame Jose Devereaux, wife of Hector. They are already

179

helping place tables and chairs."

"Oh yes, I can see them," said Laure and she waved. Odette and Jacqueline chatted before Julia escorted them to the catering tables set out in a line. To their left was a low table with the Gramophone player and a huge stack of 78s ready to play.

"Will you help me?" asked Odette, turning to Jacqueline who had just celebrated her tenth birthday two days before.

"Of course, I'd love to. Oh and by the way, you look absolutely beautiful. I love that dress. You really look like a Paris model!"

Odette giggled and mentioned that Jacqueline also looked pretty. Odette was dressed in a dark blue woven georgette midi-length dress with a star pattern print in cream. It had a cowl neck, short puff sleeves and a simple matching tie around her waist. She wore seamed dark stockings and high heels and had spent much time with powder puffs, dark pencil eyeliners and Helena Rubenstein red lipstick. Jacqueline wore a dark red skirt and a peasant-style white blouse. They were both so attractive that their mothers were nervous, knowing the place would soon be full of excitable and mischievous young men.

Odette busied herself with the record player. It was already plugged into a crude electrical wiring system and when switched on crackled into life. She tried a couple of 78s, which seemed to work without a hitch. Even the sound was loud enough for such a large room although the quality was a little daunting. Her mother and Julia were already laying out copious amounts of food. It ran in the face of all the rationing so they were surprised and delighted that the Americans had managed to persuade the local shops to help out. There were terrines of cold meats, salads, cheeses, a large tureen of soup on a heater, a large dish full of chicken Maryland, a large side of pork, bread and, for some, the first sight of butter in two years. Another table displayed endless patisserie, tarts, cakes and éclairs. The Americans had also insisted on ice cream so there was a cold box containing blocks of various flavours. Another table contained all the coffee-making essentials.

Next to all this was a very long table which held all the glasses for drinks, 5 barrels of Pilsner, endless bottles of red wine, some spirits and fruit drinks. Alan's contribution towards American tastes included Sodas, Sarsaparilla, Cola Cola and after a struggle finding it, Dr Swett's original Root Beer .

At precisely 20:00 hours, Odette placed her first 78 on the HMV deck just as a few guests started to arrive. She chose Ella Fitzgerald and the Ink Spots playing 'I'm making believe'. The first through the doors were the Americans. They were a mix of air and ground crew, smartly dressed in their uniforms. They walked in singing loudly and uninhibited, with happy, beaming faces. Most were smoking. The RAF arrived looking very smart in their uniforms, inviting good-natured boos and catcalls from the Americans. The Englishmen were generally more reserved and kept to themselves. In amongst them were Alan and Harry who joined a few friends sitting at the rear of the hall. Zac and George, already quaffing beer, joined them. Harry left Kate and disappeared towards the bar. George turned to Alan.

"Is that Harry's broad? I though he had a girl back home."

"He thought so to, until he had a 'Dear John' letter yesterday," replied Alan. "Seems she's found someone else. Doesn't take long for Harry to charm the ladies though." George and Zac laughed just as Harry returned with a collection of drinks.

"Would you like to dance?" Harry offered his hand to Kate and the two of them joined the crowd attempting the Jitterbug to the Benny Goodman song 'Peckin'.

Alan and Zac were joined by a couple of WAAFs who wanted to know if they would like to chat. The conversation lasted about five minutes until the music suddenly stopped and everyone came to a standstill wondering what had happened. There were a few attempts to re-start the music judging by some horrendous scratchy noises coming from the far side. All of a sudden, there was an announcement in poor English by a woman's voice with an attractive French accent.

"Is there anyone in the room who can mend the gramophone?"

Harry, who had returned to the table, stood up and shouted, "There's a chap over here that can do it!" He turned to Alan and said, "Off you go Al, you're our Mr Mend-it!"

Alan was horrified and turned red as he stood up. George and Zac clapped and the crowd joined in making way as he headed towards the table where the music had come from.

"Merci Monsieur! I am so grateful for your help."

Alan looked up suddenly realised that he was staring at the tall brunette he'd remembered from the Grand Place. She was smiling.

"I seem to recognise you," she said.

Alan took her hand as she helped him over a box at the end of the table and replied, "I saw you the other day as my tram passed you. I think you were with an elderly man."

"Yes, that was my father. My name is Odette. What is yours?"

"Alan, but my friends call me Al."

"Then instead, if you don't mind, I shall call you Alain. Do you think you can fix the music?"

"I'll do my best," said Alan blushing slightly.

Alan's concentration was compromised. He quickly realised that the problem with the record player was simply a short in the electrical plug, which he fixed in a couple of minutes. On the other hand, he was kneeling next to a girl who he'd already determined was the most beautiful thing he'd ever seen. Alan's palms were damp and clammy. He'd already blushed when he realised that Odette was watching him. He turned to speak but couldn't. Nothing came out. He simply looked into her eyes and it was reciprocated.

"It's working okay for now," he said. "You should have no more trouble but, if you do, just shout out for me." She touched his hand, looking at him intently whilst saying thank you in good English. Odette's cheeks were flushed just as her mother approached.

"Are you going to introduce me to our hero?" asked Laure.

"Oh yes Mama, this is Alain an English airman. He's staying in my old school at the *Ecole Normale*." Laure stepped forward and shook Alan's hand. She could not speak English, so Odette translated after her mother also expressed her thanks.

"I'd better get back to my friends over there," said Alan. "It has been really good to meet you, Odette. Perhaps we can arrange to meet again soon?"

"Yes, I'd like that very much," she said. Without hesitation he leaned forward and gallantly kissed the back of her hand before whispering in her ear, "You are charming and very beautiful." She blushed bright red.

"He's a handsome young man," said Laure to Odette. "I could tell you liked him, but please don't get your hopes up. He's English and the English are fighting a war. Anyway, maybe you are too young for that sort of thing."

"Mama, I'll make up my own mind." Odette looked determined and responded by reminding her mother that she was also very young when she met Papa.

Jacqueline joined Odette. She was curious even though still young.

"Who was that? He's a really handsome man."

"He's called Alain and he seems kind and a true gentleman."

"But you don't know what he's really like, do you?"

"No, of course I don't know him, but we are keen to meet each other soon. He's tall and I love his eyes - so intense, blue and kind." Odette could not stop smiling, particularly when she spotted Alan looking at her through the crowd.

"Harry, I've just met the girl of my dreams."

"Really?" said Harry. "Tell me about it." Kate listened in.

"Do you remember that I mentioned I'd seen a beautiful Belgian girl in the Grand Place the other day?"

"Err, yes, I think so," responded Harry.

"Well, she's here! She's the one playing the music and the girl who asked for help when the gramophone broke down. Thanks for calling me out Harry, you've done me a massive favour and I will always be in your debt."

Kate smiled and reached over to touch Alan's hand.

"She's clearly impressed you Alan and I hope things will workout. It's about time you had some luck with the ladies."

"I'd like to think so," said Alan. "We've expressed a wish to see each other again."

"Well done old chap, that's spiffing good news and you deserve a drink," said Harry.

A few others had joined them. Harry suggested that Alan should go and ask permission from the girl's mother to meet her daughter again and, "If she says 'yes', you must buy her a bunch of flowers. That's the proper way to do it."

Alan agreed that was a good idea. He could not get Odette out of his mind. He turned to Harry and said, "It's best to strike while the iron's hot!" He asked Harry to write a note in French on the back of a serviette. It read 'Will you please allow me to meet your daughter tomorrow at mid-day outside the Hotel de Ville?' Harry looked puzzled but agreed. Alan stood up and grabbed some flowers from the next table.

"That crazy man is going to do it now!" exclaimed Harry.

Alan approached the long catering table and saw Odette with her mother. He handed Laure the note and the flowers and waited for a response. Odette was looking at him and smiling.

"Odette, this young man wants to meet you tomorrow. I don't know what to say or do. Your father will not like it but he's such a nice polite man though."

Odette pleaded with her mother to persuade her father to agree. "OK, I'll talk to him but it will not be easy." Odette hugged her mother and turned to Alan.

"I'd love to meet you but it depends on Papa. He's coming to

184

meet us in about half an hour so he can walk us home."

Alan's heart skipped as he responded. "How will I know about his decision which just has to be OK or I'll be sad forever?" he asked.

"I'll come to you before we leave." She leaned towards him, her perfume hanging close, whispering so that her mother could not hear, "You are very handsome Alain. I would hate to make you sad." Odette giggled as Alan turned bright red.

He waved and blew her a kiss as he returned to Harry and Kate. Odette skipped and placed another 78 on the deck. She played a particular favourite by Ella Fitzgerald called 'I've got a feeling I'm falling.' She would have loved to dance with him but she doubted her mother would approve. Anyway, the others were so busy and who would change the records?

Alan and Harry's table finished off the food they'd fetched earlier. Some of the dancers were getting boisterous. The Americans in particular knew all about swing and showed off. It was 22:30 hours when Odette approached Alan's table with her mother and father in tow.

"I can meet you tomorrow Alain. My parents have agreed but only consented if they are chaperones. I hope that will be alright?" Alan stood up to thank Laure and Fernand in his terrible French, making both of them laugh.

"Yes of course," said Alan. "Anything to see you again."

She smiled and walked away with her parents, glancing back frequently and smiling. "See you tomorrow Alain."

With no music, the dance hall began to quieten down. People sat around chatting amicably, finishing off their drinks.

"Well, I'd say this has been a very successful evening," said Harry. Kate agreed and Alan just sat back and grinned from cheek to cheek. Several Americans came over and thanked them for helping organise the dance.

"Al, that girl is simply fantastic," said Harry. "I hope it goes well for both of you. No more broken hearts, eh!"

185

Kate looked at Harry and knew he was thinking about Daisy. She gave him a hug and asked him to take her outside for a walk. On his way out later, Alan saw them silhouetted in the moonlight, kissing under the spreading branches of a huge beech tree. It made him feel strangely very happy.

When Odette reached home, her parents persuaded her to listen to their thoughts, although she had an idea what they might be. Earlier at the Waux-Hall, her mother and father had engaged in a heated discussion, an argument that was won by her mother. However, Fernand was not too happy. He was the first to speak.

"You are only eighteen with no experience of foreign men or any men. He looks like a nice enough young man but the English are different from us. I know that, after meeting several in the last war. You may not like some of their customs and they are a different religion. Your mother has persuaded me to go easy because you have to meet men to find out what they are like and gain some experience. That's fair enough, but I will never allow any man to hurt my girl. You will need a very sensible head on your shoulders. Also, the war is not over yet. There are still many dangers and he may well get caught up in further fighting. I will allow you to see him but if things become serious, your mother and I will need to discuss matters again. For the moment, let's just say that you are friends and let's just leave it at that."

Laure agreed, although secretly she knew that both Odette and Alan had met as if destiny had brought them together. Her feminine instincts and knowledge of her daughter made it feel that their coming together was somehow natural and right.

Odette said very little but did mention that she was old enough and experienced enough to make her own decisions, especially after witnessing events in the last four years. She thanked them both and got up to go to her bedroom.

"She takes after you Fernand. She's stubborn. I know you want to protect her but I think, maybe, she has discovered love."

"Nonsense," he said, "it's much to soon for all of that!"

"We'll see!" Laure looked fondly at her husband.

The next day, a Sunday, Alan was up early. He'd hardly slept, thinking about Odette. At 08:00 hours he made his way down to breakfast. Harry was already there tucking into slices of toast and drinking coffee. Alan joined him and helped himself to a cup from Harry's Cafetière. "Oi, do you mind, get your own pal," said Harry. Alan was still beaming.

"You look like the cat who got the cream, Al! Don't tell me, you're besotted. No don't bother, I can already tell!"

"Harry, I've never been so nervous in all my life. Something tells me this girl is perfect. I can't stop thinking about her."

"Al, for goodness sake you hardly know her. A meeting at the dance and somehow everything falls into place? Life is not that straight forward. You must try and get a grip on reality. We may be whisked off to some distant place. The Japs haven't been defeated yet. We could end up in the far east."

"You're a bundle of fun this morning, Harry Silver! Anyway, how about Kate, surely it's the same for you and her."

"I guess so, but I think I'm a little more resilient with the fairer sex. It's more of a casual thing with me, at least until the war is over. You are really quite sensitive, the creative type and I wouldn't like to see you hurt. Go and have some fun. Find out what she's like and if it all works out, then fine. I'll be the first to say congratulations!"

"Christ! It sounds like you've already married us off. I'm not stupid old chap and do intend to take it one step at a time."

"Then that's fine," said Harry" giving Alan a wink

At 09:00 hours, Alan received a hand-written message via a duty sergeant. A Belgian man had delivered it.

'Dear Alan, my parents have suggested it would be much easier if you came to my house at 13:00 hours instead of meeting in the Grand Place. The address is 10, Chaussée De Beaumont. I hope you'll say yes as I'm looking forward to seeing you again.' It was signed by Odette.

187

Alan excitedly looked on a wall map for the location and realised it was only a short walk from Boulevard Dolez. From the King Baudouin statue, he had to head up the Avenue Reine Astride past the *Waux-Hall* and then climb the Avenue de Binche until he reached a sweeping right hand road called Chaussée De Beaumont.

At 12:55, the bell rang. Odette opened the front door and there stood Alan in a fashionable tweed jacket, white shirt, blue tie, dark grey trousers and polished black brogues. He was carrying two bunches of flowers and a small packet of cigars.

"Please come in and meet my parents," said Odette beaming. He thought she looked even more beautiful that the evening before.

"I'm so glad you received the letter. My father decided it was more appropriate that you come here. He delivered the note early this morning. Oh, what beautiful flowers!"

"There's some for your mother and the roses are for you." She looked at him and reached up to hug him. The smell of her perfume excited him and he blushed.

"The other flowers are for your mother and, not wanting to leave your father out, I managed to find some cigars in a Tabac in the Marche Aux Poissons." The two of them were so excited that they could not stop talking. It was obvious that they were rapidly becoming more than just friends.

"Mama, Papa, Alain is here." She took him through the hallway, across the front sitting room with impressive dark oak furniture, into the back dining room. Laure and Fernand were waiting. Alan shook their hands and presented the peace offerings.

"Oh, they are so beautiful. You are very kind Alain," said Laure.

Alan did not understand too much French but made an effort to say it was his pleasure, only it came out as 'I hope you find them with many of my pleasures'! It broke the ice. They were delighted and amused at the same time.

Fernand shook Alan's hand and Odette translated that he was very moved by Alan's kind gesture.

He motioned for Alan to follow him into the garden. Odette accompanied him while Laure went to prepare something special to eat. Alan remarked on the delicious smells coming from the kitchen.

Fernand was keen to show Alan the results of his hard work and took time to explain with Odette's translations that he'd recently managed to grow leeks, potatoes, carrots, onions, garlic and, his pride and joy, strawberries, although they wouldn't be ready until next June.

The stable fascinated Alan with its strong musty odours along with farming and gardening tools. There was even an old leather shire horse harness and halter.

"We used to have a pig called Adolf in here but we had to get rid of him," said Odette. Alan laughed out loud, so much so that Fernand was startled.

"The Englishman has got a good, hearty, amusing laugh," said Fernand. "I'm wondering what was so funny?" Odette replied that she'd told Alain the story of Adolf.

They stepped out of the stable just as Laure shouted from the kitchen. "Quickly, it's ready!"

Odette giggled and just at that moment, Misky, her dog, ran up and sat on Alan's feet. "Oh, you've woken up have you?" she said. "I guess it's feeding time." She stooped down and picked him up.

Alan stroked him and the dog licked his hand.

"He likes you," she said. "He's obviously got excellent taste!" Alan laughed and they followed Fernand into the veranda under its grape vines and into the back room. Odette brushed Alan's hand with hers and he held it and squeezed it for a brief moment. She looked at him with soft eyes and knew right then that she was falling for this gentle-natured English airman.

On the table Laure had prepared an impressive spread. Alan's eyes grew wide when he spotted four plates of Crocque Madames, some cheeses, a few galettes, plus an array of glazed fruit tarts and a fabulous lemon meringue.

189

Odette translated when Alan enthusiastically mentioned that this was much better than going to a café on the Grand Place. Laurethanked him and yet sounded apologetic saying that food was still very difficult to come by due to rationing. She and Fernand had managed to persuade some friends who owned shops to let them have a few extras. After trying out the different foods, most of which were new to him, Alan was left with nothing but praise for the chef.

"So, tell me about yourself," said Fernand. He was deliberately trying to discover something about Alan's background. Alan responded with a potted history of his adventures in the RAF, his family and life back home. Odette, although mesmerised, translated everything quickly as he spoke.

Laure made coffee and Fernand placed a bottle of Triple Sec spirits on the table.

"We should drink to peace, prosperity and friendship," said Fernand. They chinked their glasses, repeating santé four times. Alan then mentioned he was curious to know how they had managed under German occupation, adding that they must have suffered badly. Over the next forty minutes or so and more Triple Secs, Odette, with constant references to her parents, recalled the last four years.

Alan was staggered by the stories, tragedies and difficulties they had encountered. At one point, he nearly took hold of Odette's hand but though better of it.

"Mama, Papa, do you mind if Alain and I take a quick walk. I'd like to show him the Bascule and I need some fresh air." Alan smiled coyly at her.

Fernand hesitated, looked at Laure who smiled and said, "Only if it really is a quick walk otherwise we'll come and find you!"

As they left and banged the front door shut, Misky launched himself at the door and started barking.

"He's so protective of me," Odette said, "and hates it when I

190

leave. He'll be okay in a short while. I could tell when Misky took to you earlier that you like dogs and they like you."

"Yes, I do love dogs. I think they are very special. My father has a couple of black Scotties. One of them, Jamie, is over protective. He once chased the postman from the house and actually ripped a hole in his trousers. It was so embarrassing!" Odette laughed especially when Alan made an impressive growling noise.

They crossed the Avenue de Binche just as René Leonard drove past and hooted. Odette waved vigorously and smiled.

"Who was that?" asked Alan curiously.

"Oh, he's a good family friend who was with us on the march. He lives just a few doors away from here." They arrived at the Bascule and stood in silence as Alan read the inscriptions on the memorial. It paid tribute to the Canadian and English soldiers who had defended Mons during the 1st World War.

Odette turned to Alan, her dark hazel eyes looking into his.

"We have much to be grateful for. Many of your countrymen died for our freedom during the retreat from Mons in 1914 and here you are again helping us. We are in your debt."

Alan took her hand and squeezed it tightly. She smiled and did not try to extract it.

"You really are so very beautiful," said Alan drawing her closer. "I can't stop thinking about you. Oh goodness me, I've never felt these feelings before but now I'm afraid you'll think I'm being too forward and too obvious, but please will you be my girl?"

Odette took a step closer and put her middle finger on Alan's lips and whispered, "You talk too much Alain." She reached up and kissed him passionately. He felt his head spin as they held each other closely for what seemed an eternity.

"I feel the same," she said. "I have felt this way from the moment we met at the dance and now I think about you too, every moment, my English RAF man. I don't want this moment to end."

Alan felt himself welling up and knew his emotions were very

191

close to overpowering his instincts to remain calm and in control. They both wanted to speak at the same time but ended up laughing. Odette had tears of joy in her eyes and her face gave way to a flush of love that just wanted to leap out.

"We must meet again soon," she said. Alan rapidly agreed and was then reminded by Odette that they would, in all probability, have to be chaperoned by her parents.

"I don't care," said Alan. "I want to be with you as much as our circumstances will allow, no matter what or who tries to stop me."

They kissed again before Alan looked at his watch and said with regret, "Your parents may come looking if we don't hurry and get back soon."

They walked back holding hands glancing frequently at each other with giggles and smiles.

The time flew by. Alan left at 17:00 hours after thanking his hosts for a wonderful afternoon. He had arranged to meet Odette two days later at mid-day in the Grand Place. She wanted to show him the Cathedral of St Waudrau and hoped they would have time to walk to the top of the Belfry. She had a two-hour break whereas Alan had only one hour, but he was confident he could steal one more hour.

Her parents had elected to leave them alone on the doorstep. Alan put his hand in his pocket, pulled out a penny and gave it to her. At first she was puzzled, but when he said that in England there was an expression 'A penny for your thoughts', she understood and slipped it into her purse. Alan reached over and kissed her goodbye. She waved as he walked away and blew him a kiss. He reciprocated.

"I'm in love Harry, really in love!" It was Monday morning and Alan was sitting with Harry in the *Ecole Normale* canteen. Harry was reading some papers but looked up and said, "Go on then, tell me all about it." Alan described the previous afternoon's few hours.

"Sounds like the fruit trees are beginning to blossom Al." Alan chuckled at another of Harry's engaging expressions.

"I've just been reading through our next schedule. You know that gun laying system, the TRU (Transportable Radio Unit) we set up in La Roche recently? The Yanks want us to help set up four more around Malmedy and two near Bastogne. Something is in the air, pal, and I'm getting a bad feeling it's to do with potential action down in the Ardenne forests."

Alan looked puzzled. "I thought we were told that Montgomery, Patton and Bradley had got it all sewn up and driven the Jerries back beyond the border."

"They have, but it won't stop that madman Hitler from trying something! Anyway, I have our orders for the week and we have to be in meetings most of today, starting in about ten minutes. Looks like we'll be travelling to site on Friday. Alan looked at Harry's papers and noted that in the following week they'd be away at least four days, maybe five

"Not much opportunity to see Odette," he said. Harry reminded Alan that duties came first and girls came second.

"Well at least I have some time tomorrow."

"Well, yes and no," said Harry. "Don't forget Sqd. Leader Mike Rolands and the Chaplain, Rev. John Lloyd, are going to be here early. They want to inspect the facilities and maybe ensure that we are still of the faith and say our prayers!"

Alan looked thoughtful. "I'm meeting Odette in the Grand Place at mid-day tomorrow and I'll ask the AOC for an extra hour."

"Good luck pal," said Harry.

The day passed quickly enough and proved to be mind numbingly boring. Talks about radio potential, alternative detection methods, technical advancements and new calculations required to establish more accurate co-ordinates wasn't exactly on anyone's favourite list. At 16:00 hours, a few of the Americans including Zac and George, who was suffering from a cold, decided they needed to restore sanity with a few drinks and a game of darts. They'd pestered Alan and Harry for days about the English pub game and wanted to have a go. Someone noted that it was getting colder and the old heating boiler in the basement needed to be turned up.

After an evening playing darts and having a good time with the Americans who gave up darts and converted to poker, Alan and Harry retired to the mess where they wrote a few letters and read a few magazines. Alan wrote to his sister and effused about Odette, letting Barbara know he'd met the most wonderful girl and her parents. Kate joined Harry later and the two of them disappeared for a long walk.

At 10, Chaussée De Beaumont, Laure had detected a change in her daughter. She knew that Odette was serious about Alan but she harboured a secret dread. Fernand was not so aware, hoping that things would eventually subside when the RAF boys returned to England. Laure had spent an hour sitting on the edge of Odette's bed asking her how she felt. Odette always trusted her mother to keep things between them, so she simply told her that the two of them were falling in love. Laure was quite taken aback and found it hard to believe that it could happen so quickly.

"Are you positive? Are you really sure?" she asked.

"Yes Mama, I'm sure. We will of course take it easy, but Alain feels the same way."

"You've had little experience with men, ma cherie. How can you trust him?"

"We shall spend time getting to know each other, but please be assured that destiny has brought us together. I've witnessed the good and bad in men as you know, but in this case my instincts tell me it is right and proper."

"What happens if he goes back to England? How will that end up? He may have a girl over there and you may never see him again."

"Mama, let's cross one bridge at a time. Who knows, I believe we are realistic enough to understand that the war is not yet over and anything can happen. My wish is that you and Papa will understand and allow us to enjoy our friendship and love whether it turns out to be short or long term."

Tuesday morning brought a change in the weather. It was bright and unusually warm as a ridge of high pressure rapidly moved up from France. At 08:30 hours, Alan was asked to meet Sqd. Leader MikeRolands in the Officer's Mess. He greeted Alan amicably, asking if he was fully settled in and whether there were any missing facilities. Alan responded by saying he'd mended the boiler timer clock but the boiler itself was not really capable of heating the entire building.

"I hear you're a dab hand at fixing things. You might like to think about taking a look at my staff car outside. It makes the most awful racket when idling. If you can sort it out old chap, I'll think about supplying a new boiler. Now dear boy, is there anything else I can help you with even if my capacity for generating favours these days is often limited?"

"Well yes Sir, there is. I'm due to meet someone at mid-day and I might need an extra hour if that's alright Sir?" Alan purposely didn't mention he was meeting a girl, as it may not have gone down too well.

"Err, that might be bit tricky, but if it's that important you'd better take the extra hour. Mind you, I expect an excellent job in fixing my car. It's my pride and joy so treat her like a beautiful woman! And make sure you're not a minute late."

"Thanks, Sir. I'll get on to the car right away."

"Good man, Flt. Sergeant." Alan saluted and went to find Harry.

An hour later, with Harry's help, Alan had sorted out the car, a large Citroen Traction Avant Cabriolet. He'd taken the carburettor apart, the distributor and adjusted the dynamo mountings before cleaning all the parts. Harry stood idly by smoking and handing out tools until Alan told him he preferred not to be incinerated as there was a real danger with cigarette sparks and petrol.

At 10:30 hours the inspection started, but for nearly forty minutes, Rev John Lloyd kept them occupied with passages read from the bible, hoping that examples from the scriptures would help them in the coming months. Sqd. Leader Mike Rolands who wanted to thank him for his excellent work on the car embarrassingly singled out Alan. He winked at him and whispered, "The new boiler is on its way."

The town clock chimed mid-day followed by Carillon bells. Alan arrived at the Hotel de Ville a few minutes early. He watched a double carriage tram wind its way around the square and disappear up the Rue D'Enghien. He considered taking out a cigarette but thought better of it when Odette appeared and waved. She ran towards him and hugged him, planting a big kiss on his lips but then stepped back with a giggle and used her right hand to partly hide her mouth.

Alan took her hand and asked her if something was wrong.

"No, no my love, it's just that I forgot that my parents are over there in Café *Chez Saey*. They must have seen us!"

"I don't really care," said Alan. "I can't even begin to tell you how much I've thought about you and could not wait to see you again. However, we must respect your parents' wishes and, if that means being tactful and discreet for their sake, then so be it."

They walked out into the Grand Place linking arms. Odette was radiant. Her long dark hair was contained under a fashionable wide brimmed hat. To Alan she was a goddess, a Hollywood star and even a Renaissance angel. They chatted and laughed as they approached *Chez Saey*, Odette's head resting on Alan's shoulder.

Laure and Fernand were talking with some other people who they knew. Alan, apologising for his rude interruption, was the first to speak. Odette stood by ready to translate but she did not need to.

"Hello to you both. I'm so happy to meet you once again." His French, apart from a serious accent issue, was word perfect. He'd borrowed a book the night before called 'Speak French in a day' from one of the WAAFs. Odette clapped and patted Alan on the shoulder. Laure stood up and broke into a big smile before giving

196

him a big hug. Fernand was also smiling and held Alan's shoulder whilst shaking is hand warmly.

"Well done Alain," he said. "Your French is improving greatly."

"Mama, Papa, we are going to the Cathedral. Do you want to come along with us?"

Before her mother could say anything, Alan jumped in and said "I would prefer that you did, if it's okay with you?" Odette was taken aback but translated. Her parents looked at each other with approving expressions and were clearly more than happy. Before they went, Fernand asked if Alan and Odette would like to join them and Laure for an omelette aux fines herbes and a glass of red wine. They agreed and Alan mentioned he'd managed to get an extra hour off. Fernand disappeared to find a waiter.

Laure was smiling. She was impressed with this kind, thoughtful and respectful Englishman. She was also feeling great happiness after seeing the pair of them so natural and clearly in tune with each other and did not admonish her daughter over the constant touching, whispering and mutual spellbound gazes. Fernand, on the other hand, was not so impressed. On his return, he saw his daughter and Alan sneak a quick kiss whilst Laure was distracted. He caught Odette's eyes and held up a finger. She knew it was a warning sign and blushed.

After the meal they set off walking in front of Laure and Fernand but hardly dared to touch as Alan imagined Odette's father would be scrutinising their every move.

The interior of the Collegiate Church of Sainte Waudrau was bigger than Alan imagined. He was impressed with its Gothic architecture, its harmony, elegance and balance, which inspired a feeling of awe. The complex and ornate decorations and light masonry made him think of fine lace. Hidden away in a corner he saw a golden ornately decorated carriage, which Odette explained, was the centrepiece of an annual festival called the 'Dou Dou'.

"Every year the people of Mons take to the streets and converge on the Grand Place where St George kills the Dragon. It's such a joyous, happy occasion. Everyone laughs, sings and dances. It hasn't happened since 1939 because of the occupation." She grabbed his arm and pleaded, "Please, please Alain, be here next year so we can both watch it and take part in the event together."

"I'd be delighted and will do all I can my love," said Alan. Odette suddenly realised he had called her his love and making sure that mother and father were not in sight, she looked into his eyes and whispered, "I like it when you call me 'my love'."

They emerged into sunshine and decided there was enough time to visit the Belfry. Odette's father decided that climbing to the top of its eighty-seven metres was not for him and Laure. He had been given a day off work so he and Laure made up their minds to catch the 90 tram and head back home to do some gardening. Fernand was not too concerned, knowing that Alan and his daughter had to be back at work within the next hour, but he did tell Odette to be discrete.

"It's a long way up," said Alan. He was behind Odette on the narrow stone steps of the spiral stair well. They both grasped a wall rope and climbed towards the top.

They reached the top out of breath and stood looking over the landscape. Odette moved closer to him still panting from the exertion. He put his arm around her and she snuggled up to keep warm while explaining the various landmarks.

"Over there is where the Germans arrived in 1914 and over there is the Borinage and the old coal mines." Alan gently turned her head to face his.

"You talk too much, Odette," he said and then kissed her.

They merged into one as emotions took over. He could detect her heartbeat and feel her gentle hands on his face. Their tongues met in the full passion of their feelings and he let his hand slide down to caress her hips.

She pulled him closer, still looking in his eyes. "Alain, my darling, I love you."

His hands caressed her face as he whispered, "Odette, I love you too with all my heart and always will." The words flowed easily, and connecting perfectly with her own feelings.

They spent ten minutes just holding each other. There were tears in their eyes and they instinctively knew that nothing on earth would ever tear them apart and this is how it should be. They were also scared that a commitment might end up with heartbreak if the war got in the way.

Alan looked at his watch just as Odette opened his hand and gave him a piece of paper neatly folded up.

"Don't read it now my love, take it back and when you are lying on your bed tonight read it and think of me. I'll be holding your penny and thinking of you."

He kissed her and broke away when they heard voices. "There's someone coming up the steps." A minute later, a couple of young boys appeared. They politely said "Hello Monsieur and Mademoiselle" and carried on around the viewing platform.

"We must be getting back. We've got about twenty minutes," said Alan. "I'm not sure when we can meet again this week, my darling, as there is a new intensive schedule. Also, I'll be away all next week working near Namur."

Odette looked disappointed so Alan suggested they could meet on Thursday at the same place at mid-day. "I'll have something to give you and please let's exchange photographs when we meet."

They descended the stone steps holding hands. Alan took the lead and turned to see if she was all right. He could not help notice her long shapely legs, clad in dark stockings, perfect figure and beauty. These images became engraved in his heart and mind.

After they reached the Grand Place, Alan escorted Odette to her office but only after she insisted on them both rubbing the head of a small cast-iron monkey, sitting on a wall outside the Hotel de Ville.

"When we rub the monkey's head, it will bring us good luck

and make our wishes come true," said Odette. "It's a very old legend but it really does work." They rubbed the worn head vigorously and then tried again together with their hands together. Odette giggled when Alan asked her what she'd wished for. She looked into his eyes and with a huge grin said she'd tell him one day. She skipped away, waving furiously and throwing kisses, before disappearing up the stairs to her office.

She arrived at her desk, just as one of the girls, Justine Lagarde, giggled and whispered to her that some of the others had seen her looking happy with a handsome man in an RAF uniform. Odette confided in the girls that she was 'stepping out' with Alain.

Later, Alan lay on his bed and opened the note from Odette. It was a poem beautifully written in English. It occurred to him that his French was woefully inadequate and he must make an effort to understand and speak the language. He felt ashamed, but his heart was ready to burst as he read it over and over again. He would keep this poem forever.

'I see a million stars beyond the sky
But one shines brighter, I can't deny
It lights up a heartfelt love so true
A love that flows from me to you
The angels sing when you are near
Within your arms I have no fear
You make me love you in a special way
Just talking to you lights up my day
I love you my Alain with all my heart
Together, forever and never to part.'

That night, Alan went to sleep at 11:00 hours with a smile on his face and woke up the next morning at 07:00 hours with the same expression. He could not wait for Thursday.

Two days later, they met again as the carillons were chiming mid-day. They walked around the Jardins du Mayeur and found a dark corner where they embraced and chatted excitedly. As promised, Alan produced the surprise for Odette. It was a pen and ink drawing of the Belfry and written across the bottom he'd written: *'To my Odette with all my love'*. She was so moved by the picture that she wept. He held her tightly for a few moments and they kissed before Odette said they'd better go and join her father who was probably waiting impatiently at *Chez Saey*. On the way they exchanged a few photographs.

Alan and Odette met on many occasions during October and November, more often than not accompanied by her parents. Alan's duties in Mons and various sites closer to the war zones in Southern Belgium meant their time together was compromised. Whenever they met, it was a joy with emotions and passions unleashed. Odette was showing a growing concern about Alan's activities so close to the American and British attempts to roll the Germans back. He reassured her with statements like, "Our chaps are not trained for battle. They would not involve us as we'd only get in the way. Our job is simply to set up detection units to the rear of any action." Odette knew that it wasn't that simple and he was only trying to allay her fears. She was very much aware that Hitler was more than capable of ordering a counter attack at any time.

During a period of six weeks heading towards winter, the weather, influenced by Siberia, took a turn for the worst. It became colder, windy and sleet appeared towards the end of November. Alan and Odette managed to visit her wider family and friends who were more than impressed by Odette's choice of companion. It was a happy time. On a couple of occasions, Laure and Fernand hosted dinners. Fernand often expressed more than a little irritation after watching too many eager drinkers deprive him of his precious bottles of St Emilion.

For them both it was a difficult time. There were still many dangers in the outskirts of Mons, meaning they had to always be on their guard. Alan's policy was to stick closer to the town centre and avoid narrow backstreets or poorly lit areas. On one occasion, as he was walking with Odette along the Rue de Nimy towards the Grand

Place, they heard shutters banging in the wind and heard what Alansaid was the click of a bolt action rifle. They put it down to the banging shutters, but two days later there was an incident near the railway station that brought the dangers closer to home and worried Alan about Odette's safety.

One morning in early December, Harry and Alan were handed a report by a duty Sergeant. The news was quite startling. Sqd. Leader Mike Rolands had ordered all personnel to remain grounded for two days whilst American military police and soldiers from the 3rd Army scoured the town after it was discovered that a sniper had shot and killed three servicemen.

"That's rotten luck," said Harry. "I was hoping to take Kate to the cinema. It's just re-opened after four years."

"The films will be in French," said Alan grinning.

"That's right, but as you know Kate and I can speak French, although not perfectly."

"I must try to learn French," said Alan. "I've only got a basic schoolboy ability and it isn't good enough. Odette's friends think it's amusing when I try, but it's embarrassing."

"OK," said Harry, "I will converse in French with Kate when you are around. It's the best way. You'll soon pick it up." Alan showed his gratitude by offering Harry a cigarette.

"No swearing though," said Alan. "I wouldn't know if you threw one in. Can you imagine the egg on my face and what Odette would think if I unknowingly dropped one into the conversation?" Harry laughed and winked mischievously at Alan.

"Can't promise I won't," said Harry. He laughed out aloud as Alan stuck up two fingers.

The next day, more news emerged. According to a local courier employed by the RAF, the sniper was a German who was living with two Belgian accomplices. He was soon found and caught hiding in the Rue Du Cappucins but committed suicide when cornered. It seems the two women are strong Rexist supporters. They were shamed in public before being bundled into a wagon and taken away by the Gendarmes.

Alan and Harry met up with Zac and George for a quick lunch in the canteen. They were due to travel to the Florennes air base to pick up much needed replacement equipment but, being grounded, they decided to spend the day playing cards, darts and table tennis. Alan took some time drawing more pictures of Mons, using newspaper photographs as a reference. His reputation as an artist grew particularly when he showed them a portrait of Odette. She'd spent twenty minutes modelling for him a few days before, during one of their mid-day breaks.

"You really do love that girl," said Zac. "I'm so pleased for you and hope it all works out." Alan thanked him and turned as Harry walked in with Kate. She'd just finished exercising with a keep fit class and wanted to go and change, but Harry held her arm and started speaking in French. Alan smiled and tried to respond when asked a question. Harry attempted to get Alan to role his R's. The resulting noise from Alan was a cross between a gargle and a growl. Harry and Kate burst into laughter before she disappeared.

"It's no wonder you make them laugh. Your French is almost incomprehensible!"

In the first week of December temperatures plummeted to -8F. Alan, Harry and a few Americans, including Zac, installed additional radar and detection masts near Sainte Hubert, Rochefort and Tenneville. On the December 16th, all hell broke loose.

The RAF's 109 Squadron, which included Alan and Harry plus 72 Signals, were once again confined to quarters in The *Ecole Normale*. News arrived that the Germans had spearheaded a major offensive in the Ardennes. Hitler, against all advice from many of his senior generals including Walter Model and Gerd von Rundstedt, was determined to break through with his Panzers and cut the Americans off and push the allies west in a race for Brussels and Antwerp. Initially, the American 3rd Battalion 119th Infantry Regiment suffered badly from surprise attacks by the German Sixth

Panzer Army lead by SS-Oberstgruppenführer Sepp Dietrich.

Zac and George plus the other Americans at the *Ecole Normale* were called to their divisional HQ in Dinant. Alan and Harry never saw them again. Stories spread of the massacre of soldiers and civilians at Malmedy and Stavelot, of paratroopers dropping behind the lines and of English-speaking German soldiers, disguised as Americans, capturing critical bridges, cutting communications lines and spreading rumours. For those who had lived through 1940, the picture was all too familiar. Belgian townspeople in the southern Ardennes put away their allied flags and brought out their swastikas.

On Monday December 18th, after some pleading with the Sqd. Leader, Alan was able to escape the confines of the *Ecole Normale* and spend that afternoon and evening with Odette and her parents at their home. He did not bring good news. The battle in the Ardennes was bad enough but he'd received a letter from his sister with the news that George, his father, was very ill and the family wanted Alan to try and spend Christmas in Nuneaton on leave. He asked and was reluctantly granted compassionate leave for two weeks although he hated the idea of leaving Odette behind.

Fernand and Laure had already come to the conclusion that their daughter and Alan were joined together in a deep natural friendship and love. It scared them but they did not show it. Alan had constantly proved that he respected their sensitivities and wishes, which they both greatly appreciated. He'd grown very close to them and they to him. In some ways, he was the son they had lost. "How long will you be away, my love?" enquired Odette. They were standing close together in the veranda under the canopy vines. It was 16:30 hours and over towards the east, the agitated sky took on a dark complexion. Alan looked up and quoted from Shakespeare's Richard III but with more than a hint of distortion, play acting and downright unsophistication.

"Now is the winter of our discontent, made glorious summer by this sunny Belgian beauty. And all the clouds of a war torn land are discarded in such a beauteous passion."

204

He spoke the words with the intensity and the hand-waving gestures of a professional actor as he watched her dark hazel eyes. She was impressed, knowing a little of Shakespeare from school days and she smiled at the well-meaning corruption. He cradled her face in both hands and kissed her with all his built up emotions. Her response was equally intense and a memory he would carry with him whilst they were apart. He then reluctantly replied to Odette's earlier question.

"I'll be away for two weeks," said Alan, "but I'll be back as soon as I can." He whispered in her ear, "I'm going to go crazy missing you my darling, but I'll write as often as I can." She started to cry so Alan held her tightly and was moved by her tears as they were caught in the half-light of the evening sky, sparkling like tiny jewels as they fell upon his shirt.

"Please promise to come back to me, my Alain. Please remember that I love you." She gazed up at him, stepping higher on tiptoes and holding the lapels of his jacket. "Please stay safe and take my love with you wherever you go and let it make you happy every day." She was clearly nervous that something might happen to him. After all, the war was still dragging on.

"I will and remember that there is nothing on this earth that will stop me loving you and nothing will keep us apart."
Misky ran towards them and sat on Alan's shoes looking up at him. He bent down and gently stroked the dog's head. "I'll be back for you too and I'll bring you a special treat," he said. Alan stood up and Odette held him tightly. She was still tearful when he pulled her close and kissed her again. Her dark eyeliner started to smudge in the moist warmth of tears that transferred to Alan's cheek. He tasted her lipstick as they held hands and intertwined their fingers, whispering sweet words of longing in each other's ears, the words that countless lovers express in moments of emotion and passion.

Laure and Fernand had deliberately given them time together andso had disappeared upstairs. When they reappeared, Alan gave them and Odette personal Christmas cards he'd made himself and in each one there was a small, gift-wrapped postcard size drawing. They were not to be opened before Christmas Day. Five minutes later, after emotional goodbyes, Christmas best wishes and warm hugs all round, they stood at the front door waving furiously as Alan slowly walked back towards the Chaussée de Binche, constantly turning to see Odette being comforted by her mother. That evening, he promised himself that on his return he would ask her to marry him.

Chapter 12: A Marriage Made in Mons

Alan climbed into an old USAAF Dakota at Chièvres air base. It was Wednesday morning on December 20th 1944 and the weather was rough. Temperatures hovering near 34°F made hanging around very uncomfortable. There was also a strong gusting cross wind that would make takeoff tricky. The twin Pratt and Whitney engines burst into life and the pilot taxied to the end of the runway waiting for permission to take off by the control tower.

He settled down as the Dakota, or 'Gooney Bird' as the USAAF crews called it, accelerated and after some hairy yawing motions, took off without incident. Once airborne, Alan decided to approach the navigator who was drinking hot coffee from a flask. He was a chatty friendly man from California and was interested to know about Alan's experiences with radio navigation and radar. He offered Alan a swig from his flask, which Alan discovered, contained more than just coffee. "Good old Tennessee Bourbon, just to keep the spirits alive!" the navigator kept repeating.

Alan returned to his seat where he looked out of a window and day dreamed. Visibility was poor, so he took out photographs of Odette and thought about her. The monotony, vibrations and noise stopped him from sleeping but after almost three hours, the Gooney Bird descended and landed at RAF Gatwick where he was able to spend a couple of hours writing to Odette, before taking off again on the last leg to RAF Bramcote. On this trip, three army officers as well as an RAF Lancaster rear gunner who had been wounded in both legs joined him. The conversation was jocular and spirited as all four men were on leave for Christmas and looked forward to seeing friends and family at home. Alan was the only one who didn't, for although he wanted to see his family, particularly his father, he wished his Christmas could have been spent in Mons.

"Alan, thank goodness, it's so good to see you!" It was Barbara who opened the front door of 195 Higham Lane. He'd already passed on his ETA in a phone call from Gatwick to Helen Cross next door. She had installed a telephone after qualifying as a midwife.

"How is he?" asked Alan, referring to his father.

"He's better than a couple of weeks ago, but he's weak. The doctor says that with care and lots of rest he'll be okay."

Alan stood in the hallway amongst his kit bags and breathed a sigh of relief. He had imagined coming home to the worst-case scenario, arriving too late. Alice came down the stairs and greeted him with a warm hug and a kiss on the cheek.

"Oh Mum, I've got so much news to tell you all."

"It's been a long time but before all that, I'll make us all a cup of tea whilst you go and see your father."

George was lying in bed in his pyjamas, propped up on several pillows reading a book. In the old fireplace an electric fire kept the room warm. Smells of carbolic soap, *Germaline* and freshly aired bed sheets hung in the air.

"Hello Dad, how's it going?"

George looked at Alan and smiled. "Glad to see you back safely, son. I'm dying to know all about your adventures in Belgium. Barb tells us you've found a girl. Can't be much of a war on if you can go gallivanting around with the ladies. I'll be down as soon as I can get dressed and then you can tell us all about it." He coughed loudly and spat out sputum and slight traces of blood into a bowl. "Damned lungs need replacing," he said with a chuckle.

Barbara reappeared and said she'd help him with his dressing gown and escort him downstairs.

"Don't fuss girl, I know how to do these things," said George.

She looked at Alan and raised her eyebrows and shrugged in a way that acknowledged their father's independence and stubborn nature. As George struggled to get out of bed, Barbara helped Alan carry his things into the single front bedroom. He lay on the bed for a few minutes and made up his mind to put on a happy face for the sake of his family and in any case it was the season of good will.

Downstairs, Alan walked into the dining room whistling 'Hark The Herald Angels'. Norman, Barbara's boyfriend stood up.

"Hello Alan, good to see you've arrived safely. How's the war going out there?"

"It's not going anywhere really, Norman. It's brutal, cruel and demoralising but the allies are winning despite the best efforts of Adolf Hitler in the Ardennes. I understand that you've managed to help Dad out by working in the Scala."

"Yes that's right, he can't do it all. Gordon has also helped on occasions but he's now got a lady friend called Bess and he's trying to settle down in Rugby. I'm not sure if and when your father will be able to carry on for much longer."

Alan noticed that Norman had piles of magazines and leaflets about Latter Day Saints and Salt Lake City spread on the dining table. He was about to say something when Barbara and George walked in. Alice, carrying a tray of teacups and a large china teapot covered with a brightly coloured woollen cosy, followed them in.

"Goodness me, it's chilly," said George. "I think we are in for a very cold winter."

In the corner, a skinny threadbare spruce Christmas tree had been decorated and it reminded Alan of his childhood. He stood up to help his father who slumped in an armchair and coughed profusely for a few minutes. Norman lit a fire in the grate and wafted the initial smoke away muttering that the chimney was very sooty and needed cleaning.

"Soon have you warm again Dad," said Alan. George commented that if they didn't freeze to death, the smoke would probably asphyxiate them anyway.

"It's the bloody malaria," said George. "It comes back to revisit and annoy me."

He wiped his mouth and asked Alan all about his time in Belgium. They were all dying to know about the Belgian girl and her family. Alan noticed he was getting a sore throat but still managed speak copiously and enthusiastically about Odette and her parents.

He showed them a couple of photographs before carrying on with the war news from Belgium.

"You need a rest son," said Alice, "but I'm happy and pleased that you have found a nice girl."

Barbara spoke out for everyone when she mischievously said, "When are you going to pop the question?"

Alan simply said, "When I go back."

Not expecting that answer, everyone expressed surprise and George said, "You'll find it more difficult than you envisage. Think about the problems. She's a foreigner and doesn't understand our ways. Also, remember she'll have a strange accent and the simple people around here can't tell the difference between a French, German or a Japanese one. Nuneaton folk don't like the Germans one bit after they dropped bombs on the Oaston fields and killed six cows. One bomb dropped on the sewage works over in Camp Hill. According to reports in the Tribune, it caused one hell of a mess and a stink for hundreds of yards."

Alice turned her nose up and said it was disgusting. Everyone laughed. She disappeared into the kitchen saying she'd be some time preparing an evening meal.

Alan looked outside at the back garden. Nothing had changed in over a year. He saw the familiar stonewall and pond dividing the top flower garden from the vegetable patch. The greenhouse and the pear tree were still there. He daydreamed and thought about what Odette might think of his family, if he managed to persuade her to marry him.

The next few days were uneventful. George seemed to rally particularly after Alan managed to sneak him the odd tot of Whisky. Christmas arrived and although it was a happy occasion, for Alan he had to force himself to join in with the games and celebrations. The food and the gifts reflected the austerity of rationing. All he wanted to do was to speak with Odette but telephoning was out of the question. Gordon and Bess along with Graham, Florence and Geoffrey turned up on Boxing Day. They spent most of the time drinking and playing on an upright untuned piano in the front room and singing pub songs.

On December 28th, Alan received a letter from Odette in which she had included a few scented dried flowers from her collection. She'd received his letter and on the 25th had opened his card and the gift. Inside was a colour drawing of her and Misky based on a photograph. She adored it and in reply she'd attempted a little sketch of her and Alan holding each other with a message saying 'My love forever'. There was an imprint in lipstick of her lips and it was signed off with a row of kisses. She also mentioned she'd gone to bed with his drawings tucked under her pillow.

The winter temperatures dropped rapidly during the first week of January 1945. It had snowed for several days, keeping everyone indoors. Alan managed to walk across the road to see if Bill had managed to arrive on leave. His parents said he was stuck at an airfield in France due to severe weather conditions. Alan trudged back home disappointed but decided to drop in next door and ask Helen Cross if he could telephone RAF Bramcote to check on outgoing flights. The news was not so good but there would be a flight to Gatwick on the 12th January, if the weather improved.

On the morning of the 12th, the weather suddenly changed for the better. There was still snow and ice but a thaw was well on the way. Alan had already packed his kit bags the night before which included a number of gifts. The most important of these by far, was a stunning but simple 18-carat gold engagement ring clasping a beautiful solitaire diamond.

After protracted goodbyes with his parents and sister, Alan left for Belgium and his Odette. He was now full of joy, expressing happiness with every breath. It did not go unnoticed by his brotherGordon who had unexpectedly turned up and offered him a lift to Bramcote. Once at the airfield, Gordon hugged his brother and shook his hands after they discovered that the scheduled flight was on time. He expressed a wish to meet Alan's Belgian girl soon and wished him luck. Alan pulled up his greatcoat collar against the cold wind, walked towards the parked Dakota and waved to his brother as he climbed on board. Gordon waved back and waited till the aircraft took off.

"Flights to France, Belgium and Holland are delayed by five hours due to severe weather in Europe." The announcement at Gatwick was met with disgruntled looks and angry comments by a number of British and American military people pacing up and down. With nothing better to do, Alan decided to rest up and found a bench next to a small but busy refreshments kiosk. He was just about to fall asleep when he felt a poke in his back.

"Alan, this is spooky. Fancy seeing you here!" It was Leon, the Frenchman from Rodel and his Scottish lass Birdie. Alan jumped up startled, but delighted.

"What a lovely surprise! So what are you doing here and where are you off to?"

"I have to go back to France. My mother died five weeks ago and father is not coping with it very well."

"So sorry to hear that old chap. Here, sit down the pair of you. I'll go and get some cups of tea and sandwiches." He left Leon and Birdie on the bench as they hugged and stared out of the windows.

"Are you still in Rodel?" asked Alan, after returning with a tray of teas and sandwiches. With all the seats taken, he sat on the floor in front of them, propped up by his kit bags.

"No, they moved us all to Benbecula for some odd reason. Since you and Harry left, there's hardly been anything to do. Birdie and I have some good news. We are going to have a baby. It's just a shame that mother will not see her grandchild." Birdie smiled coyly at Alan.

"So what have you been up to?" asked Leon. "Have you found romance yet and why are you off to Belgium or is it all hushed up?"

Alan ran through the past few months and mentioned Odette. He took out her photo from his wallet. Both Leon and Birdie were delighted and wished him luck. An announcement on the Tannoy alerted Alan with news that an RAF flight to Brussels had been rescheduled and passengers should go to the main terminal. After shaking Leon's hand and hugging Birdie, he wished them lots of happiness with the forthcoming addition. With little spare time, Alan ran with all his kit towards the terminal, showed his RAF pass and, within thirty minutes, was airborne.

After a horrendous flight through sleet and snow with threats of being diverted to other airfields, Alan's plane finally arrived in Brussels, two hours late. The airfield was a blanket of snow with just the runways clear. However due to a stroke of luck, he managed to organise a lift to Mons with two US army officers in their Ford army staff car. Over towards the east, dark clouds were gathering. One of them looked skywards before making a comment.

"Looks like more godamned snow heading this way. Our boys are fighting hard and winning down there in those forests, despite terrible conditions."

"Will you be joining them at some point?" enquired Alan.

"We're hoping to catch up with Patton's 3rd Army near Bastogne. We are engineers from the 1st US Cavalry Division, sent to manage the repairs of his damaged Shermans. My name is Lieutenant Brad Swarovski and my buddy here is Captain James Blackhawk. His father was a Cherokee Indian, but I'm happy to say he's thrown away his bow and arrows and now prefers an M4 Sherman. What about you buddy?" He turned to face Alan who found this American highly amusing.

"I'm one of the RAF radar operators, stationed in Mons. I've just spent Christmas with my folks in England so I'm not sure what the situation is back here."

The rest of the journey proved difficult as the snow built up and the road became treacherous. Inside the Ford there was very little heating. The three of them eventually reached Mons at 18:00 hours and Alan mentioned he would enquire to see if his two companions could bed down for the night. They turned down the offer as they were late and had to try and drive on despite the road conditions.

"Harry, good to see you old bean." Alan walked quickly across the mess towards Harry who jumped up and greeted him with a big smile. He was limping noticeably.

"Good to see you Al. Hope you had a reasonable flight. I only got back two days ago and believe me it was a nightmare. How is your father. Hope all is well back home?"

Alan grabbed a cup of coffee, noting the place was warm meaning the boiler had been replaced and was working well.

"He's fine. The old goat is as strong as an iron girder but he's got to take things easy. Good to see the family again although I have really missed Odette. So, what's happened to you? I noticed that you're limping."

"Oh nothing much. I had an altercation with a sharp metal post at the airfield. The entire country is covered in deep snow. God knows how I got here on those icy roads. The taxi driver was petrified and even asked me to drive. It's not that easy with a gammy leg! He lifted his left trouser leg to reveal an eight-inch gash with dark blue bruising around his kneecap.

"God! That looks bad Harry," said Alan. "Hope you've had that seen to by medics."

"There's no need, I've got my Kate. She's better than all the doctors and nurses put together."

"Oh that reminds me, I've got a note from Odette delivered yesterday. She asked if I knew when you would be coming back. She's looking forward to seeing you but don't go thinking you can just walk up to her place right now in all that snow and ice. It's down to 10F and the roads and paths are impossible, even the trams aren't running. There have been several accidents, mostly involving broken bones. A chap from the Observer Corps had to be rescued from a snowdrift two days ago. Stupid ass thought he could drive to Brussels. He was close to death with exposure when they found him. Now look here Al, I know what you are thinking so forget it. I know you can be crazy at times but not completely nuts!"

Alan seriously thought about it but dismissed the idea. He opened the note from Odette. It read:

'*My Darling Alain,*

I have missed you so much and cannot wait to see you again. I trust you had a happy Christmas with your family and are now safely back in Mons. My parents and I have been prisoners in the house for five days as we cannot venture out in this awful weather. I don't even know whether it will be possible to deliver my note as it may be too risky in the snow and ice. I will try and hopefully get through so that Harry can pass it on when you arrive.

Please try to let me know that you are safe and well. I've thought about you every hour of every day and held your penny before going to sleep. I also pray that the weather will get better quickly so that I can travel to work and we can arrange to meet as we used to in the Grand Place. If you feel it's safe enough to walk, I'll be here at home until things improve. My parents would also be happy to see you again. Take care my darling.

Your Odette.'

The next day, the weather deteriorated even further, making Alan frustrated. He made up his mind that he would try his best to make it irrespective of weather conditions. On 14th January, two days after he'd arrived in Mons and dressed like Scott of the Antarctic, he ventured out at mid-day. He was surprised because although the snow was piled high, and the paths were still treacherous, the temperature had risen and he was constantly being hit by cold drops of water from melting ice that had collected on rooftops and guttering. The slow hazardous walk dragged on and was not without a few falls. Alan skidded along the Chaussée de Binche, passing the Waux-Hall, which had been turned into a fantasy winter wonderland. Alan marvelled at the quietness as he struggled up the hill towards the Bascule before eventually arriving at the Moreau's house.

He rang the bell and Odette opened the door. She squealed with delight and pulled Alan into her arms. They held each other, whispered sweet endearments and kissed as though their lives depended upon it.

Fernand and Laure appeared in the hallway as Alan stepped inside and closed the door. They were overjoyed to see him and ignored his apology for not warning them. Misky arrived on the scene wagging his tail furiously and jumped into Alan's arms.

"It's wonderful to see you again Alain," said Laure. "You are very brave walking through all that snow and ice."

Fernand agreed and then mentioned that a certain somebody would now be very happy. Alan turned to Odette. She was blushing, grinning and chuckling.

"Come into the warm," said Fernand, "I'm sure we'd all love to hear about your trip to England."

Odette came to sit next to Alan. He explained he'd love to tell them but before that, he had a few gifts to hand out. They were items he'd either acquired from people in the know or saved during his Christmas break back in Nuneaton. From deep inside his bag, he withdrew chocolates, cigars, perfume, and pearl earrings for Odette. Last but not least a bright blue rubber chew ring for Misky who ran around in circles wagging his tail furiously.

Odette then disappeared and returned with a small box for Alan. "This is my gift to you."

He opened the box to find a pair of gold cufflinks with an onyx plaque on which A&O had been inscribed. Alan was delighted and suddenly reached over to kiss Odette. He realised at the last moment he shouldn't have tried and, when trying to recover from reaching too far, he overbalanced. Everyone laughed. Fernand suggested they should celebrate Christmas and Alan's safe arrival.

"We're hoping you'll stay for something to eat with us," suggested Fernand. Alan enthusiastically accepted the invitation and Laure, still singing, disappeared with Odette into the kitchen to prepare food.

Fernand, picked up *La Derniere Heure* newspaper, lit a cigar and went to sit in his favourite chair by an old radio. He turned it on and tuned into Edith Piaf singing some well-known songs. That triggered Laure in the kitchen to join in with 'L'Accordéoniste'.

Odette appeared in the dining room doorway laughing and apologised for her mother's impromptu rendition. She blew Alan a kiss and he reciprocated. She watched him for a few minutes and giggled at his laugh as he played tug of war with Misky. She had never felt so happy and excited even though the war was not yet over and there were still many uncertainties ahead.

January seemed to go slowly. The weather improved allowing the allied forces in the Ardennes to halt the German offensive and relieve Bastogne. Aircraft were finally flying after being grounded for a month. By the end of January, the enemy had been defeated and were being pushed back by Patton, Bradley and Montgomery.

Back in Mons, the RAF, Signals and USAAF surveillance personnel, although still on standby, had more free time. This suited Alan and Odette. They met nearly every day in the town centre and, as the weather became warmer and the town safer, they ventured further to meet up with Odette's family, numerous cousins and friends. Many had endured the agonies and horrors of the return march to the coast four years previously. The two of them were becoming popular and recognised in whispers as 'Les Amants Heureux' (the happy lovers).

On Saturday February 10th, Alan met Odette in the gardens of the Waux-Hall. It was unusually warm, reaching 63F. The recent bad weather had damaged much of the exotic shrubs and flowerbeds but they were happy to find a secluded bench next to the widespread branches of a conifer. Alan turned to Odette.

"You are my best friend and the woman I want to spend the rest of my life with." Odette reached out and caressed his face. He took her hand before kneeling on one knee and reached into his pocket and took out the little black box.

"My darling Odette, will you do me the honour of becoming my wife?" He opened the box to reveal the ring.

"Oh Alain! YES yes yes!" She started to cry with tears of happiness. Alan was also tearful and held her face so they could see into each other's eyes.

"I have thought of nothing else. It would be my greatest wish to become your wife and the mother of our beautiful children. I love you, my Alain, with all my heart."

Alan took out the ring and placed it on the third finger of her left hand. It was a perfect fit as he watched a teardrop fall on the sparkling diamond. For once, Odette was lost for words. She threw her arms around Alan's neck and kissed him. He could taste the salty tears and at that moment knew that their love was indelible and decreed by a force far greater than he was able to contemplate. To them both, in this moment, it was an unbreakable commitment they wholeheartedly wanted to cement in marriage.

"I thought we could get married on your birthday, August the 8th, so long as there are no complications." Odette clapped her hands and said that would be perfect.

"We must go and break the good news to my parents. They will be so excited."

Fernand and Laure's reaction was predictable. On the outside, they expressed happiness for their daughter and Alan. However, the smiles, the laughter and the joy were tempered by feelings of trepidation. Fernand in particularly was feeling sad and had already spoken to Laure about the possible outcome of the relationship. Clearly he feared losing his precious daughter if she decided to followAlan to England. Laure was more sanguine, believing that distance should never get in the way of true love. Nevertheless, she also realised that it would become an emotional exigency should it come to that. Despite the thought of losing her daughter, she was excited about the preparations for the wedding. What would she wear? Also, a new hat was needed but for now she insisted they must organise an engagement party preferably in early March.

Two days later, at the *Ecole Normale*, Alan announced his engagement but the reaction he received was not what he expected. Harry and Kate were happy, but counselled Alan about the hurdles that lay ahead.

"You really should be thinking more about how Odette's

218

parents will be feeling," said Kate. "They stand to lose their only daughter if you take her back to England."

Harry butted in. "Don't forget the RAF will not necessarily be on your side. Chances are, whilst the war is still on, they'll try to convince you that it's a bad idea. They can't stop you, of course, but I'd have a word with the CO and the Chaplain. Make no mistake pal, we are really happy for you both, but we don't want to see either of you hurt."

Others soon got to know, many of them friends who Alan had known for some time. They, too, cautioned him against any rash decision. Alan, still happy and jocular, dismissed them all and refused to be intimidated by negativity. He preferred to follow his instincts rather than someone else's interpretation of right and wrong. He somehow knew this was his destiny.

The next day, before meeting Odette at *Chez Saey*, Alan spent two hours chatting with the Mike Rolands. It was almost as Harry had predicted. The Sqd. Leader did try to steer him away from marriage but added that once the Germans surrendered, he'd give him his full blessing. Later, in his chat with the Chaplain, Alan discovered there may be complications regarding Odette's Catholic faith. She would have to make a big decision but he was determined support it.

"It's not impossible though," said the Padre. "I can marry you here so long as she renounces her faith for the Church of England. That marriage would be recognised in England. You may also both decide to have a civil wedding afterwards for her relatives and friends, but that ceremony alone would not be recognised in England. You should regard it as a blessing. It's not uncommon to have both but you'd have to talk with the Mayor and his staff."

Alan was still reeling from the potential difficulties when he met Odette. They ordered two croissants and coffees.

"Alain, you look worried. What is the matter my love?" He shifted uncomfortably on his seat and took her hand gently fondling the ring. She carried a concerned frown as she studied her fiancé's eyes and listened intensely.

"In order for us to be married, it appears you'd have to renounce your Catholic faith and adopt the Church of England."

Odette, looked shocked and anxious. She remained silent for several minutes. Alan knew she was struggling with her response.

"Let me make this easy for you, my darling," he said. "There is another way. I could become Catholic. I'm not that concerned about faith so long as we are together. I don't mind staying here in Belgium after the war. I'd learn French and we can make a home here in Mons."

Odette smiled, wiped a tear from her eyes and took his hand.

"I cannot let you do that," she said. "It's a beautiful noble thought but how would you find work? I think it would take a very long time for you to find something acceptable. After all, Belgium is still recovering from five years of war and it will take time. No, I've made up my mind. I will change my faith and I'll go to England with you when we are married even though my parents will be very sad and it may break their hearts. It's where you know how to find a future in these difficult times."

Alan was shocked and surprised that his fiancée would make such a huge decision. He realised just how much she was prepared to sacrifice in her deep love for him. However, being cautious by nature, Alan asked her to think hard about it and to talk with her parents before making a final decision. He was quietly excited and thanked her for such a demonstration of love. They kissed and hugged, just as Harry and Kate joined them.

"We've just climbed to the top of that damned tower," said Harry, breathing hard.

"You mean the Belfry," replied Odette smiling.

"Yes, that's the one and now we're knackered!"

Odette asked Alan what 'knackered' meant. He tried to explain but got it all wrong and they all burst into spontaneous laughter causing others in the café to glance over.

Odette became embroiled in much discussion with her parents

over the next few days. It did not go well. They protested that the war had taken their daughter away from them and at one point blamed Alan for the hurt they felt. Odette was heart broken. She tried to make them see that he was a good man and had offered to stay in Mons after the war. Her parents took nearly three weeks to come to terms with the situation. It all came to a head one Friday afternoon. Odette had returned home early from work after decorators had moved in to her offices. She found Alan with her parents. They were all smiling.

"Odette, please come and sit down," said her father. "Alan arrived an hour ago and has spoken to us about your future together. We are now more at ease with the situation. Your fiancé is a very kind and respectful man. I don't think your mother and I could wish for a better son-in-law. He understands that going to England will be hard for you and ourselves but we are not to think of it as a separation but as an opportunity to spend holidays together either here or in England. He's keen to make sure we meet as often as possible, maybe several times a year, particularly if decide to have children. I suppose it will not be so bad after all. We are confident that Alan will take good care of you."

Laure was smiling broadly and Odette jumped up and hugged both her parents, thanking them over and over again.

"It's not us you should thank, it's your fiancé."

She looked at her mother and father with a wink and a chuckle before planting a big wet kiss on Alan's lips. Her parents said nothing and realised that from now on, chaperoning would no longer be necessary.

"This house is now your home here in Mons, Alain," said Fernand. "You are welcome here at any time."

Alan walked over to Laure and embraced her. He then shook Fernand's hand and in French said, "Thank you, Father." Fernand gulped and hugged Alan. He said something which Alan did not quite understand but when translated later by a tearful Odette became 'Please take care of her. She'll always be our little girl'.

Over the next few months, Alan, Odette and her parents spent time planning the wedding which had been put back two weeks due to RAF paperwork. They had already celebrated a fabulous engagement party with family and friends in March, so knew what kind of reception Odette's mother was capable of organising. Rationing was still a big problem but Fernand's connections made things easier and friends had promised them extra chairs and tables. They also had time to celebrate in style on VE Day with street parties and dancing the day after Germany's surrender on May 7th. The entire Moreau family, including distant cousins and all their friends, converged on the Grand Place. Within two weeks, the entire population of Mons once again gathered in or near the Grand Place for the *Ducasse*, affectionately called the *Dou Dou*. This annual festival where the 'Montois' celebrate St George slaying the Dragon takes place on Trinity Sunday. Alan had promised Odette he would be there for the event, the first one since 1939. It may still be regarded as the most poignant and popular Ducasse ever, since it came to signify victory over the enemy after five years of hardship.

In between times, Alan had finally organised all the formal paperwork and visas for his forthcoming marriage, including the necessary papers for Odette from the Rev John Lloyd. He'd written letters to his parents explaining his intentions but was sad to learn that, due to his father's illness, they had declined the invitation, as it would be risky for him to travel. None of the Whites would be attending duet o prior commitments, but Barbara said they would all organise another reception when the happy couple arrived in Nuneaton. With none of Alan's relatives attending, Odette and her parents were also sad but looking forward to meeting them as soon as possible after the wedding.

"Harry, have you got the ring?"

"Yes Al. Don't worry; it's all going to be OK! Try to smile, she's going to look better than Greta Garbo."

Downstairs in the tiny Chapel, Alan's witnesses and RAF friends including Sqd. Leader Mike Rowlands were all gathered. It was just before mid-day on 20th August 1945 and it was a hot day. Rev. John Lloyd was standing in front of a blue draped alter on which two lit candles stood flanking a silver crucifix. On the wall a large embroidered tapestry denoted the RAF Motto 'Per Ardua ad Astra'. Alan and Harry walked in and took their places on the front row. Alan was dressed immaculately in his uniform.

Laure was sitting one row behind next to two WAAFs. She was wearing her favourite summer pale blue floral dress and a dark blue floppy brimmed hat. She constantly smiled at Alan and Harry.

At precisely five minutes past twelve, the Chaplain asked everyone to stand. Someone at the back opened the twin oak doors and revealed Odette with her father. She looked stunning in a beautiful sheer ivory chiffon dress with scalloped tulip short sleeves, a narrow V neckline and a wide waistband of intricately swirled piping. Her long wavy swept-back dark brown hair cascaded from under a small angled dark blue velvet crown topper hat, fringed with lace.

Fernand, beaming as a proud father does, walked proudly with her arm in his. Alan turned and smiled. He whispered to Harry that an angel had just walked in. Odette joined Alan and they held hands as they looked into each other's eager young faces. Their wide liquid eyes reflected the warmth of an inner beauty, the secret longings and the emotions that cradle the passions of desire. He squeezed her hand and whispered to her that she redefined 'beautiful', which made her blush.

Rev. Lloyd spoke eloquently of a love that conquers all despite adversity, quoting passages from the Gospel of St Matthew. In less than twenty minutes, Alan and Odette were married. Everyone cheered as they walked out of the *Ecole Normale* into the bright warm sun. Harry, Laure and Fernand joined them for a few photographs and a showering of rice before jumping into a taxi. Next stop would be a short drive to the Hotel de Ville and their Civil Ceremony in front of a huge crowd already gathering outside. Inside, Maraine Lea Manderlier and her sister Maraine Fernande Renson, Odette's aunts had decorated the main reception area with a lavish display of flowers. The latter's daughter, nine year old Monique, was the bridesmaid. Sixty-four chairs had been laid out in a wide arc of eight rows. Facing the seated guests and those standing at the back were six of Odette's close work friends from the office where she worked. They had volunteered to sing during the ceremony. Leading them was Madame Marie Adélaïde Clotilde Fremont, the lady with a secret from the past and whom Odette had helped and come to admire. She was now the new mayor's personal assistant. To their right, the Mayor had organised a pianist, a cellist and clarinetist as a gift to Odette.

Amongst the guests, apart from Harry as best man, Daisy and Mike Rowlands, there were many from the RAF and a smart looking captain representing the USAAF. Needless to say, the majority of guests were made up of Odette's entire family and many friends.

Laure spent some time with her daughter and Fernand in an anteroom making sure she was feeling all right after the taxi ride. However, Fernand's bow tie and high wing collar had become detached causing a few expletives to be launched. Odette and her mother burst into fits of stifled laughter. Laure disappeared and went to sit next to Julia, Jean-Baptiste and Jacqueline on the left. Monique, the bridesmaid, joined Odette and held her spare hand. In her other hand Odette carried a bouquet of pink roses and ivory Calla Lillies. It was a gift from her godmother, Maraine Lea Renson the mother of the pretty six year old bridesmaid. She walked shyly behind the bride carrying a posy made up of Lilleys of the Valley.

"Are you ready?" The Registrar knocked on the door.

Fernand smiled at his daughter and said they were ready. Choking back his emotions he spoke to Odette telling her that he loved her and was deeply proud of her. Odette, with tears in her eyes, hugged him and kissed his forehead.

Alan was sitting nervously with Harry on the right who had the unenviable task of guiding Alan's hand into his top pocket to reassure him that the ring was intact and safe. Both wore very smart full dress uniforms with their officer's peak caps which they removed as they stood. Prompted by the returning registrar and her assistant, the choir and musicians started with Jo Stafford's 'Ev'ry Day I Love you, just a little bit more'.

At the end of the ceremony, Odette and Alan where overwhelmed by the number of people wanting to congratulate them. They were showered with kisses, hugs and unfettered happiness. Odette, as tradition would have, turned her back on the guests before throwing her posy backwards. Kate somehow managed to avoid all the eager out-stretched hands and caught it. Harry, shouted something mildly rude and embarassing in French before giving Alan a sly wink.

Family, friends and strangers gathered outside the Hotel de Ville, clapping as the newly married couple emerged into the bright sun on the Grand Place. They waited for a few moments as the taxi reappeared, waving and blowing kisses to the crowd. Without any warning, she grabbed Alan around his neck, pulled him closer and kissed him full on his lips. He held her waist, detecting her trembling body and felt the fires of emotion and passion running through his veins like never before. He knew instinctively that, like him, she could not wait to be alone - to consummate their love.

The journey time from the town centre to Chaussée De Beaumont and the reception was not long enough. Alan and Odette spent the entire ten minutes wrapped in each other's arms, kissing touching, laughing and whispering words of love. It could have gone on forever.

Some time after, Alan remarked that he could not believe how many people were able to fit into his new in-law's house, although most preferred to stay out in the garden and take advantage of the warm weather. Others relaxed in the veranda's new wicker chairs. There were 35 people milling around, mostly close family. Little Monique, the cute bridesmaid, spent most the time playing with Misky and feeding him naughty morsels from the wedding table. Harry and Kate were always at hand to help which was much appreciated by Laure in particular. The Moreaus and a few friends, despite rationing, had organised some excellent food and a wedding cake bearing the British and Belgian flag. Fernand, in charge of the wine stock, had brought up twenty bottles of his treasured Bordeaux and Champagne from the cellar. Fearing that someone might be tempted to explore his wine racks, he made sure the cellar door was locked. Music played constantly whilst the smell of cigar smoke drifted amongst the guests.

The speeches were really an extended opportunity for many toasts. Harry, as the best man, described some of the qualities, irritations and habits that Odette would discover in her husband - the very same ones he'd had to endure in over three years of friendship. It was a very funny speech in French that reduced the crowd to tears of laughter. He also apologised since he realised he could say anything he liked about Alan who probably would not understand a word. Once again people laughed. However, he left those listening with no doubts that Alan was a lovely fellow and that Odette was a lucky girl.

Fernand spoke eloquently about his daughter, her loveliness, her caring nature, hard work and bravery. He also thanked Alan for coming into their lives and emphasised that he and Laure were finally blessed with a wonderful son. His speech included a wish for many grandchildren, which received a cheer. Alan put his arm around Odette and kissed her.

One of Odette's relations had gifted them the services of a semi-professional photographer dressed all in black with a top hat. Alan made Odette laugh when he mentioned the man must also be in big demand for funerals. After much shuffling around at the front of the house, swotting away a persistent wasp and tripping over his huge Gandolfi plate camera, he managed to take a number of photos.

Alan and Odette did manage to slip away from the crowd for half and hour. They ended up in her bedroom, specially decorated with flowers for their first night together. However, it seems that time waits for no man. They once again reignited the passions of love but, on their return to the party, Laure noticed that her daughter's cheeks were flushed. She said nothing but smiled one of those mother's knowing smiles and went to find her husband. The reception finished at midnight after a few friends mucked in and helped Laure and Fernand tidy up and wash the crockery. Some of the older people had departed earlier. Harry and Kate thanked Odette and her parents as well as teasing Alan about the night ahead. They decided to walk back to the *Ecole Normale* under a bright moon lit sky, singing to each other some of the party songs they'd found to their liking.

After thanking Laure and Fernand for a very special day, the happy couple took a walk in the moonlit garden before Alan decided he'd like to carry Odette to her bedroom.

Two days later, the newly married couple travelled by train from Mons to Ostend via Brussels. Laure and Fernand, as a wedding present, had arranged a four-day stay in a top hotel and then a further three nights staying with Laure's cousin Paul and his wife Celine in their very well appointed apartment.

It was a time of great happiness for them both. They enjoyed each other's company and shared many interests. They made each other laugh and Alan's ability to tell a good story kept her entertained. More importantly their love for each other grew each day. In a letter written by Paul to Fernand, he stated that he and Celine had never before seen a couple so much in love.

Alan, encouraged by Odette, and during moments they were not entwined in each other's arms, spent time painting pictures around the old harbour paint set in an artists studio and shop in Mons two weeks before.

On September 2oth, Alan's 24th birthday, Odette, Laure and Fernand organised a trip to the recently opened theatre in Mons where Ruggero Leoncavallo's 'Pagliacci' was being performed by a Brussels operatic society. It was followed up with dinner at a local restaurant run by one of Fernand's relations.

The balmy summer running into a warm autumn and the joys

of new married life helped everyone relax. Odette continued working at the Hotel de Ville and Alan was busy dismantling radar units with his colleagues in the *Ecole Normale*. Then one day, things changed dramatically with some good news.

"Alan, I've just returned from the doctor. We're going to have a baby!" It was an unusually warm October 20th 1945. Odette had suspected she was pregnant for a while. She had waited for confirmation before excitedly announcing that the new arrival was due in July 1946. After the honeymoon in Ostend, she and Alan had returned to Mons and had put into motion the preparations for flying to England, later in October.

"Oh my darling, you have made me so happy. Are you okay, is everything all right?" He couldn't get the words out quick enough but still managed to kiss Odette many times. He experienced a feeling of such intense joy that he ran up and down the veranda doing a sort of crazy waltz routine. Odette laughed at his antics but all Alan could see in that moment was his radiant, beautiful and happy pregnant wife. The noise alarmed Fernand and Laure who were attempting a rest in the dining room. When they discovered they were going to become grandparents, they both welled up. Alan had never seen Fernand weep who was a little embarassed but seeing him do so made him shed a few tears too.

"I'd better start knitting," said Laure. "The baby will need bootees mittens, bonnets and a shawl if we have another cold winter."

Her remark made them all laugh. Laure and Fernand were ecstatic which meant they had to celebrate with something special. Out came the 'Picon Amer', a bitter sweet herbal liqueur which Laure carefully poured into three large wine glasses, topped up with sweet white wine, plus generous shots of Grande Marnier. It played havoc with Alan who quickly felt the effects of the powerful alcohol. Odette preferred her favourite, Lambic Gueuze beer, with a dash of Grenadine syrup. She referred to it as 'Brussels Champagne.'

Alan had already obtained and filled in the necessary but tedious paperwork pending being demobbed. Operations for the

RAF and Signals units had been suspended and were no longer required. Everyone would be going home. Odette had managed to acquire her first passport and obligatory references, along with the marriage certificate. She'd also handed in her notice at work, which had been half expected by the rest of the girls.

"It's been a hell of a ride but at least we are alive and kicking and we've experienced a few adventures," said Harry.

Distance would soon separate Harry and Alan, once they had made their way back to their homes in England. Kate decided she would go back with Harry and move to the east coast. They too were becoming more romantically involved. Alan asked him to make an honest woman of her. Harry smiled and winked at him.

"We'll see old chap but it's highly likely but only if you'll be my best man so we must stay in touch." Alan agreed. They both laughed and decided to go for a beer.

"I've written to my parents back in Nuneaton and they are more than happy to meet Odette. They've also managed to persuade Barbara to sleep in my old single bedroom and give up her double bed for us. Best news is that I had a word with the top brass and they have managed to find a flight for us from Brussels to Gatwick early on the 28th."

At 07:00 on the morning of the 28th October, Alan, Odette and her parents travelled to Brussels airport by train. They all felt a deep sadness and hardly spoke. At Brussels Midi Station, Fernand and Laure disappeared to the lavatories and then queued to buy breakfast with large cups of Chat Noire filter Coffees. The conversation brightened up when Alan mentioned he'd arrange with his parents for Laure and Fernand to visit for a holiday within a few weeks. Alan's sadness was partly due to leaving Belgium, the place he'd met his wife and partly due to leaving Harry and the rest of the lads. It was also because he knew that Odette's parents would miss her terribly. He felt guilty and something inside him resented what he was doing. Odette sensed his feelings and took his hand. She pulled him close and whispered in his ear.

229

"Don't be troubled, my Alain. I'm frightened and I'll miss my parents and that makes me very sad, but I love you so much that being with you means much, much more."

Alan choked and suppressed a tear. He whispered, "I love you my darling. You are more precious to me than anything else. I promise to keep you safe and look after you forever." He placed his hand on her tummy and added, "Our child too."

They arrived at the airport and waited for an hour before their flight was called. Because it was a military aircraft and she was a Belgian, Odette had to undergo a short security check before they were both allowed to embark. They'd spent some time in tears saying goodbye to Laure and Fernand and although they attempted to put on a brave face, it was impossible. They sat uncomfortably in the old noisy Dakota just snuggled up in each other's arms. It was Odette's first flight and despite her trepidation, she was also a little excited. Questions kept flooding through her head. What lay ahead? What would Alan's family think of her? Would their baby be all right? Would she be able to make herself understood in conversation despite her accent? The cold in the aircraft made her shiver. She pulled herself closer to Alan who wrapped his RAF flying jacket around her.

They landed badly at Gatwick in strong winds under a grey sky. After some confusion and a number of immigration formalities, they caught a train from Gatwick to Victoria station and then Odette was treated to the wonders of the London Underground. She was full of childlike amazement, marvelling at the posters, the people, the distinctive pungency of the electric trains and above all the speed as the carriages rattled along towards Euston Station. The train to Stafford, calling at Rugby and Nuneaton Trent Valley, was due out in one hour at 3.30pm. Alan left Odette with a coffee at a table outside WH Smiths while he visited the lavatory. On his return, she'd gone. He panicked for a second until he saw her walking back from the ladies' lavatory. She'd smartened herself up with cosmetics and now wore a wide brimmed hat that complimented her dark red military style coat. She was also wearing fashionable shoes. Alan smiled and hugged her.

"I had to leave the coffee, it tasted very odd." He realised that she'd never experienced Camp Coffee before.

"Sorry my love, English food and drink may take you a while to get used to."

Odette chuckled and reached for his hand.

They got up to go after a last call for passengers travelling on the Stafford train. Alan found a porter to carry her heavy suitcase and his big kit bag to platform 12 where the train was waiting. He turned to Odette and above the noise of the engine blowing steam he shouted, "We'll be in Nuneaton by 5.00pm." They found a deserted compartment and settled down. Odette rested her head on Alan's shoulder and they held hands as the guard blew his whistle and the train pulled out.

The English countryside flew past as the darkening evening slowly rolled in across the sky. Thy both woke from a deep sleep as the train slowed and jerked as it came into Rugby station. Alan decided to get out and buy a newspaper from a platform vendor. He only just made it back as the train pulled out. Odette laughed and wondered what she would have done if he'd missed it.

"I'm still thinking about my mother and father," she said to Alan. "They must be feeling so lonely. They were used to having me around for nineteen years and now they are on their own."

"I know my love, it occurs to me too. I wrote to my parents and Barbara two weeks ago to inform them about our plans. In their reply, they understand what you and your mother and father must be feeling." He pulled out Barbara's letter and handed it to her.

"Read this. It will make you feel better."

Odette read that Barbara was so excited and looked forward to meeting her. Everyone was thrilled to know there was a baby on the way. She added that they hadn't wasted any time, which made Odette smile. She laughed when she read that after suffering the torments of three elder brothers for too many years, she was looking forward to a new sister friendship and fully appreciated that Odette would be anxious and sad after leaving her parents. Barbara offered her help and guidance until such a time that Odette became accustomed to English ways. Odette suddenly felt a lot better. She reached for Alan's hand, chuckled and said she felt loved and safe.

"I'm looking forward to a happy future in England and to meeting Barbara. I have a feeling we will become good friends." She stood up, took some cosmetics out of her handbag and despite the swaying coach motion, looked in the mirror whilst tinkering with her makeup.

"I must look smart for your family."

Alan stood up behind her, held her waist and helped her stay upright. He could not help notice how beautiful and radiant she looked in the mirror's reflection. She giggled as he kissed the nape of her neck while she finished tracing her lips with red lipstick.

"I love you, Alain," she said in her attractive French accent.

"I love you too my darling," he said.

The door of the compartment slid open and a ticket collector stood there with his machine slung around his neck.

"Ticket's please!" he shouted. "And a little less of that nonsense," he remarked, smiling at them.

He then said to Odette with a cheeky grin, "You must be foreign young lady. Hope you ain't one of them Germans." Odette blushed as Alan passed him the two tickets. After dinging the bell, he handed them back with holes punched in them. The train started to slow down as it approached Trent Valley Station, Nuneaton. Alan leant out of the window and spotted a porter. After a struggle, they stepped down from the train. Odette was finally in Nuneaton after a long and tiring journey. This was the town that Alan had grown up in, where his family lived and where she would make her home. However, her imagined dreams and hopes of arriving in a beautiful place evaporated rapidly.

As they walked down Platform 2 watching the train disappear, Odette could not help notice how grey and scruffy the station looked.

There was the most awful pungent stench of fish and decaying meat wafting in the breeze, which Alan balked at and apologised for. He embarrassingly explained it probably came from an animal waste factory called 'De Mulders'.

Odette's first impressions of Nuneaton as she walked along the platform, smartly dressed, were not good. She couldn't help shed a tear and wondered what she had come to. Alan guided the porter towards the exit and soon found a taxi. The drive home was a revelation. Odette had never experienced being driven on the left and giggled as they passed through the town centre, which she thought looked, rather grey and neglected.

Alan and Odette finally arrived at 195, Higham Lane in the evening just before the grandfather clock in the hallway struck 5.30pm. Their taxi honked its horn and they climbed out to be greeted by Alan's entire family. Even the neighbours were keen to see the Belgian girl who they'd heard so much about.

It was a joyous occasion and went a long way to reversing Odette's initial impressions of Nuneaton. Barbara was laughing and smiling. She hugged Odette and an immediate bond of friendship was formed, just as Odette had imagined would happen. Gordon and Graham kept clapping Alan on the back congratulating him and Alice was tearful as she hugged her daughter-in-law. George tried hard to remain impassive but took both of his new daughter-in-laws hands and welcomed her into the family. She bent over and kissed his cheeks surprising him and causing him to remark,

"Well I never, that must be the way they do it over there."

Within an hour of arriving, and after an introduction to some 'interesting' English cooking, Odette felt as if she was more than accepted here in the bosom of Alan's family. She started to embrace their humour and although perturbed by a local accent which she had some difficulty understanding, looked forward to a new and exciting future in Nuneaton.

233

That future held many ups and downs, good times, times of sadness and adventures but one thing that encompassed all of this, was the love that Alan and Odette shared and which so obviously formed a basis upon which their family life would develop. It was a marriage that defined happiness that lasted for over 50 years.

Epilogue

After their return to England, Alan and Odette lived for a short time in the family home in Higham Lane with Alan's mother, father and sister. George White died in 1949 after a long struggle with illness. Alan was faced with taking over the management of the Scala Cinema in Nuneaton after his father's death. In 1946, eleven months after being married in Mons and just before her 20th birthday, Odette, gave birth to Richard, her first son who would eventually become the author of 'The Belgian Bride'.

In late 1947, Alan, Odette and their one-year-old son moved to Trinity Walk in Attleborough, a suburb of Nuneaton. They moved back to Higham Lane after Alice White's death in 1953. She had left the house to them in her will.

Barbara, Alan's sister married Norman in 1948. In 1952, they emigrated to Salt Lake City and adopted the Mormon Faith. They had four children; Robbie, Mandy, John and Lynwood.

Robert George White, the author's brother, was born in April 1951. He went on to manage plantations in South East Asia. Here he met and married his wife Jennie Ah Moi. They have a daughter, Alexandra.

Alison, the author's sister was born in 1957. She married Michael Goodwin in 1980 and they have two children; Catherine and Robert. Catherine is married and living in Salt Lake City and Robert lives and works in Paris.

Over the years and before taking up writing, Richard Fernand Alan White, the author of 'The Belgian Bride', was a photo correspondent, graphic designer, artist and tutor. He married Daphne Moore in 1971. Their two children, Christopher and Abigail were born in 1979 and 1981 respectively. Abigail is married to Robert Edmunds and they have a daughter, Artemis. Abi is the owner of a successful ladies high fashion shop in Stratford upon Avon. Christopher is a surveyor and a world class archer. He represents Great Britain at many International events. In 2010 he won Gold and Silver medals at the Commonwealth Games in Delhi. In 2001, Daphne (Daf) tragically died of Lupus in Warwick hospital after a tragic six year battle with a failing immune system.

In May 2009, Richard married Clare de Galleani in Stratford upon Avon. Clare's daughter Charlotte is a lawyer in London and a highly accomplished Clarinetist.

Laure and Fernand sold 10 Chaussée de Beaumont and came to live in England so they could contribute towards a new family home in Fenny Drayton. They stayed for a few years but returned to Mons after the house was sold. However, their health started to fail and so once again they returned to live with the family in Nuneaton. Laure passed away in 1987 after suffering blood circulation issues and a leg amputation. Fernand, broken hearted at losing his wife, lived on for another two years. Both are buried in Nuneaton.

Harry and Kate married but separated six years later. They have a son who joined the RAF. Alan would never be reunited with Harry again or his former RAF colleagues other than Bill Bennett, despite attempts to set up a reunion.

Veronique del Haze, the pregnant girl from Mauberge who had befriended Odette during the march in 1940, was reunited with John Lucas in 1946 after he came to look for her. By this time and still single, she had a six-year-old son who accepted John as his father. They still live in Mauberge.

Jacqueline, Odette's friend and 2nd cousin, married in 1956 but was tragically killed in a car accident 10 years later. Her mother Julia never got over it and a few years later committed suicide.

Marie Adélaïde Clotilde Fremont, Odette's former supervisor and secretary to the Mayor of Mons is a fictitious name. There is little known about the real person but it is said in gossip that she never married after failing to re-establish contact with her German lover. There are unconfirmed rumours that she never got over it and committed suicide by throwing herself in front of a train.

Alan died in January 1996 after suffering from a crippling form of rheumatoid arthritis for 40 years. Despite this and throughout his life, he maintained his promise to look after Odette and the family. In 1955, after managing the Scala Cinema in Nuneaton, he trained and became a skilled engineering draughtsman, eventually dedicating most of his working life to the Massey Ferguson Company in Coventry. He also developed into a brilliant artist, well known in the locality and could have gone further with his creative abilities. However, Alan considered his responsibilities lay with a guaranteed income from his full time work to ensure his promises were maintained. He also kept his promise to ensure that Laure and Fernand were reunited with their daughter as often as possible through the years.

Odette died in June 2010 after a short-term struggle with pancreatic cancer. In the end, her last words were "I will be with my Alain once again." During her life in England, she continually found unbounded energy helping others and was an inspirational, caring and gentle mother to her three children and five grandchildren. During the early years, Odette took on voluntary nursing work with the Red Cross before finally dedicating herself to teaching. She was a popular, well-loved and respected member of the local community with many friends. She also developed a love of amateur theatre and opera, based at her school where she was recognised as a brilliant French teacher. Apart from teaching French she spent many hours behind stage helping actors with costume design. Significantly, Odette could not forgive the Germans until just a few years before her death. As she approached her 80s, she grew close to the Church, which gave her an added inner strength and peace. It was because of this that she finally forgave the Germans for all the suffering they had put her and her family through, years before.

Footnote by the author:

This historical novel is based largely on actual events and facts contained in notes, archived documents, or records. As well as recalling personal experiences, it also relies on stories conveyed by my parents and grandparents. The book is mostly non-fiction except on occasions when corroborated facts cannot be established and memories have proved unreliable. Therefore, in trying to retain a sense of reality and continuity, I have occasionally resorted to artistic licence, imagination and distorted historical narrative. This was necessary to add a sense of realism and a better understanding of life under occupation and the horrors of war, when factual research was unable to reveal the differences between rumour and fact. There are some passages where people's names, events and detail have been invented or may have been used in the wrong context or unintentionally misinterpreted. Should any of these details cause concern or offence to any person alive, or the relatives and friends of those now deceased, the author apologises unreservedly.

Being the eldest, born in 1946, I naturally have a longer record of memories spent in Mons in the late 1940s and early 1950s. I even attended school there as a four year old and met many of the people mentioned in this novel. As a family, we frequently holidayed at our Grandparents home and were made aware of the war years and the unending stories from that period. It was a joyful time when the people of Mons were rebuilding their lives and were continuously grateful to the English and Americans who they saw as liberators. Trips to Belgium continued until the late 1970s when my grandparents sold their home in Mons and came to live in England with their family.

As an aside, amongst the first Americans to arrive in Mons during the towns liberation in September 1944 was the crew of a Sherman tank affectionately called 'Fish & Chips'. In 1946, the US army kindly donated 'Fish & Chips' to the town, where it still resides in the Jardin du Mayeur beyond the Grand Place and a few yards away from where Odette once worked in the Hotel de Ville.

It is my hope that the story of Alan and Odette White and my grandparents Fernand and Laure Moreau, along with those mentioned in the book will help readers understand that within the ordinary lives of people there exists an extraordinary spirit that determines the will to overcome suffering.

This story is mostly about my parents, grandparents, relatives and family friends, who overcame fear and remained resolute in the face of tyranny and occupation. To my living family particularly my two children Christopher and Abigail and my granddaughter Artemis, as well as all future generations to follow, it is my dearest wish that this book will help to keep you closer to family members now departed and all the wonderful memories they have left us in which love for each other conquers all adversity.

Acknowledgements:

- My wife Clare for all her time proof reading, support and love
- Family papers, documents, photographs, notes, and memoirs
- My brother Robert and sister Alison for checking facts
- 'My Heritage' for family history archives - Salt Lake City, USA.
- The Royal Airforce Association.
- The Royal Airforce Museum.
- Forces War Records.
- 'Dark December': Robert E. Merriam.
- 'First Light' – Geoffrey Wellum
- 'The Quest for Freedom': The Yvonne de Ridder Files.
- 'Histoire de la Ville de Mons, ancienne et nouvelle': Gilles-Joseph de Boussu.
- 'Belgium in the Second World War': Jean-Michel Veranneman.
- Searches in archives held in Mons and with others dedicated to the history of Mons.
- The BBC – 'WW2 People's Lives'. An archive of WW2 memories, written by the public and servicemen and gathered by the BBC.
- Radar explained: www.beyourfinest.com/radio-detection-finding.
- 'Belgium in the Second World War: Jean-Michel Veranneman De Watervliet
- 'Nuneaton: A History': Ted Veasey
- 'Agent for the Resistance': A Belgian Saboteur in WW2: Herman Bodson.
- 'Collaboration in Belgium': The Rexist Movement: Leon Degrelle.
- 'Find a Way Home': Michael Vaal
- 'Americans in Occupied Belgium' Ed Klekowski & Libby Klekowsky.

Printed in Great Britain
by Amazon

53506560R00138